The Birth of Japan's Postwar Constitution

The Birth of Japan's Postwar Constitution

Koseki Shōichi

EDITED AND TRANSLATED BY
Ray A. Moore

WestviewPress
A Division of HarperCollins*Publishers*

To my grandchildren, Nicholas and Kelsey

Copyright © 1997 by Westview Press, A Division of HarperCollins Publishers, Inc.

Published in 1997 in the United States of America by Westview Press, 5500 Central Avenue, Boulder, Colorado 80301-2877, and in the United Kingdom by Westview Press, 12 Hid's Copse Road, Cumnor Hill, Oxford OX2 9JJ

Library of Congress Cataloging-in-Publication Data
Koseki, Shōichi, 1943–
    [Shin Kenpō no tanjō. English]
    The birth of Japan's postwar constitution / Koseki Shōichi ; edited and translated by Ray A. Moore.
        p.   cm.
    Includes bibliographical references.
    ISBN 0-8133-3162-5 (hc)
    1. Constitutional history—Japan.   2. Japan—Politics and government—1945–   I. Moore, Ray A., 1933–   .   II. Title.
KNX2101.K6713   1997
342.52′029—dc21   97-4511
                                                                                            CIP

The paper used in this publication meets the requirements of the American National Standard for Permanence of Paper for Printed Library Materials Z39.48-1984.

10   9   8   7   6   5   4   3   2   1

Contents

Translator's Preface and Acknowledgments

Throughout the translating of this book I have benefited from the support of colleagues at Amherst, Mount Holyoke, and Smith Colleges and Doshisha University in Japan. I wish to thank in particular Uda Yoshitada and Wako Tawa for numerous suggestions for translating difficult passages and Tadanori Yamashita for assisting me with the text on many occasions and for translating the "Constitution songs" in Chapter 10.

The author, Koseki Shōichi, has spent many hours with me in Japan and Massachusetts going over passages, events, and names. His willingness to share his notes on his sources, including many in English, saved me many hours of searching and translating. He also helped secure a foundation grant to defray the costs of publication. John Dower and Kyoko Inoue not only offered personal encouragement but wrote letters of recommendation for the publishing subsidy. I owe a deep debt of gratitude to Charles Kades and Donald Robinson whose knowledge and understanding of the origins of Japan's postwar constitution have been a constant challenge to me. And I wish to thank my wife, Ilga, for her constant assistance and moral support.

I must thank Japan's Association of 100 Titles for the grant that made the project possible, as well as the Tokio Kaijo Kagami Kinan Zaidan (Tokyo Marine Kagami Memorial Foundation) for the publication subsidy. A special word of gratitude is due Cynthia Gralla for her careful reading of Chapters 1 through 7 and editorial suggestions and Mark Vanhoenacker for help in the final stages of preparing the electronic manuscript. Finally, I am grateful to my copyeditor, Jennifer Barrett, and to the editorial staff of Westview Press, especially Susan McEachern and Carol Jones, who have helped at every stage. For whatever errors and deficiencies remain, I alone am responsible.

Ray A. Moore
Northfield, Massachusetts

A Note on the Translation

Japanese names in the text are given in Japanese order, that is, surname first and given name second. In the transcription of Japanese words, macrons are used to indicate long vowels except in the case of common place names. In some English sources Konoe Fumimaro is referred to as Konoye.

All material in brackets has been inserted by the translator. Unless otherwise noted, brackets in the original Japanese have been changed to parentheses by the translator. Whenever possible the translator has used the original sources in English rather than retranslated from Japanese.

Preface to the English Edition

When I was finishing the writing of this book at the beginning of 1989, the Shōwa period (1926–1989) came to an end. The death of Emperor Shōwa revealed to me clearly that the Japanese people's feelings toward their emperor had not changed much since before the war. With the emperor's death all the television channels were offering programs related to him. All the employees of Japanese automobile companies, which represent Japan, were shown on television bowing most reverently toward the imperial palace.

For most Japanese intellectuals and especially for those who had put their faith in democracy, the half year surrounding the emperor's death was without doubt a melancholy time. Needless to say, I was holding my head in my small study.

Until at least the 1970s most of the books written by Japanese, both those on postwar Japanese history and those on postwar legal history, depicted Japan's prewar and postwar political systems as completely different, that is, depicted a sharp break between the prewar and postwar periods. Many of the books published between 1945 and the 1960s especially emphasized this break in modern Japanese history. I recall clearly as a student being taught by a progressive professor that "there is only a very slight difference between the symbolic emperor system and a republican form of government."

Certainly the reforms carried out by the American occupation forces immediately after the war rivaled the Meiji Restoration in Japan in terms of their significance. Of these reforms, the Japanese Constitution drafted by General Douglas MacArthur's staff was epoch-making and was greeted by most Japanese with great surprise. But for about ten years after it was adopted, the constitution was not an important political issue. Those in the conservative camp were unhappy with this constitution but, being under a foreign military occupation, were unable to raise their voices in protest; they also had no political ideas for preparing a different constitution to replace this one. Those in the progressive camp under Marxist influence had much greater interest in a "people's revolution" than in this constitution. Most people who belonged to neither camp had little concern for the constitution. From their experience with the Meiji Constitution, the new constitution was not something that had to do with their own human rights and consequently the Japanese Constitution was far removed from their lives.

The constitution only became a central political issue after Japan signed peace and security treaties in 1951 and became a member of the western camp and after the Korean War (1950–1953), when proposals were made under a conservative government to revise the constitution to make rearmament possible, to strengthen the emperor's position, and to restore the traditional family system.

These ideas for revising the constitution responded to the American demand that Japan rearm and, at the same time, included Meiji period constitutional values, which were based on the nationalism that the Japanese people had carried over from the prewar period. When ideas for revision were set forth, nationalist feelings appeared clearly in the argument that, because the constitution had been imposed on Japan by the American occupation, a new "independent constitution" should be written by the Japanese people themselves.

By contrast, the progressives took the position of opposing rearmament and protecting the Japanese Constitution, thus making the constitution the point of contention and setting up a conflict over Article 9, which prohibited the maintenance of military forces.

Because of the strength of those conservatives who wished to revise the constitution, the protectionists opposed revision of any part of the constitution and developed a great respect for it, greater than that for the Meiji Constitution. It was quite natural therefore that they came to see a sharp distinction between the prewar and postwar periods. That was due to the fact that in Japan the historical materials necessary for doing careful research had not been made public, but due also to the fact that most Japanese intellectuals of this period cherished the new values that were the products of the postwar reforms and did not wish to see a revival of prewar values.

During the 1980s, however, this kind of distinction began to seem less clear. One reason for this was that during the 1970s the SCAP records in the U.S. archives began to be opened to scholars. As research on the occupation advanced, the continuity between prewar and postwar gradually became evident. A second reason was that the conservative government holding power throughout the postwar period had, without amending the new constitution, gradually revived institutions of the Meiji Constitution in areas where the occupation reforms had been incomplete. The "end of the Shōwa period" was a symbolic event that presented clearly to the Japanese people an objective view of an emperor system that has continued from the prewar into the postwar period.

Some American and European Japan specialists, of course, have emphasized this continuity between prewar and postwar Japan for a long time. Japanese scholars, including myself, were first strongly impressed by this interpretation, I believe, when we attended the International Conference on the Occupation of Japan at Amherst College in the United States in 1980. Shortly after this conference, articles began appearing in Japan on the theme of "continuity and discontinuity." Interest in the problem then began gradually to shift from the issue of postwar Japan's sharp break from its prewar past to what had actually continued and what had not. And the new Japanese Constitution is certainly one of the things that has broken sharply with the prewar Meiji Constitution.

I myself had believed that the basic principles of the Japanese Constitution were completely different from those of the Meiji Constitution. But in carefully relating the details of the framing process of the constitution in this book, I have pointed out both the continuities and discontinuities. The Japanese Constitution that is a symbol of "postwar democracy" has an aspect of continuity with the prewar Meiji Constitution. And the Japanese Constitution that is generally regarded as being a product of General MacArthur's staff during the U.S. occupation was actually "Japanized" by conservative officials of the Japanese government. I emphasize these two facts because they are essential to know if one is to understand postwar Japan.

I am delighted that an international audience will have an opportunity to read this book, thanks to this English translation by Professor Ray A. Moore, the organizer of the 1980 Amherst conference, the first international conference I ever attended.

Koseki Shōichi

Introduction:
Seeking a New Perspective

It is now half a century since the end of the Pacific War and Japan's adoption of a new constitution in 1946. Throughout that fifty-year period the constitution has been the center of controversy in Japan's postwar political system. To be sure, the controversy over the constitution goes well beyond the "postwar system" to broader and deeper principles that constitute the pillars of Japan's postwar democracy.

Everybody regards his or her own research topic as important and some may even become obsessed with its significance. My concern has been that the nature of Japan's "postwar democracy" has been reduced to the question of how the constitution was made, the issue that defined the point of departure for postwar Japan. Among the many reforms of the occupation period (1945–1952), the making of the constitution is one on which research is comparatively well advanced. In spite of this, however, I continue to have the uneasy feeling that much of the previous research has been unable to escape the ideological framework of the Cold War.

It was probably through Mark Gayn's book, *Japan Diary*, which was published in Japan at the end of the American occupation in 1951, that the Japanese people first learned the truth about the constitution being "imposed" on Japan during the drafting process.[1] However, this did not become widely known until later, in April 1952, shortly before the San Francisco Peace Treaty took effect, when the journal *Kaizō*, freed from occupation censorship, published an enlarged issue with the title, "The Secret History of the Secret History of Occupied Japan." But knowledge of the event at that point came primarily from Ashida Hitoshi, a cabinet minister when the constitution was being drafted, who talked about his own experience at a roundtable discussion;[2] and from discussions of the book *The Political Reorientation of Japan*, which the Government Section of MacArthur's headquarters (GHQ) had published in 1949. Even though this book was indeed a "secret history," the true facts surrounding what was called the "imposition" of the constitution on Japan were still not completely evident. Nor had these facts been incorporated into the framework of current Japanese politics as a major topic of debate.

The constitution became a political issue in July 1954 with the testi-mony of Matsumoto Jōji, former minister in charge of constitutional re-form in the Shidehara cabinet, at the Liberal Party's Constitutional Inves-tigation Commission, which had been established in March under the chairmanship of Kishi Nobusuke.[3] The purpose of the commission was to make the constitution consistent with the existence of the Self-Defense Forces (established in 1954), which Japan was required to maintain under the 1953 Mutual Security Agreement with the United States. With Mat-sumoto's testimony, interest in how the constitution was written mush-roomed and led in 1956 to the establishment of the government's Com-mission on the Constitution.

In short, interest in and research on the framing of the constitution was prompted by the effort in 1954 to amend it. And for that reason, the focus of that interest has always been on whether or not the constitution was imposed on Japan. Although several conclusions have been reached ("yes, it was imposed"; "no, it was not"; and, "yes, but it was unavoid-able"), whatever the conclusion, the making of the constitution has in-variably been presented as a confrontation between two nations or as a struggle between the United States (that is, General Douglas MacArthur as Supreme Commander of the occupying army) and the government of Japan. I myself cannot help thinking that, at least in terms of procedure, the constitution was indeed imposed on the Japanese government by MacArthur. Yet depicting the framing process and the interest that has been shown in it according to this analytical scheme has made it difficult to understand the real process by which the constitution was produced and, therefore, the true significance of the constitution itself.

In a fundamental sense, the Japanese Constitution rests on principles of internationalism. Both the pacifism expressed in the preamble ("We have determined to preserve our security and existence, trusting in the justice and faith of the peace-loving peoples of the world") and the re-spect for human rights contained in Article 97 ("The fundamental human rights by this Constitution guaranteed to the people of Japan are fruits of the age-old struggle of man to be free") distinctively reflect an interna-tional perspective that transcends national boundaries.

Thus despite the fact that the Japanese Constitution contains a denial of the absoluteness of nationalism, which can be called a characteristic of post–World War II constitutions, and an international perspective,[4] the enactment process through which such international concepts were man-ifested has been studied from the extremely nationalistic perspective of a confrontation between nation-states.

Moreover, this nation-versus-nation approach suggests that the out-come should be depicted as constitution-making by the use of force since, concretely, it was a case of the victor nation "imposing" a constitution on a defeated nation. Accordingly, the revisionists have appealed to the re-maining proud subjects of the Great Japanese Empire to "make our own constitution," while, on the other hand, protectors of the constitution have battled to defend the "peace constitution." Constitutional reform was certainly required of Japan in 1945–1946; it could not have been avoided under a military occupation. But neither can we deny that, intel-lectually, the historical significance of the process that produced the con-stitution has been studiously ignored for that very reason. Yet the process that gave birth to the Japanese Constitution was in fact complicated, var-ied, and rich, going well beyond the actions of any state.

The Japanese side was not of one mind about constitutional reform, nor was the U.S. government or MacArthur's staff. With respect to con-stitutional ideas, one can see major similarities between the constitution that MacArthur's staff drafted (the SCAP draft) and those drafts pre-pared by Japanese civilian organizations. Even among the members of the Japanese government's Committee for Study of Constitutional Prob-lems, there were some who wrote opinions similar to those found in the SCAP draft. Or again, organizations and individuals did not maintain their views on constitutional reform unchanged throughout the framing process. There were cases in which major changes took place in long-held views, such as the Socialist Party and the famous constitutional scholar, Miyazawa Toshiyoshi.

On the other hand, MacArthur, who "imposed" the constitution on the Japanese government, was harshly and continually criticized by his own government (the State Department) and by the Far Eastern Commission (FEC) for the high-handed procedure he used. Eventually, to be sure, the U.S. government ratified all of MacArthur's actions. But by that time he was completely isolated. The process by which the American draft was written was in fact a complicated one. For example, the original draft of the women's rights section, which was written by a woman in Govern-ment Section, contained many details that were ultimately cut out by men. However, when the Japanese government's draft, based on MacArthur's, was presented to the National Diet, Japanese women legis-lators of the lower house offered an amendment that was almost exactly the same as the original draft written by the woman on MacArthur's staff. And just as had happened on the American side, their amendment was ignored by their male colleagues in the Diet.

In other words, the framing process of the Japanese Constitution cannot be elucidated simply by an analytical scheme that pits one nation-state against another. Only with a constitutional perspective that goes beyond the nation-state and with an approach that stresses the clash of legal ideas can we begin to clarify that process.[5] In the Japanese Constitution there are provisions, for example, that were merely products of compromise, inserted without sufficient discussion; other provisions that are vestiges of the Meiji Constitution that Japanese legal bureaucrats, unnoticed by the Americans, succeeded in retaining; completely new provisions, not in the American draft, that Japanese officials or Diet members inserted; and provisions that, even though they were important in retrospect, ran counter to the trend of the times and disappeared at the early drafting stage. In short, the Japanese Constitution had the appearance of a mosaic.

Furthermore, trying to understand the constitution by peering through the lens of two nation-states confronting each other has made it extremely difficult to see the real continuity between prewar and postwar Japan. Both the revisionist school, which sees the Japanese Constitution as having been imposed, as well as the protectionist school, which values the constitution highly, ignore this element of continuity in the constitution. It would be going too far perhaps to say that the structure of the new constitution bears a close resemblance to that of the Meiji Constitution. But in the midst of the postwar reforms, unaccompanied as they were by a social revolution, the bureaucrat in the cabinet's Legislation Bureau who wrote the Liberal Party's draft constitution (which said that "Japan is a Monarchy") six months later became the minister in charge of defending and interpreting the government's bill to revise the constitution as it made its way through Diet deliberations. Or again, the bureaucrat in the Ministry of Education who at the end of the war served as director of the Student Mobilization Bureau one year later became director of the Administrative Affairs Bureau of the Society to Popularize the Constitution, with the responsibility of familiarizing the populace with the "peace constitution." These are examples of continuity between prewar and postwar Japan. Is it not precisely here that the present state of the constitution, with its fairly hollow peace and human rights articles, becomes blurred?

If we reexamine the origins of the new constitution from this angle, it is difficult to regard the date on which it legally took effect—May 3, 1947—as its real date of birth. Accordingly, this study treats the period from September 1945 to May 1949 as "The Birth of the New Constitution." Early in 1947, just months before the constitution took effect, MacArthur informed the Japanese government that there would be an opportunity to review it within a year or two. In August 1948, therefore, the National Diet established a committee to review the constitution. But there was no subsequent effort to propose amendments, and the opportunity for doing so was lost during the second Yoshida cabinet. Thus two years later, in May 1949, the constitution was established without being amended or even reviewed. When examining the thesis, therefore, that the constitution was "imposed" on Japan, this fact raises a very important question. It is for this reason that I deal with the issue until May 1949.

Finally, I wish to explain why I chose to call [the original volume] "The Birth of the New Constitution." By the end of the 1960s the expression "new constitution" had generally fallen into disuse. It was about that time that the constitution, after the passage of some twenty years, had become fixed in people's minds, and consequently the events of its framing were receding into the past. From the late sixties the new constitution generally came to be called "the present constitution," or simply "the constitution."

In spite of this, my reason for using "the new constitution" here is because I wish to single it out as a new document, completely different from the Meiji Constitution. The people, liberated from war and oppressive government, were delighted when the constitution took effect. They sang and danced; young people in remote mountain villages organized groups to study the constitution. The sight of them entering essay-writing contests about the constitution had never before, or since, been seen in modern Japanese history. Not only that. While one cannot ignore the role of government officials in the framing process, civilians not in government service and laymen without special legal training or knowledge also played a significant part in that same process. The wellspring of the Japanese Constitution, which still retains its modern significance today, is the extremely large role those laymen played (with the exception of the provision on the renunciation of war). No single Diet member or constitutional scholar came close to exercising the influence of those few laymen. The writing of proposals for constitutions that ultimately influenced the American draft, the clear statement of popular sovereignty, the making of normal education compulsory, and the writing of the whole text of the constitution in colloquial Japanese—all of these were contributions by laymen.

On the occasion of the 150th anniversary of the U.S. Constitution in 1937, President Roosevelt said that "the American Constitution is a layman's document, not a lawyer's." The constitution of a modern nation indeed has that feature as its essential character.

Throughout Japan's past "law" was the monopoly of government officials and legal specialists. In that sense the Japanese Constitution opened up new horizons, if even in a modest way. When we consider the constitution in this way, it still seems appropriate to bestow on it, despite its age, the appellation of "new constitution."

Notes

1. Mark Gayn, *Nippon Nikki* (Tokyo: Chikuma Shobō, 1963), p. 356.
2. Symposium, "Kenpō wa nishūkan de dekitaka," *Kaizō* (April 1952). Participants included Ashida Hitoshi, Iwabuchi Tatsuo, Suzuki Yasuzō, Miyake Kiyoteru, and Abe Shinnosuke.

3. From Matsumoto Jōji's testimony, "Nihonkoku kenpō no sōan ni tsuite," in Kenpō chōsakai jimukyoku, *Kenshi: Sōdai 28* (October 1958).

4. Higuchi Yōichi, *Hikaku kenpō*, rev. ed. (Tokyo: Rinsei Shoin, 1984), pp. 503 ff.

5. Tanaka Hideo, "The Conflict Between Two Legal Traditions in Making the Constitution of Japan," in *Democratizing Japan*, ed. Robert E. Ward and Yoshikazu Sakamoto (Honolulu: University of Hawaii Press, 1987).

1

The Probing Begins

Konoe Fumimaro Calls on MacArthur

The first person to suggest the revision of the Japanese Constitution was General Douglas MacArthur. At 5 P.M. on September 13, 1945, Prince Konoe Fumimaro, prime minister three times before the war and minister without portfolio in the first postwar Higashikuni cabinet, made his way to the Customs Building near Yokohama Harbor, where MacArthur's general headquarters (GHQ) was located. On September 17 MacArthur would move to the Daiichi Insurance Building in Tokyo, across from the Imperial Palace, and on October 2 would establish his headquarters as the Supreme Commander for the Allied Powers (SCAP).[1] Meanwhile, however, he was commander of the United States forces in the Pacific. At the time, none of this was known to the Japanese, nor did it matter much, for Konoe needed to meet with MacArthur in any case.

Tomita Kenji, chief secretary in the Konoe cabinet before the war and later a close adviser to Konoe, has said that Konoe made the trip to Yokohama on September 13 because "MacArthur summoned him."[2] To the Japanese, however, Konoe's reasons for the visit were not that simple. The political critic and adviser to Konoe, Iwabuchi Tatsuo, thought that "the Japanese side felt it necessary to inform MacArthur of conditions in Japan," and later explained that the "request for the meeting was made" by Konoe.[3] Obata Toshishirō, a minister in the Higashikuni cabinet who had worked with Konoe during the war, agreed with Iwabuchi's view of events.[4] Konoe's position in the Japanese government certainly justified his request to meet with MacArthur. Konoe had exceptionally rich international experience: He had been appointed to the House of Peers at the age of twenty-five while still a student at Kyoto University; he had served roughly three years as prime minister during a long political career; he had attended the Paris Peace Conference in 1919 as an aide to the Japanese delegation; and he had later traveled to the United States and other countries.[5] It was precisely for these reasons that he was appointed to the cabinet in August 1945 and given the rank of deputy prime minister under Prime Minister Prince Higashikuni.

Konoe thus proceeded to MacArthur's headquarters in Yokohama, acting as the unofficial representative responsible for probing MacArthur's intentions. This was two days after the Supreme Commander had issued an order to arrest Tōjō Hideki and others as suspected war criminals. Konoe's meeting ended after only about an hour primarily because, it was said, MacArthur's American interpreter was unable to perform his duties adequately.

Konoe and MacArthur met a second time on October 4. The location this time was the waiting room next to MacArthur's office on the sixth floor of the Daiichi Insurance Building in Tokyo, the headquarters of the U.S. occupation. This time the interpreter was Okumura Katsuzō, a Foreign Ministry official who had also served as the interpreter at the first meeting of MacArthur and the Japanese emperor just a week before. The time was 5 P.M., the same time as their first meeting in Yokohama. Konoe first met MacArthur's chief of staff, Lieutenant General Richard Sutherland. Then, after waiting about twenty minutes, he entered the room where, besides MacArthur and Sutherland, George Atcheson, Jr., the political adviser to the Supreme Commander, was also waiting. On the Japanese side were only Konoe and his interpreter, Okumura.

The reason for the twenty-minute delay, according to Okumura years later, was that "Atcheson, who was in Japan as the representative of the State Department, also wished to hear what Konoe had to say. In order to summon him suddenly from the Mitsui Building in Nihonbashi, where he had set up his office, it must have taken some time."[6] This is quite a shrewd observation, since it would have taken Atcheson about twenty minutes to drive from Nihonbashi to Hibiya. But it seems unlikely that this was the only reason for the delay. For on this day at 6 P.M., MacArthur had issued a very important directive to the Japanese government. Usually referred to as the "human rights directive," this document ordered the immediate release of political prisoners, the abolition of the Special Police, the abrogation of repressive laws, and so forth. Because of this directive, on the following day the Higashikuni cabinet resigned, and on October 10 some three thousand political prisoners—including Tokuda Kyūichi and other members of the Japan Communist Party—were released. It is clear now that MacArthur was finalizing approval of the human rights directive at the very moment that he was to meet with Konoe. It seems reasonable to surmise, therefore, that this was probably the reason for the delay. Meanwhile, Konoe had no way of knowing that a directive was being issued while their talks were in progress.

When the meeting finally got under way, Konoe, according to Okumura, launched into a monologue on the causes of the war. He spoke of the militarists and Marxists and their responsibility for the war. "Cooperating with the militarists and nationalists, the Marxists were the ones who provided theoretical backing; and this union of militarists and leftists is what led Japan down the path to destruction."[7] No matter how staunch an anticommunist MacArthur was, it is easy to imagine his astonishment when he heard Konoe's assertion that responsibility for the war lay with those leftist political criminals whom he himself was about to release from prison.

In any case, after talking at length, Konoe, "with a slight change of tone," asked MacArthur (Okumura reconstructs the conversation in the following way): "I'd like to know whether you have any ideas or suggestions regarding the organization of the Japanese Government and the composition of the Diet." On hearing this, MacArthur—suddenly sitting erect and speaking in a certain military tone—said in a loud voice, as if reprimanding him: "First of all, the Japanese Constitution must be revised. It is essential to introduce into government sufficient liberal elements through constitutional revision."[8]

Whether or not MacArthur in fact said "constitutional revision" on this occasion was later to become a major point of contention. The Foreign Ministry's record of the meeting, probably written by Okumura, indicates that MacArthur used these words.[9] Furthermore, Atcheson's dispatch to the secretary of state on October 10 corroborates that the October 4 meeting was one "at which I was present and at which the General told Konoe that the Japanese Constitution must be revised."[10] Thus it appears certain that MacArthur did in fact utter these words. Okumura states that in the car returning from the meeting Konoe said to him, "Today we heard something remarkable."[11]

It was not only Konoe who thought that MacArthur had said "something remarkable." In fact, Atcheson thought so too. When he returned to his office, he quickly sent the following short telegram to the secretary of state:

> As there appears to be considerable discussion among politically-minded Japanese in regard to questions of the revision of Japanese Constitution, it is suggested that completion of the directive on this subject be expedited as much as possible. Meanwhile please telegraph outlines of draft so that we may know direction which American Government thought is taking in the matter.[12]

For both Konoe and Atcheson, "something remarkable" had happened. They each began moving in earnest toward constitutional revision; Konoe, especially, moved quickly. As the Higashikuni cabinet had already resigned, Konoe would lose his cabinet post as soon as the next cabinet was formed. Determined to move ahead without delay, Konoe, still formally a cabinet member, went to see Atcheson on October 6. This time at his side were Takagi Yasaka, Tokyo University professor and Japan's leading authority on U.S. political history; Matsumoto Shigeharu, chief editor at Dōmei News Service during the war and a close associate of Takagi; and Konoe's private secretary, Ushiba Tomohiko.

Atcheson had not yet received a reply from the secretary of state; nonetheless, he expressed his own views quite explicitly, while careful to remind Konoe and his associates that he spoke "unofficially." According to Takagi's memorandum of the meeting, Atcheson named nine points of revision to the Meiji Constitution,[13] while Atcheson's own report to the secretary of state mentioned seven points, organized as special features of the Meiji Constitution.[14] Although at a glance they may appear to differ, the contents of both reports are largely the same. The basic change that was discussed would make the Diet a representative institution elected by the Japanese people. The cabinet would be responsible to the Diet, and consequently the House of Peers and the Privy Council would be abolished. The major points were that the powers of the emperor, beginning with his right of supreme command of the army and navy, would be reduced; the legislative power of the Diet would be expanded; human rights would be guaranteed; and centralized control of police and education would be abolished. Nothing was said about the position of the emperor as sovereign.

The Struggle for Authority over
Constitutional Revision

As soon as the meeting had finished, Konoe quickly called on the Lord Privy Seal, Kido Kōichi. Kido and Konoe agreed that Konoe would undertake the work of constitutional reform as a special appointee in the Office of the Privy Seal. The formation of the Shidehara cabinet was to take place the following day. Konoe, accompanied by Takagi, went directly to the home of Hosokawa Morisada, Konoe's son-in-law and private secretary. Over dinner they refined their plans for revising the constitution. They agreed to ask Professor Sasaki Sōichi of Kyoto University, with whom Konoe had studied, to direct the work of revision. Hosokawa hurriedly departed for Kyoto to meet with Sasaki.[15]

On October 9, Konoe had an audience with the emperor to explain events of recent days, and at noon on October 11 received as planned his appointment as special assistant in the Office of the Privy Seal. On the same day at 5 P.M., the new prime minister, Shidehara Kijūrō, called on MacArthur at his office. It was on this occasion that MacArthur issued instructions to Shidehara regarding what came to be known as the "five great reforms directive." Two days later MacArthur's judgment, introduced as "the General's view," appeared in the morning papers: "In carrying out the Potsdam Declaration, the traditional social order under which the Japanese people for centuries have been subjugated will be reformed. This will unquestionably involve a liberalization of the Constitution." Following this the "five great reforms" were presented.

Briefly, these were emancipating women, encouraging labor unions, liberalizing and democratizing education, abolishing secret and oppressive organizations, and democratizing economic institutions. In short, although MacArthur had already made clear that it was essential to revise the constitution, the revision itself was not to be included among the five great reforms mentioned in the directive to the Shidehara cabinet. Moreover, the directive was not mentioned in the lead articles of the newspapers. Instead, the top news stories reported the emperor's appointment of Konoe to the Office of the Privy Seal. With the appearance of these news accounts, the Japanese people first learned that Konoe would be involved in constitutional reform. Without information on the contents of the two MacArthur-Konoe meetings, the news reports gave two distinct impressions: that the emperor had ordered Konoe to revise the constitution, and that MacArthur had ordered Shidehara to carry out five major reforms.[16] Years later Takagi gave the following testimony at the Liberal Party's Constitutional Investigation Commission on the background of how the events of this momentous day, October 11, were reported:

> Since we predicted that the problem of constitutional reform would definitely come up in Shidehara's meeting with MacArthur, we tried to develop a preliminary strategy by consulting with Brigadier General [Bonner] Fellers. That is, for us it was undesirable that constitutional reform should be included among the political reforms which we fully expected MacArthur would demand when the new Prime Minister went to see him on October 11. We called the attention of the other side to our hope that constitutional revision could be undertaken in a different way. We secured an understanding that no demand for constitutional reform would be made along with, for example, the issues of raising the status of women, reforming the system of labor unions and education and the other reforms suggested by MacArthur. On the basis of that understanding, Shidehara met with MacArthur. . . . In short, we on the Japanese side were trying to devise a way by which we could independently consider constitutional reform.[17]

The Japanese strategy seemed feasible in view of the fact that all newspapers were subject to daily American censorship, and because Takagi— a specialist on U.S. political history—had long had good connections with the American side. At the same time, it is clear that MacArthur and his staff were eager to accommodate the Japanese desire to revise the constitution themselves.

At the cabinet meeting on October 13, immediately after his meeting with MacArthur, Shidehara moved quickly to set up the Committee to Study Constitutional Problems, with State Minister Matsumoto Jōji as its chairman. Consequently, it appeared at the time that the decision to establish this committee was taken because MacArthur, in his meeting with Shidehara, had directed that the constitution be liberalized. In fact, however, Shidehara's decision seems to have been motivated by other factors. Judging by Matsumoto's own testimony later at the Constitutional Investigation Commission, during the cabinet meeting on October 11—the very day Shidehara met with MacArthur (probably immediately before the meeting with MacArthur)—Privy Seal Kido called Shidehara to say that "Prince Konoe was being entrusted with revision of the Constitution." On October 13 Konoe and Shidehara met with Matsumoto, who told them there was "no possible reason for excluding the Cabinet from constitutional reform. We too have already begun thinking about that."[18]

When viewed in this way, it appears that behind the Shidehara cabinet's sudden decision to appoint the Committee to Study Constitutional Problems was the desire to prevent Konoe from seizing the initiative on constitutional reform. On October 13 Sasaki Sōichi, accompanied by Konoe's messenger Hosokawa, arrived from Kyoto, went to the palace to receive the imperial appointment of special assistant in the Office of the Privy Seal, and continued on to Konoe's private residence in Ogikubo. Newspapers published editorials commenting on constitutional revision, *Asahi* under the headline "Democratization of the Present Constitution" and *Mainichi* under "The Urgency of Revising the Constitution." Thus by the middle of October, conditions were ripe for taking the first steps toward constitutional reform. It was also the beginning of a period of rivalry between the Office of the Privy Seal and the Shidehara cabinet. Beginning with Chairman Matsumoto's speech on October 15, the rivalry developed into a public dispute and confrontation.

> Constitutional revision is an important State matter. At the time that Prince Itō (Hirobumi) drafted the Constitution, there was no clear distinction between the Court and the Privy Seal. Now, however, since the Constitution has been created by the Emperor, the Government must carefully investigate the matter, and it is the responsibility of a State Minister to advise on the exercise of the Imperial power to amend the Constitution. Who bears responsibility in this important State matter? Since the Emperor has no responsibility for it, obviously offering advice is the responsibility of a State Minister. Presently, in the Office of the Privy Seal research on the Constitution is being conducted by Prince Konoe. But I consider that merely preparation for the purpose of studying the Government's proposed constitutional amendment when it is presented for the Imperial consideration.[19]

The newspapers reported the speech the following day. *Mainichi*, for example, treated it in a special edition under the headline, "Round One in the Issue of Constitutional Reform," printing, above Matsumoto's statement, comments of a similar nature by Professor Miyazawa Toshiyoshi of Tokyo University and by Rōyama Masamichi. Miyazawa criticized the Office of the Privy Seal's work on constitutional reform more harshly than had Matsumoto:

> That it is improper for both the Government and the Privy Seal to prepare a draft amendment of the Constitution is abundantly clear. I believe that misinterpreting the present Constitution and understanding constitutional reform as something that should be done behind the scenes, unrelated to the Government's advice and responsibility, is to ignore the very principles of constitutionalism enshrined in our Constitution.[20]

In response to this, Sasaki Sōichi quickly published a rebuttal in the *Osaka Mainichi* of October 21. He argued that advice by the Privy Seal and the government were essentially different:

> The Government's advisory role with respect to constitutional revision is to request that the Emperor undertake the actual act, or not undertake the actual act, of amending the Constitution. By contrast, the role of the Office of the Privy Seal is to bring the Privy Seal's knowledge of the matter to the attention of His Majesty and to be a source of information and assistance in reaching a proper Imperial judgment when the Emperor expresses the Imperial wish with respect to amending the Constitution.[21]

A basis for both arguments could be found in Article 73 of the Imperial Constitution of Japan (the Meiji Constitution), an article whose wording could be interpreted in various ways. It provided that "When it becomes necessary in future to amend the provisions of the present Constitution, a project to the effect shall be submitted to the Imperial Diet by Imperial Order." Until this time, the question of amending this "Code of Immutable Laws" had never arisen, even as a matter of discussion, since the promulgation of the Meiji Constitution in 1889. Only with Japan's defeat in the war had amending the constitution become an issue. Therefore, it is not surprising that dissension arose over the proper course of action.

Sasaki's interpretation, however, was contrary to the principle of responsible government, which holds that "State affairs ought to be conducted responsibly and openly by the Cabinet." Sasaki himself cannot avoid the charge that he lacked a critical attitude toward the institution of the Privy Seal.[22] Constitutional revision by the Office of the Privy Seal was also criticized by, among others, an editorial in *Asahi* on October 18.

Generally, most critics favored granting the cabinet the authority to re-vise the constitution.

As concern mounted in Japan over constitutional reform by the Privy Seal, strong criticism of Konoe's involvement appeared abroad, espe-cially in the United States. The *New York Herald Tribune*, after reporting the story in a dispatch from Tokyo by its correspondent, Frank Kelley,[23] sharply questioned MacArthur's actions in the following editorial:

> Among the foolish mistakes the United States has made in the Far East, the most egregious was selecting Prince Konoe as the drafter of Japan's new constitution. . . . If the Prince were already in prison awaiting trial as a war criminal, there would be absolutely no reason to object. For him to be ap-pointed the drafter of Japan's democratic constitution with the formal ap-proval of the American side is foolish in the extreme.[24]

The notion of Konoe being in charge of constitutional reform was from the outset subject to criticism at home and abroad. In spite of this, Konoe and Sasaki proceeded with their revision plan to amend the constitution. They could do so because of the personal guarantee provided by MacArthur's October 4 suggestion to Konoe. But, as they were to learn, that suggestion was an unreliable guarantee at best.

The Konoe Group Begins to Write a Draft

Konoe and Sasaki eventually commenced work on their draft on October 22, 1945. For their place of work, they chose a remote mountain inn in Hakone Miyanoshita, in the foothills of Mount Fuji some sixty-five miles west of Tokyo. Sasaki and his assistant, Ritsumeikan University Professor Iwasaki Tatsugorō, occupied the whole third floor of the inn as they went about their work. At the same time, Konoe, living in a summer house in Odawara not far from Miyanoshita, engaged in almost daily discussions with Sasaki about the draft.

One wonders why Konoe had to take Sasaki and others to Hakone, a secluded mountain resort, to prepare a draft constitution for the nation. Matsumoto Jōji had said earlier, when criticizing constitutional reform by Konoe and the Office of the Privy Seal, that the historical circumstances of the framing of the Meiji Constitution had made a strong impression on Konoe. Although there were several drafts of the Meiji Constitution, the one that most resembled the final version was the so-called Natsushima Constitution. In 1887 Itō Hirobumi, under imperial command to prepare a draft constitution, began deliberations on the draft at the Azumaya Inn in Yokohama-Kanazawa, accompanied by Itō Miyoji, Kaneko Kentarō, and later Inoue Kowashi. Unfortunately, the Azumaya Inn was the object of a burglary; a package containing money and the draft constitution was stolen. The money in the package was never found, but the draft was successfully recovered from a nearby field, where it had been abandoned. After this unsettling incident, Itō Hirobumi and his associates moved their quarters to a lodge that had been built on Natsushima, an isolated, uninhabited island off the coast of nearby Kanazawa (now the site of a factory's company housing; a memorial stone marks the spot). There they continued their work and soon produced a finished draft of what has come to be called the "Natsushima Constitution."[25] It appears that Konoe's decision in 1945 to take his drafting committee to the mountain resort of Hakone was an effort, in short, to use Itō's experience of framing the Meiji Constitution as a model for his own work.

While Sasaki pursued his work on a draft at Hakone, Takagi Yasaka tirelessly conducted his liaison with SCAP in Tokyo. According to Takagi's subsequent testimony: "On October 25th when we met with [John K. Emmerson], we heard in somewhat more detail that 'recent information from Washington supplements' earlier information."[26] Perhaps it would be more accurate to say that rather than coming "from SCAP," the information they obtained in the conversation with Emmerson was directly from the State Department in Washington. Two of Atcheson's subordinates, Emmerson and Robert T. Fearey, were present at the meeting. It seems unexceptional that Emmerson and his colleagues "provided more details" at this meeting. Takagi and Emmerson had had a close relationship before the war. Moreover, Emmerson had received from the secretary of state on October 17 the special instructions already mentioned. Based on this, Emmerson put together his own views on constitutional reform and submitted a memorandum to MacArthur on October 23.[27]

The instructions from the secretary of state stated very concisely:

Attitude of the Departmental officers who have been giving consideration to this matter may be summarized as follows: There should be assurances that the Japanese Constitution is amended to provide for government responsible to an electorate based upon wide representative suffrage. Provision should be made that the executive branch of government derive its authority from and be responsible to the electorate or to a fully representative legislative body. If Emperor institution is not retained constitutional safeguards against that institution will obviously not be required but provision should be made for (1) Complete control by an elected congress of financial and budgetary matters, (2) Guarantee of fundamental civil rights to all persons within Japanese jurisdiction, not to Japanese only, and (3) Any action by head of state only pursuant to authority expressly delegated to him.

If Emperor is retained, following safeguards in addition to those enumerated above would be necessary:

(1) A cabinet to advise and assist the Emperor should be chosen with advice and consent of and responsible to representative legislative body, (2) No veto over legislative measures should be exercised by other bodies such as House of Peers or Privy Council, (3) Emperor should initiate amendments to constitution recommended by cabinet and approved by legislative body, (4) Legislative body should be permitted to meet at will, and (5) Any ministers for armed forces which may be permitted in future should be civilians and all special privileges of direct access to throne by military should be eliminated.[28]

From his meeting with Emmerson, Takagi drew the conclusion regarding the emperor system—the most important issue in constitutional reform—that "in the final analysis, this should be determined by the will of the Japanese people; that is, it will not be dictated by outside authorities."[29] He so informed Konoe.

At this juncture, in short, the basic ideas of constitutional reform that the Konoe side had elicited from the United States through Atcheson and his staff were the establishment of popular sovereignty and the reform of the emperor system. These were ideas that Konoe could accept. Thus at this stage of Konoe's efforts to revise the constitution, prospects for "protecting the emperor system" looked good.

MacArthur Repudiates Konoe

On the evening of November 1, SCAP suddenly announced in a public statement that "Prince Konoe was not selected by Allied authorities for that purpose [revising the constitution]." The full SCAP statement, published in the newspapers on November 3, said: "Prince Konoe as Deputy Prime Minister representing the Prime Minister [Higashikuni] was informed that the Japanese Government would be required to revise the Constitution." Since the Higashikuni cabinet had already resigned, Konoe had no official position, and therefore "the Supreme Commander informed the new Prime Minister, Shidehara, of his directive to revise the Constitution."[30]

At a news conference held in the afternoon of November 2, Konoe repeated his contention that MacArthur had indeed suggested constitutional reform to him on October 4, but added: "I personally have not received any order or commission in particular. It is due entirely to the decision of the Japanese side that I came to undertake this important task."[31] MacArthur's statement was nevertheless deeply disturbing to the Konoe group. With extensive press coverage of the event, on November 4 Takagi and Ushiba sought a meeting with Emmerson, despite the fact that it was a Sunday. According to Ushiba, "Emmerson's attitude this time had undergone a very sudden change, a very sudden change indeed. In a matter of a few minutes [the talks] were broken off."[32]

That was not surprising. MacArthur's attitude toward Konoe was undergoing a radical shift. Atcheson had already ordered E. H. Norman to investigate whether Konoe might be charged with war crimes. Norman presented his findings and recommendations to Atcheson on November 5, the day after Takagi's and Ushiba's hasty Sunday meeting with Emmerson.[33]

Norman, the son of Canadian missionaries who had lived in Japan until he was fifteen years old, was a specialist on modern Japanese history with many publications to his credit, the most important of which was *Japan's Emergence as a Modern State* (1940). After Japan's defeat in 1945, he worked as a diplomat in the Canadian Foreign Ministry handling the repatriation of Canadian civilians from Japan and, at the same time, served as the chief of SCAP's Research and Analysis Branch, Counter-Intelligence Division. Norman ended his lengthy report to Atcheson with the following evaluation of Konoe:

> Reviewing Konoe's record of public service gives the strong impression that he fits the description of a war criminal. More than this, however, he intrudes himself into public life and with a well-educated group of political specialists conspires to gain more power and to gain access to the central offices of government. It is intolerable that he attempts to find an escape route for himself by intimating to the Supreme Commander that in the present situation he is the indispensable person. One thing is certain: while he is allowed to occupy an important position, he will block and frustrate the latent possibilities of the liberal democratic movement. So long as he is directing the committee to revise the constitution, he will make a mockery of all serious efforts to write a democratic constitution. Whatever he touches turns to dust.[34]

Konoe's fate began to take a decidedly negative turn. On November 9 he was summoned by the United States Strategic Bombing Survey and subjected to hours of interrogation by Paul Baran, a member of the survey, aboard an American ship in Tokyo Bay. The interrogation on his responsibility for policy decisions leading to the invasion of China in 1937 and decisions on American-Japanese relations on the eve of the war was quite harsh. Yet Konoe persisted throughout in laying the blame on the Japanese military and General Tōjō Hideki.[35]

Nevertheless, the interrogation appeared to have affected him adversely, for he became deeply pessimistic and is said to have told Hosokawa Morisada that "if the United States comes here with such ideas, the Japanese Imperial House is finished."[36]

SCAP's statement of November 1 repudiating Konoe was obviously not consistent with the facts, for even after the formation of the Shidehara cabinet on October 9, SCAP officials met with the Konoe group and offered suggestions on constitutional reform. It seems plausible that MacArthur suddenly changed his mind about Konoe because he had been severely criticized for suggesting that Konoe take the lead in revising the constitution.

Years later, after the occupation, a story spread that an interpreter's error was to blame for the belief that MacArthur had urged constitutional reform at the MacArthur-Konoe meeting of October 4. The source of this story appears to have been H. E. Wildes's book, *Typhoon in Tokyo* (1954). Wildes wrote:

> Perhaps the most famous translation incident concerned the Constitution. Soon after arrival in Japan, MacArthur held a consultation with former Prime Minister Prince Konoe Fumimaro. In discussing Occupation requirements Konoe asked if MacArthur had any suggestions concerning changes in the "make-up of the Government," meaning the relations of the military and naval Cabinet ministers to the civilian officials. The interpreter, however, translated "make-up" by its English equivalent "constitution," which MacArthur understood as a proper noun. Although heretofore little attention had been given to the thought that a new Constitution should replace the Meiji Constitution of 1889, MacArthur replied that Constitutional changes would indeed be necessary.[37]

This seems like a plausible story. Moreover, when we consider that Wildes was a member of the legislative and political branch of Government Section and was one of the group that later prepared the SCAP draft constitution, the so-called MacArthur Constitution, it seems increasingly credible. But Wildes was not a party to the events of October 4. As we have seen, the records of those present at the meeting—not only the interpreter Okumura's but Atcheson's as well—state that MacArthur did say that constitutional revision was required.

Where, then, did Wildes hear this story? Surprisingly, the notion that there had been a translation error seems to have originated with George Atcheson. On November 5 (that is, on the very day he received from Norman the report on Konoe as a war criminal), less than a month after he had telegraphed the secretary of state that "General of the Army MacArthur said that the Constitution must be revised," Atcheson wrote in a letter to President Truman:

> There is a curious story behind the activities of Prince Konoe which have caused press criticism in the United States and in Japan as well. I was present on October 4 when he called on General MacArthur on his own initia-

tive. The General mentioned that the "administrative machinery" of the Government should be reformed and Konoe's interpreter (who verified this to me later) could not think of the correct Japanese translation and passed the statement off [translated the General's statement] with the only thing that came to his mind—"the constitution should be revised."[38]

The conclusion seems inescapable that Atcheson was the source of the wrong-translation thesis. Wildes, who was at the time a member of Government Section, somehow must have learned of Atcheson's letter to Truman. In short, Atcheson, aware that MacArthur had made an error in judgment in assigning to Konoe responsibility for revising the constitution, shifted the blame for that error to a mistake by the Japanese interpreter. We know that this was a dishonorable and shockingly false charge against the interpreter Okumura Katsuzō.

Konoe rushed to finish his draft revision in the midst of growing despair. Just as SCAP's attitude toward Konoe underwent a sudden change, he was notified that the Office of the Privy Seal itself was to be abolished on MacArthur's orders. Moreover, there were differences between Konoe and Sasaki over constitutional reform, making it difficult for them to write a joint draft constitution. Konoe, with assistance from Takagi and others, was contemplating a draft that would take American ideas into account, whereas Sasaki disliked such political considerations. Accordingly, Konoe avoided writing out a full text of provisions and instead prepared only an "outline." The Konoe draft, after presenting "reasons for the need to revise the Imperial Constitution" ("in view of Japan's recent defeat, it is necessary to revise the Imperial Constitution for the purpose of planning future reconstruction of the nation; one should not rely only on its interpretation and application"), listed in nine provisions the "essential points of revision." Of these, the following were considered most important:

1. Make clear in particular that the Emperor in exercising the right of sovereignty shall rely on the support of the people.
2. Under the principal purposes for restricting the Emperor's constitutional prerogatives are: a) the Imperial Diet shall be able to propose its own dissolution; the Constitutional Provisions Deliberative Committee (composed of members of both houses) acting for the Imperial Diet, shall be able to petition the Throne directly to convene the Diet; and dissolution of the Diet shall not be repeated recklessly. b) With regard to urgent Imperial ordinances, they shall be referred in advance to the Constitutional Provisions Deliberative Committee. . . .
3. It shall be made especially clear that the command and organization of the armed forces are affairs of State.

4. Under the principal purposes of respecting the freedom of Japanese subjects: a) It is necessary to dispel the impression that under the present Imperial Constitution subjects have freedom of action only within the limits of the law. b) It shall be made especially clear that as a basic rule foreigners shall receive the same treatment as Japanese subjects.[39]

As is obvious at a glance, the influence of Atcheson's suggestions and advice from the secretary of state are clearly reflected in this document, although the basic structure of government established in the Meiji Constitution remains.

Meanwhile, Sasaki drew up a complete set of articles and provisions for a "draft constitution." The Sasaki draft comprised one hundred articles in all, using the Meiji Constitution as a model, and added a new chapter on "self-rule" (the autonomy of local groups). The basic structure of Sasaki's national government, however, was much closer to the Meiji Constitution than was Konoe's draft.

Article 1. The Empire of Japan shall be reigned over and governed by a line of Emperors unbroken for ages eternal.

Article 2. The Imperial Throne shall be succeeded to by Imperial male descendants, according to the provisions of the Imperial House Law.

Article 3. The Emperor is sacred and inviolable.

Article 4. The Emperor is the head of the Empire, combining in Himself the rights of sovereignty, and exercises them according to the provisions of the present Constitution.[40]

These four articles concerning the emperor are identical to those of the Meiji Constitution. Furthermore, in regard to human rights provisions such as freedom of speech, the Meiji Constitution states in Article 29: "Japanese subjects shall, within the limits of law, enjoy the liberty of speech, writing, publication, public meetings, and associations." Compare this to the Sasaki draft: "Japanese subjects shall have freedom of speech, writing, publication, public meetings and associations. For the benefit of the public necessary limits shall be determined by law." This did no more than define as public benefit or interest the broad legal reservations of the Meiji Constitution; as before, legal restrictions were provided.

The same was true with respect to freedom of the person (arrest, search, and seizure), and provisions regarding freedom of personal expression and religion. The draft does indeed contain a new right-of-life provision—"the right to enjoy the necessities of human life"—that the

Meiji Constitution definitely does not include. Generally speaking, however, Sasaki's draft never ventured beyond the basic framework of the Meiji Constitution.

Konoe presented his "outline" to the emperor on November 22; Sasaki followed two days later with a lecture to the emperor on his own "draft Constitution." For the moment, then, both Konoe and Sasaki had accomplished their immediate objectives. On the very day that Sasaki delivered his lecture at the palace, however, the Office of the Privy Seal was abolished on MacArthur's orders. The completion of Sasaki's special service meant, at the same time, the death of the Office of the Privy Seal itself. Konoe's fate was even crueler: On December 6 he was designated a war criminal suspect and ordered to surrender to the American military police. Ten days later, in his Ogikubo home, he ended his own life by taking potassium cyanide.

Premodern Soil

Konoe's scheme for constitutional reform thus collapsed. During the two months of his efforts, Konoe was made aware of the magnitude of Japan's "war crimes." The conclusion is hard to avoid that Konoe and his associates seemed only dimly aware of the fact that Japan had accepted the Potsdam Declaration as the basis of surrender and was under Allied military occupation, and that Konoe himself was soon to be designated a "war crimes" suspect.

The Potsdam Declaration promised clearly to eliminate "the authority and influence of those who have deceived and misled the people of Japan into embarking on world conquest" and to punish "all war criminals." Even so, Konoe believed that he had the qualifications and authority to assume responsibility for revising the constitution. Yet he was sadly lacking in an understanding of the urgent need to reform the emperor system. Neither Sasaki nor Takagi possessed much critical understanding of the nature of the imperial system included in the Meiji Constitution. There was no room in their minds for doubts about the system; to them it was eternal and immutable. Takagi, a "liberal," was Japan's leading authority on American political history. Of all the later constitutional reformers in the Japanese government or in civilian groups, only Takagi could have succeeded in drawing out the Americans' own ideas on reform. Perhaps for this reason alone he should be judged positively. But for Takagi as well as Sasaki, the emperor system was without question a fixed entity, even after the war. In December 1945, one month after Konoe's draft was presented to the emperor, Takagi noted in a lecture delivered at the Foreign Ministry:

This very system [emperor system] is socially the center of our people's lives; politically the foundation of our *kokutai*; and, it must be said, forms the pivotal idea of our constitutional system of government. There can be no doubt that its preservation is the collective desire of our people.[41]

The fact that the major articles of Sasaki's draft concerning the emperor replicated those of the Meiji Constitution indicates that for Sasaki, too, the emperor system was immutable. It is therefore surprising that a prominent scholar of constitutional law and a strong defender of the new constitution, Tabata Shinobu, former president of Dōshisha University, has said that it is unacceptable to view Sasaki's 1945 draft as reactionary. Tabata wrote:

Of course, one cannot deny that on the question of preserving the Emperor system, which runs throughout it, Sasaki's draft revision is conservative. However, one must also acknowledge that there are not a few points in the draft that are considered [by Sasaki] for the purpose of perfecting constitutionalism and democratization. In that sense it is unacceptable to consider [the draft] reactionary.[42]

When Sasaki received the imperial command from the Office of the Privy Seal and began collaborating with Konoe on revising the constitution, those who openly opposed the project—Matsumoto Jōji, Miyazawa Toshiyoshi, and others—were members of the Committee to Study Constitutional Problems. Most of the principal positions on this committee were held by graduates of Tokyo University, all of whom considered Sasaki's draft reactionary.

Tabata, on the other hand, had studied with Sasaki at Kyoto University. Furthermore, behind Tabata's exaggerated praise of Sasaki's draft is the undeniable fact that all those working with Konoe on constitutional revision were, like Tabata, alumni of Kyoto University: Konoe, of course; Privy Seal Kido, with whom Konoe discussed the selection of those who would assist him with the revision; and Hosokawa Morisada, who went to Kyoto to meet Sasaki. Of those on the Konoe team, only Takagi attended Tokyo University, and was a graduate not of the law department, as were many members of the committee, but of the political science department.

At the time, there was virtually no intellectual exchange between Tokyo and Kyoto; the gap between the two universities was figuratively equivalent to the distance between the eastern and western sides of the Pacific Ocean. There was not even a common forum for discussion. Konoe's initiative was like that of a feudal lord of one small province attempting to write a constitution for the whole country. Not until 1948 was there formed a national scholarly organization, the Japan Association of Public Law Scholars. Konoe's ideas for constitutional reform thus revealed quite by accident the premodern nature of Japan's scholarship on constitutional law.

MacArthur's meeting with Konoe and suggestion that he take the lead in revising Japan's constitution was the first indication of probing by both sides. In this first encounter, MacArthur misjudged the other party. Moreover, he never imagined that Konoe's involvement in the revision of the Japanese Constitution would produce such a strong negative reaction in the United States. After this abortive effort, MacArthur turned to his own trusted staff for advice on constitutional reform and excluded from the process his State Department political adviser, George Atcheson.

Atcheson wrote in a letter to the undersecretary of state on November 7: "General MacArthur, or his Chief of Staff and other members of his Bataan Club who act as his Privy Council or genro—wish if possible to keep the State Department out of this matter."[43] Rather than sending a telegram, Atcheson dispatched the letter by airmail, as the cable traffic was controlled by the U.S. military and a telegram would have been read by MacArthur's staff. One can judge the seriousness of this matter by noting Atcheson's reliance on communication that took a week to reach its destination.

On the Japanese side, amidst the collapse of Konoe's effort at constitutional reform, the government's Committee to Study Constitutional Problems now assumed leadership. Although the Shidehara cabinet had won its struggle with the Privy Seal, at the moment of victory the cabinet stood at an important crossroads for choosing the future direction of constitutional reform. This was an excellent opportunity to analyze the ideas for reform that the Konoe group had solicited from the Americans and to learn what had caused Konoe's failure.

Notes

1. Takemae Eiji, *GHQ* (Tokyo: Iwanami Shoten, 1983), pp. 45–46.

2. Kenpō chōsakai, *Kenpō seitei no keika ni kansuru shōiinkai dai kyūkai gijiroku* (hereafter, Kenpō chōsakai, *Kenpō seitei*), p. 3.

3. Zadankai, "Kenpō wa nishūkan de dekitaka," *Kaizō* (April 1952), p. 14, statement by Iwabuchi.

4. Sumimoto Toshio, *Senryō hiroku* (Tokyo: Mainichi Shinbunsha, 1965), p. 78.

5. Oka Yoshitake, *Konoe Fumimaro* (Tokyo: Iwanami Shoten, 1972), pp. 20 ff.

6. Okumura Katsuzō, "Konoe kōshaku to MacArthur gensui," in *Himerareta shōwashi,* ed. Hayashi Masayoshi (Kagoshima: Kagoshima kenkyūsho shuppankai, 1965), p. 268.

7. Ibid., p. 272.

8. Ibid., p. 276.

9. "Konoe kokumushō MacArthur gensui kaidanroku," Gaimishō gaikō bunsho, gaikō shiryōkan, microfilm reel no. A'0092.

10. The Acting Political Adviser in Japan (Atcheson) to the Secretary of State, October 10, 1945, *Foreign Relations of the United States* (hereafter, *FRUS*) (1945), 6:739.

11. Okumura, "Konoe kōshaku," p. 279.

12. The Acting Political Adviser in Japan (Atcheson) to the Secretary of State, October 4, 1945, *FRUS* (1945), 6:736.

13. Takagi Yasaka, "Nihon no kenpō kaisei ni taishite 1945 nen ni Konoe kō ga nashita kiyo ni kansuru oboegaki," (Kenpō chōsakai jimukyoku, *Kenshi: sō dai sanjūroku gō,* 1959), pp. 2–3.

14. The Acting Political Adviser in Japan (Atcheson) to the Secretary of State, October 10, 1945, *FRUS* (1945), 6:739.

15. Saitō Makoto and others, *America seishin o motomete: Takagi Yasaka no shōgai* (Tokyo: Tokyo Daigaku Shuppankai, 1985), p. 100.

16. *Asahi Shinbun,* October 13, 1945.

17. Kenpō chōsakai, *Kenpō seitei,* p. 45.

18. Matsumoto Jōji kōjitsu, "Nihonkoku kenpō no sōan ni tsuite," (Kenpō chōsakai jimukyoku, *Kenshi: sō dai nijūhachi gō,* 1958), p. 4.

19. *Mainichi Shinbun,* October 16, 1945.

20. Ibid.

21. Satō Isao, *Kenpō kaisei no keika* (Tokyo: Nihon Hyōronsha, 1947), pp. 20–21.

22. Ibid., p. 23.

23. Frank Kelley, *New York Herald Tribune,* October 26, 1945. Frank Kelley, a war correspondent, reported that he was not criticizing MacArthur, but questioning whether Konoe could advance the democratization of postwar Japan.

24. Sodei Rinjirō, *MacArthur no nisen nichi* (Tokyo: Chūō kōronsha, 1964), p. 164.

25. Inada Masaji, *Meiji kenpō seiritsushi no kenkyū* (Tokyo: Yūhikaku, 1979), p. 249.

26. Kenpō chōsakai, *Kenpō seitei,* p. 37.

27. John K. Emmerson, *Arashi no naka no gaikōkan,* trans. Miyaji Kenjirō (Tokyo: Asahi Shinbunsha, 1979), p. 227.

28. The Secretary of State to the Acting Political Adviser in Japan (Atcheson), October 16, 1945, *FRUS* (1945), 6:757.

29. Kenpō chōsakai, *Kenpō seitei,* p. 19.

30. *Asahi Shinbun,* November 3, 1945.

31. Ibid.

32. Kenpō chōsakai, *Kenpō seitei,* p. 39.

33. Baba Nobuya, "Senryō to Norman," *Shisō* 634 (April 1977): 58.

34. *Herbert Norman zenshū* (Tokyo: Iwanami Shoten, 1977), 2:345.

35. For a summary of the interrogation, see Thomas A. Bisson, *Nihon senryō kaisōki,* trans. Nakamura Masanori and Miura Yōichi (Tokyo: Sanseidō, 1983), pp. 208 ff.

36. Takahashi Hiroshi and Suzuki Kunihiko, *Tennōke no mitsushitachi* (Tokyo: Gendaishi shuppansha, 1981), p. 20.

37. H. E. Wildes, *Tokyo senpū* (Typhoon in Tokyo), trans. Inoue Isamu (Tokyo: Jiji Tsūshinsha, 1954), pp. 53–54.

38. The Acting Political Adviser in Japan (Atcheson) to President Truman, November 5, 1945, *FRUS* (1945), 6:827.

39. Satō Tatsuo, *Nihonkoku kenpō seiritsushi* (Tokyo: Yūhikaku, 1962), 1:212–213.

40. Tabata Shinobu, ed., *Sasaki kenpōgaku no kenkyū* (Kyoto: Hōritsu bunkasha, 1975), p. 311.

41. Gaimushō gaikō bunsho, microfilm reel no. A'0092.

42. Tabata Shinobu, *Sasaki hakase no kenpōgaku* (Kyoto: Ichiryusha, 1964), p. 161.

43. The Acting Political Adviser in Japan (Atcheson) to the Secretary of State, November 7, 1945, *FRUS* (1945), 6:837.

2

Restoration of the People's Rights Ideology

The Constitutional Research Association

Constitutions are always born at major turning points in history. In that sense, it was unprecedented that Konoe, representing Japan's old guard, drafted a constitution. It is more common perhaps for a constitution to be written by those who represent the new era. But postwar Japan was not a time of revolution. Because the old guard was still in power when many of the constitutional drafts were being written, the drafts are usually classified either as written by "government officials" or prepared by the "people," the latter being designated "private drafts."

It is uncertain when the phrase "private draft" began to be used. In Japanese constitutional history there were draft constitutions being produced by the People's Rights Movement of the 1880s well before the Meiji government wrote its own constitution. These were called *shigi kenpō*. If one is considering the process by which the Japanese Constitution was enacted during the course of Japan's modernization, it might be better to call private drafts *shigi kenpō*. But today the word shigi, much like the People's Rights Movement, has been forgotten; it is a dead word that is not even included in one of the most inclusive dictionaries, the *Kōjien*.

It is difficult to compare the Meiji Restoration and the postwar reforms in terms of popular participation in the reform of the state or in terms of the attempts of the masses to participate in this process. But if we consider only the private constitutions that were drawn up, the postwar period cannot compare with the late nineteenth century. Some sixty-eight private constitutions written in the Meiji period have been discovered,[1] whereas private constitutions in the postwar period number only in the teens. The scholar of children's literature, Samukawa Michio, has written about an apparently incomplete "Draft Constitution for the Building of a New Japan" that was produced by a labor union in a former munitions factory.[2] Although it is possible that anonymous private drafts have yet to be discovered, like the nineteenth-century versions discovered by Irokawa Daikichi one hundred years after they were written, it seems unlikely that they would ever surpass in number the "shigi kenpō" of the Meiji period.

The person who invariably comes to mind when we think of private constitutions in postwar Japan is Takano Iwasaburō. Takano became a faculty member at Tokyo Imperial University in 1906. Under the influence of his older brother, a labor movement activist, he became interested in labor, resigned his university post, and in 1920 founded the Ōhara Institute for Social Research, serving as president of the institute himself. Born in 1871, he was already at the advanced age of seventy-four when the war ended in 1945, but liberated from political oppression, he began the most active period of his life. In September 1945 Takano, along with Abe Isō and Kagawa Toyohiko, issued a statement calling for the reconstruction of the Socialist Party of Japan and organized the League of Japanese Men of Culture to build a democratic society and culture.[3]

The Socialist Party convened a general preparatory conference on October 25 for the purpose of rebuilding the party. It was at this conference that the question of revising the constitution was raised.[4] While the Japan Communist Party published its "Outline of a New Constitution" on November 11, Takano was behind the Socialist Party's attempts at constitutional reform at this very early stage. Furthermore, it was Takano who, at the founding meeting of the league, approached the young constitutional scholar, Suzuki Yasuzō, and proposed that he "do the research for private citizens that is needed to prepare for enactment of a new constitution." Takano's proposal certainly made a deep impression on Suzuki, who had continued his research on constitutional history despite considerable political repression. He recorded in his diary on that day: "The old doctor's vigor is indeed rejuvenating."[5] This was the point of departure for the Constitutional Research Association. Although consisting of only a small group of intellectuals, the association produced a draft constitution that is known to have influenced Government Section in MacArthur's headquarters when it later began work on a new constitution in early 1946.

Suzuki was forty-one at the time, young enough to be Takano's son. They met for the first time at the league's founding meeting, introduced by the literary critic, Murobuse Takanobu. Suzuki later recalled in his memoirs that Murobuse was present when Takano proposed the matter to Suzuki, and remembered Murobuse's words: "You should do it right away. You can use space at the Shinseisha [New Life Company]."[6]

Murobuse was a writer and editor of the newly established Shinseisha publishing company. Located in a corner of a building in the Uchisaiwaichō section of Tokyo, the company had just started publishing the monthly magazine *New Life* in November 1945. This period was indeed one of "new life" for Japan; some twenty-odd journals and magazines were published under this name during the early days of the Allied occupation.[7] Not only the name but the style and size of these monthly magazines were new.

Thus the Constitutional Research Association worked out of the conference room of the Shinseisha and received some financial support from the president of the company. The direction and activities of the association were not solely determined by Suzuki's connection with Takano; in fact, although Suzuki emphasized only this connection in his memoirs, his writings at the time suggest that another factor was the contact he had with members of the Allied occupation. In "The Fundamental Problem of Constitutional Reform," an editorial that appeared in the first issue of *Shinsei*, Suzuki wrote: "I frankly confess that I myself was alerted to the depth of this issue (constitutional reform) by conversations on two occasions with gentlemen of the Allied powers."[8] He told of meetings with a "certain diplomat" and a foreign "war correspondent" that had caused him to reflect carefully on the fundamental problems of constitutional reform.

Although he did not mention the identity of the "certain diplomat," it is likely that he spoke of the Canadian diplomat, E. H. Norman, then a member of General MacArthur's counter-intelligence division and the author of the memorandum denouncing Konoe Fumimaro as a war criminal. Norman, in a visit to Suzuki's home on September 22,[9] told Suzuki: "I think that making a thorough and fundamental criticism of Japan's 'kokutai' [national polity] is the basic prerequisite for the democratization of Japan."[10]

In his meeting with Suzuki the unknown war correspondent "asked whether it was not necessary to revise" Article 3 of the Meiji Constitution, which said that "The Emperor is sacred and inviolable." Suzuki replied that "this provision is natural for the head of the State, and especially considering the Japanese people's nationalist feelings, it would be best not to abolish this article." The correspondent countered with the argument that "leaving this article in a new constitution which ought to guarantee the right of the people to criticize everything, including the emperor, would be a contradiction."[11] In short, before initiating the work of the association, Suzuki had the opportunity to learn SCAP's basic thinking about a key provision of Japan's constitution.

In addition to Takano, Suzuki, and Murobuse, Sugimori Kōjirō, Morito Tatsuo, and Iwabuchi Tatsuo participated at the first gathering of the association on November 5, 1945. Suzuki Yoshio, Imanaka Tsugimaro, and Kimura Kihachirō were also present at every meeting, but the others were the principal members of the organization. Of the principal members, Suzuki Yasuzō was the only constitutional scholar (although as we shall see later, he was an outsider and far from being accepted in the legal academic community as a "scholar") and the first among the principal members.

Suzuki recorded in his diary on October 2 that he "wrote a draft of a revised constitution" immediately after he had met Norman.[12] On October 15 he was interviewed by the Dōmei News Service (presently the Kyōdō News Service), and on October 18 an interview with him appeared in an article in *Tokyo Shinbun* under the title "How Should the Constitution Be Changed?" Although the article was critical, we must consider it an expression of disapproval of the work on constitutional revision being done by Konoe and Sasaki, not by Suzuki. At the time Suzuki was considered to be an objective constitutional scholar, an image that is perhaps difficult to discern as we review the first half of Suzuki's life.

Members of the Association

Suzuki was born in Fukushima prefecture in 1904. He entered the Faculty of Letters at Kyoto University to study philosophy with Nishida Kitarō, but as his interest in Marxism grew, he joined the university's Social Science Research Institute and participated in what was then known as proletarian education. Before long he transferred to the Faculty of Economics. Continuing his Marxist activities, he was soon convicted of involvement in the "Gakuren Incident," the first case tried under the Peace Preservation Law (passed in 1925), and withdrew from the university. While in prison Suzuki continued his study of nation-states and after his release immersed himself in research on the history of constitutions. In 1933, while still in his twenties, he published *A Historical Study of Constitutions*, a critical examination of the constitutional history of France, Germany, and Japan. He then continued his research on the history of constitutions and comparative constitutional history. In 1937, with the appearance of his book *Problems of Modern Constitutions*, he was interrogated for violating the Publishing Law. Nevertheless, until 1945 Suzuki continued his study of the People's Rights Movement of the Meiji period, publishing in 1939 his book *People's Rights and Promulgation of the Constitution*.[13] Without a university appointment during any of this time, Suzuki was never more than an unaffiliated researcher.

For Suzuki, Japan's defeat in the war meant not only a restoration of the freedom of speech but also an opportunity to move toward the reality of revising the Meiji Constitution, which had long been the object of his criticism. The historical significance of the defeat was especially clear to Suzuki, a student of constitutional history who had particular interest in the private constitutions written during the years of the People's Rights Movement in the Meiji period. With his background Suzuki was certainly an apt talent for Takano.

The fact that Murobuse brought the two together might at first glance be considered surprising. A political critic, Murobuse had quite a different intellectual background than Takano and Suzuki. He had made his debut as a critic in the 1920s, a time when democracy in the Taishō period (1912–1925) was all the rage and capitalism was greatly admired. In the wartime atmosphere of the late 1930s he cooperated with the movement to create a new political structure [to replace existing political parties]. He also translated Hitler's *Mein Kampf* (1940) during this time. But the conditions of war seem not to have been to his liking and he quickly assumed an antimilitary stance, the penalty for which was that he was prohibited from publishing his writings from 1942 until Japan's defeat in 1945.[14] With the war at an end Murobuse could again become politically active. It is plausible that he judged that a period of democratization was at hand after Japan's surrender and—being quick to seize an opportunity—approached Takano and Suzuki at this time for the purpose of revising the constitution.

Murobuse did not, of course, forget to bring into the association Iwabuchi Tatsuo, who was known in prewar Japan as a behind-the-scenes operator in the political world. Iwabuchi, as we have seen, persuaded Konoe to meet with MacArthur in September 1945 to discover SCAP's policy toward Japan. Yet Iwabuchi held no official position and, in the spirit of a true outsider, later sharply criticized Konoe's effort at revising the constitution. On the other hand, Iwabuchi has since explained his motive for joining the Constitutional Research Association as follows: "I thought there was no alternative but to arouse interest in the private sector" if the Shidehara cabinet had no intention of [revising the constitution].[15]

Another of the association's first members was Morito Tatsuo. He and Takano had been comrades ever since the so-called Morito Incident in 1920, when Morito [who had been accused of advocating anarchism] had been forced to resign from Tokyo University. Found guilty in this incident and expelled from the university, he joined Takano's Ōhara Social Research Institute. Responding to a call from Takano after the war, he joined in the organization of the Japan Socialist Party. Subsequently, he won election to the House of Representatives of the Diet and in 1947 became minister of education in the Katayama cabinet. Having worked cordially with Takano most of the time before Japan's defeat, it was quite natural that he would become a member of this new research association.

Finally, there was Sugimori Kōjirō. Sugimori was of the same generation as Suzuki, though a bit older. After graduating from the philosophy department of Waseda University, he became a faculty member there and lectured on philosophy. Yet it was as a critic that he became known to the world. According to an admiring evaluation of Sugimori, "In the 1920s Sugimori was the biggest star in the world of journalism. His powerful individual style, creative thought and wide-ranging scholarly views were unmatched by anyone in the field. . . . His contemporaries included Murobuse Takanobu, Tsuchida Kyōson, Hasegawa Nyozekan and others, but compared to his their styles were flat and insipid."[16]

Soon after the war Sugimori published *Principles of World Human Rights* (1947), in which he made public his personal "Outline for the Building of a New Japan."[17] The outline contained fifteen principles, the first being "the best world view, namely, the desire to establish a sociological theory based on racial pride." By this Sugimori did not advocate the supremacy of the Japanese race, but rather "basically superior culturalism"—that is, the willingness to accept "all kinds of modern ideas."

He explained that by modern ideas he meant "science, individualism, democracy, socialism, and racialism [*minzokushugi*]." Sugimori's conception of the state recognized a fairly diverse set of values. Consequently, he thought very highly of the doctrine of respect for human rights set forth in the Potsdam Declaration, remarking that respect for fundamental human rights involves deep understanding and complete tolerance of humanity. The "power of creative thinking" that Sugimori spoke of connected in the final analysis with the "building of a world republican government." As Sugimori's ideas suggest, the association was a fairly liberal organization that included a conservative group along with its core of left-wing intellectuals.

The Association Writes a Draft Constitution

The second meeting of the association was held on November 14, 1945, and thereafter meetings took place every week on Wednesday afternoons. By the third meeting, held on November 21, the discussion of principles had ended, and Suzuki proceeded to put together a "Basic Outline for Enacting a New Constitution," the first draft based on the group's discussions of the previous weeks.[18]

On the question of the procedure for enacting a constitution, Suzuki proposed that "the Japanese Constitution should be abolished and a new democratic one adopted instead. When this is done, of course, the existing Constitution will not be an issue. The decision on a new constitution will be made by the people themselves at a conference convened to enact a constitution." That is, the procedure he proposed would not involve revising or amending the Meiji Constitution. Rather, a special constituent assembly, quite separate from the National Diet, would meet and enact an entirely new constitution.

Suzuki's proposal denied the emperor's sovereignty, asserting that sovereignty "proceeds from the people," but on the delicate issue of the monarchy his proposal provided for its reform, not its eradication. He wrote: "We think that it is desirable that Japan be made a republic. But considering the realities of the present stage of transition we are in, we believe that a temporary compromise on a constitutional monarchy with a strong democratic character" is in order. The emphasis on "a democratic character" was strengthened by several provisions; for example, concerning imperial succession, "while adopting a system of hereditary succession, the emperor's accession to the throne shall be subject to the approval of the Diet, and he shall take an oath to the Diet that he will respect and defend the Constitution." One can see here the clear influence of the various draft constitutions produced by the People's Rights Movement in the Meiji period. In an article submitted to *Shinsei*, Suzuki wrote that "in considering revision of Japan's Constitution, what we should reflect on today are the constitutional views of the People's Rights Movement." He called attention to the Risshisha's "Provisional Draft Constitution" of 1881, which provided that "after accession to the throne, the Emperor would take an oath to the people to preserve the tranquillity of the country by protecting the Constitution."[19]

Suzuki proposed to change the human rights provisions in the Meiji Constitution, under which the people were nothing more than "subjects" of the emperor. But he argued that "it is only natural that the concept of 'the people' ought to be established," and that all the reservations about people's rights in the Meiji Constitution, such as "within limits of the law" and "without violating their duties as subjects," should be entirely eliminated. At the same time, he argued, articles providing unfettered human rights should be incorporated into a revised constitution. However, he did not touch on provisions on participation in government, the right of spiritual freedom, or freedom of the individual person. He described in the following way the human rights that should be incorporated:

> I think that the new and concrete rights as those listed below ought to be provided for, not merely just freedom and rights in general.
>
> 1. The right to establish a new government.
> 2. The right to work and the freedom of association based on the right to work, and the right to be employed.
> 3. The right of rest and relaxation.
> 4. The right to protection when elderly, sick or unemployed.
> 5. The right of livelihood for workers, farmers and the middle class. A provision of equality of men and women in marriage, like article 119 of the Weimar Constitution, is especially needed in Japan with its strong feudalistic tradition.
> 6. A provision for freedom and protection of the arts, scholarship and education.
> 7. A guarantee of the equality of men and women.
> 8. A guarantee of the right of complete equality and complete abolition of racial discrimination.

I also think it is essential that there be a provision like article 148 of the Weimar Constitution to state clearly a fundamental policy of promoting education and culture.

As one can see from even a cursory reading of Suzuki's proposal, the Weimar Constitution was taken as a model and special emphasis was placed on social rights and the right of existence. In the items on legislation, administration, and finances, very large reforms were included, but none were very unusual. The special characteristic of the proposal was in the section on the judiciary, which specified that "judiciary officials shall be elected," and "a complete jury system shall be established." A jury system did exist under the Meiji Constitution—indeed, a Jury Law was passed in 1923—but the law was suspended in 1943 and has never been reinstated.[20] A complete jury system was a special characteristic of this draft constitution, a feature not to be found in others.

This initial draft underwent further changes in a meeting on November 29, 1945. Discussion and debate first centered on the position of the emperor. Further clarification occurred in the second draft with the adoption of two phrases: "The Sovereignty of Japan proceeds from the people" and "The Emperor is the source of honors and performs State rituals." In the section on the rights of the people, a clause was added as a general explanatory provision of the right of spiritual freedom: "No law shall be promulgated that places any restriction on academic and religious freedoms or the freedom of expression." Other provisions define the obligations of the people, noting especially "the obligation of perfecting the human personality based on democracy and pacifism and the establishing of social morality."

With respect to the judiciary, the first draft provided that "judges shall be elected." But Morito proposed a modification, pointing out that "if only the supreme court justices are to be elected, then there ought to be another provision that determines the laws that regulate the other parts of the judiciary." On the procedure for enacting a constitution, another suggestion by Morito was adopted. He proposed that

On the question of formality, it is necessary that the current Constitution be revised. Revision is necessary because even a bad law is still a law, and based on this premise we can then make a new Constitution. In other words, it will be necessary to revise the Constitution in two stages.

According to this procedure, the revised draft would be a temporary measure. Its first heading, "Outline Draft of a New Constitution," would change to "Outline of the Revised Constitution," and the constitution would be enacted by "reconvening the constitutional assembly ten years later." Although Suzuki agreed with this method of revision, he later wrote with deep emotion that "I myself believed that if such a constitution were to become law, the Japanese people would inevitably advance intellectually within ten years to the point where they would demand a republican form of government!"[21]

On December 1 this second draft was sent to members of the association. Ōuchi Hyōe responded with comments on the clauses dealing with public financial matters. A professor of public finance in the faculty of economics at Tokyo University, Ōuchi had been suspended at the time of the Morito Incident. Although he was reinstated, he was dismissed again two years later in another incident and had only returned to his post shortly after Japan's surrender. Ōuchi's proposals for strengthening the financial provisions of the draft were accepted and a third and final draft was produced.

The final draft included a number of other changes. The words "the right to establish a new government," adopted in the human rights provisions of the first draft, were omitted from the final draft because Murobuse believed that they were "not quite right."[22] The "prohibition of torture" was added as the basis of freedom of the individual person, and the provision on livelihood that provided that "the people shall have the right to maintain a standard of wholesome and cultured living" was made brief and to the point. This provision was later added to the postwar constitution by a proposal of the Socialist Party and survives in much the same form today as Article 25. Ōuchi's proposals on "accounting and public finance" were incorporated into the draft as provisions on the budget and fiscal-year system and a board of audit. The inclusion in the draft of a fiscal-year system reflected many years of painful experience with multiyear budgets for military spending.

At last the final draft emerged in clean copy. At this point the name was changed again from "Outline for a Revised Constitution" to "Outline for a Draft Constitution." Suzuki wrote as follows about the period from the completion of the work to the publication of the draft:

> The events stand out vividly in my mind even today. Unlike today, the one room of the building where we worked had no heating system and was very cold. We had no secretarial help, and whenever there was a change in wording or a revision, we had to recopy the whole thing from the beginning. Even though I was young, it was a very burdensome task.
>
> Sugimori, Murobuse and I carried two clean copies to the Prime Minister's office, as had been suggested at one of our meetings. We were told the Prime Minister wasn't in, so we strongly insisted on leaving a copy with his secretary, went straight to the press room, released it to the press, and returned to our office.

We asked Sugimori, who knew some English, to take a copy to MacArthur's headquarters. When we got back he reported that he had handed it over to an information officer at MacArthur's office. Since we had not made an English translation, he had presented the Japanese version.

At the time the press was under strict [U.S.] censorship, but two days later, on December 28, every newspaper carried our full draft constitution on page one.[23]

Suzuki says two important things here. One is that the date of publication of their draft was December 26. The date is often reported, even in scholarly works, as December 27. In other books that he has written Suzuki has stressed that it was indeed December 26.[24] That he would emphasize the date in this way is not unreasonable in light of the fact that some have continued to insist on December 27 as the publication date.[25] However, the English translation that was presented to SCAP is dated December 27. Suzuki wrote in *Kenpōgaku sanjūnen* that "an English translation was not made," and so it has been generally believed. But Alfred Hussey, who played a major role as a member of SCAP's Government Section in preparing the American draft, included in his papers, surprisingly, both Japanese and English versions of the "Outline for Draft Constitution" written in pen by someone who must have been Japanese. Moreover, they are both dated December 27, 1945.[26] Given the existence of these documents, it appears certain that the Suzuki group thought it better to prepare an English translation to present to SCAP.

Was the English translation the work of Sugimori? It is hard to believe that the translation—written in a quick, cursive style—was done by MacArthur's Allied Translation and Interpreters Section (ATIS). A comparison of the association's English translation and one by MacArthur's political adviser's office reveals how different were their views on constitutions. Before analyzing these views, however, let us first have a look at SCAP's evaluation of the final draft prepared by the Suzuki group.

SCAP showed a strong interest in the association's draft. On December 26 (or perhaps December 27) Americans were enjoying their Christmas vacation, the first Christmas after a long war. Despite this, SCAP was not taking a vacation. ATIS, after all, finished its translation of the draft on December 31. On January 2, 1946, George Atcheson, the political adviser, submitted a report on the draft to the secretary of state with a translation of the document attached.[27] Meanwhile, Government Section made a detailed analysis of the document and reported its findings to MacArthur on January 11.[28] We will look at the contents of this report in a moment, but first let us introduce the Japan Anarchist League, another organization that was paying close attention to the association's work.

The Anarchists' Declaration of Human Rights

According to Suzuki's recollection, Iwasa Sakutarō, chairman of the Japan Anarchist League, was present when the association held its meeting on January 16. Iwasa announced that "we would like to offer our Declaration of Human Rights as a preamble to your draft constitution, and I have brought a printed copy of it with me." Born in Chiba prefecture in 1879, Iwasa graduated from the Tokyo Institute of Law (now Chūō University) before going to the United States and becoming a socialist. At the time of the 1910 plot on Emperor Meiji's life, Iwasa sent an open letter from the United States to the Japanese emperor and government. In 1914 he returned to Japan and joined the anarchist movement. He was different from Ōsugi Sakae and others in the league, however, preferring to lead the movement as an activist rather than engage in theoretical disputes. He became the league's chairman in 1947. The draft, which Iwasa presented under the title "The Japanese People's Declaration of Human Rights," declared:

> We totally abolish the self-serving state organization which is founded on the control of people by people and on the exploitation of people by people, and in its place offer an example to the world that we can welcome the emergence of a new life and new society based on free initiative and propositions and free association of individuals who depend on humanity.
> We are human beings.
> We depend on our humanity and are absolutely free. We shall neither control nor exploit other people.
> We are all equal.
> Mother Earth does not say because you do not work, you shall receive no milk. And the Sun does not say because you are lazy or have sinned, you shall be given no light. To all brothers and sisters bread shall be given equally.[29]

Originally, anarchists did not recognize the state, or authority, and therefore law. Iwasa himself wrote as follows in "The Life of the State and Social Revolution," an essay composed immediately after the "Human Rights Declaration":

> Japan is at the crossroads of revolution or national ruin. I am a Japanese. I love Japan. I do not wish to see it die. Therefore, I propose that we should abolish not only the government which steals our food and clothing but the state which fetters the people with authority and laws, casts them into the extremes of suffering and continually puts the fatherland in imminent danger, and resolutely abolish constitutional government.[30]

It is clearly a logical contradiction for a man who said that "constitutional government ought to be resolutely abolished" to propose the preamble of a constitution. Yet, for Iwasa, the beginning of the postwar period was a time of such a powerful feeling of liberation that he wished to issue a "human rights declaration." And perhaps it was the association's draft constitution, a so-called charter of rights, that concretely expressed his feeling of liberation.

Takano Iwasaburō and His Draft Constitution

The association had certainly brought together a broad array of intellectuals, not all of whom were satisfied with the final draft. Takano Iwasaburō, "a republican to the core," found it difficult to embrace the group's draft because it did not reject the emperor system. To him it was a matter of regret that the draft, which he had taken a leading role in developing, was in conflict with his own views. From the end of November, when the draft constitution was nearing completion, Takano began writing his "Outline of a Constitution for the Japanese Republic." The date on the handwritten outline, which has been preserved at the Ōhara Institute at Hōsei University, is November 21, 1945. The date December 10 also appears on the document, but this seems to indicate a date of revision. As the association's draft had not yet been published, Takano handed his own outline draft to Suzuki with the comment, "I won't publish it for a while."[31]

The outline began with the fundamental principle of "abolishing the emperor system and adopting a republic with a president as the head." It is for this reason that the outline is known as the "Presidential System Constitution." It continues: "The Constitutions of the United States of America, the Soviet Union, Switzerland and the German Weimar Republic have been consulted." Takano included in his consultations the principal types of republican constitutions that existed at the time.[32]

Takano publicly announced his outline in early 1946 in the February issue of the journal *Shinsei*. First called a "private or personal outline," the name was then changed to "Outline of a Personal Proposal for a Revised Constitution," and a number of changes were made to the articles themselves. The significance of Takano's announcement was that it contained a rather long explanation of why a founding member of the association, who had already signed the group's outline draft, would then publish his own personal draft constitution. Moreover, a section with the heading "The Imprisoned Masses" began with the following sentence:

> The Japanese people appear in the eyes of the American Occupation forces as by and large unredeemable, imprisoned masses. It may sound arrogant of me to say so, but they appear the same way to me. Why is this so? On

this point please allow me first to explain the background of my own family.[33]

He recounted how, after his father's death, his older brother, to help support the family, had gone in 1888 to the United States, and while working as a laborer at various jobs under extremely difficult conditions, had thrown himself into the labor movement. Takano then wrote: "My late brother's labor union activities developed quite naturally. In precisely the same way, my views of democracy have developed naturally." He described his own intellectual experience. "During the years of my childhood and youth [he was born in 1872], French-style ideas of freedom and human rights were at their peak, and voices demanding the opening of a national assembly filled the land." In other words, raised in a period before the emperor system was firmly established, Takano believed that democracy was a very natural thing. In the period from about 1910 to the Japanese surrender in 1945 it was indeed the emperor system that departed from the norm. It was by no means strange, therefore, that Takano thought the masses had been imprisoned forever by the emperor system. It was natural for Takano to favor abolishing the emperor system, but he did so for reasons that were quite different from those of the Communist Party.

> Ours is a time of rapid change. The old ways have suddenly disappeared, and the new age of democracy has spread over the whole country. Why must we say we are so satisfied with this new age of democracy? In spite of everything, the majority of the people of our country still have not understood the true meaning of democracy. Their clinging as before to the notion of a kind of superstitious idol worship is something that, to someone like me who embraces a view of democratic government as developing naturally, is weird and painfully difficult to understand. It is for that reason that I must proclaim that the masses are imprisoned.[34]

For Takano, securing the Japanese people's agreement with the association's proposed constitution was a practical matter. Unlike Morito, Ōuchi, or Suzuki, who had known only the period of Taishō democracy and not the People's Rights Movement of the Meiji period, Takano possessed a different kind of passion in the postwar period. He conceived of postwar democracy not as Taishō democracy but as an extension of the People's Rights Movement of an earlier era. On one occasion Ōuchi agreed with Takano's proposal for a republican form of government, but then said that, seen from the people's perspective, it was premature. Takano replied with a sad, pained smile: "For you, too, Ōuchi?"[35]

The Communist Party aside, at a time when all the people were "imprisoned" by the "notion of a kind of superstitious idol worship," only Takano offered a "private draft constitution" calling for the abolition of the emperor system. His draft, first of all, established the principle of popular sovereignty, that "sovereignty resides with the Japanese people." Next, the people would elect their president, and he would be prohibited from standing for a third term of office. On the issue of the people's civil liberties, no limits would be set by law. And the plan envisioned the introduction of a jury system. These features suggest that Takano used the U.S. Constitution as a reference. On the other hand, one can also see the influence of provisions of socialist constitutions in passages such as "the land shall repose in the state" and "the means of production essential to the common welfare shall gradually be nationalized by vote of the Diet," and especially the influence of the constitution of the Soviet Union in provisions on the right of rest and recuperation and the eight-hour work day.

Takano wrote of his draft: "That defects abound is something that I myself am fully aware of." And, moreover, "I was considering the same kind of blueprint for Japan that I had learned from the book published in 1920 by the Webbs, *A Constitution for Socialist England.*"[36] Takano was appointed chairman of NHK (Japan Broadcasting Corporation) at the end of the year, however, and never had the opportunity to develop his "blueprint for Japan" before his death in April 1949.

The Socialist Party's Draft Constitution

In connection with Takano, it is essential that we look at another draft constitution, that of the Socialist Party. As we have already mentioned, the Socialist Party confronted the issue of constitutional reform shortly after the war. But preoccupation with the problem of forging a united front with the Communist Party prevented the socialists from completing work on their own draft constitution until January 18, 1946. The drafting committee was led by Hara Hyō and included such names as Takano and Morito of the Constitutional Research Association, Katayama Tetsu, Suzuki Yoshio, Unno Zenkichi, Kuroda Hisao, Nakamura Takaichi, Mizutani Chōzaburō, and Matsuoka Komakichi.[37]

Their "Outline of a New Constitution" was published on February 23.[38] At the beginning of the outline were "three criteria for enacting a new constitution," the first of which was "to state clearly the establishment of a democratic government and resolute action toward a socialist economy." Unfortunately, this statement was far from clear. First, as regards establishing democratic government, "sovereignty and governing power" were defined in the following way: "Sovereignty shall reside in the State (a cooperative body of the people, including the Emperor). Governing power shall be divided, the more important part shall be assigned to the National Diet and one part shall be assigned to the Emperor (broadly limiting the Emperor's prerogatives). The Emperor shall be retained."

In other words, the statement even denied the doctrine of popular sovereignty. There was no concrete provision for the right to participate in government nor for participation in the judicial system. Rather, the special feature of the draft is evident in the following statement: "The people shall have the right to live. Their livelihood in old age shall be protected by the State." We should note that these words suggest the influence of the constitution of Weimar Germany. This "right to life" provision and the abolition of capital punishment are seldom seen in other drafts.

The outline also called for the "resolute action toward a socialist economy," which is far from being indicated "clearly" in the draft. In fact, the draft devoted very little discussion to economic issues. It only singled out property rights in one article, stating that "property rights shall be limited for the common welfare." Compared to Takano's private draft, the Socialist Party draft provided relatively little depth or detail.

The Socialist Party draft is no more than a product of compromise between the left and right wings of the party. Especially where the emperor system is concerned, the draft is so fluid that one cannot imagine any agreement within the party on the concept of the people and the emperor sharing power as described in the "governing power" section of the outline. As we shall see later, according to Inada Masaji, who wrote the draft constitution of the Constitution Discussion Society (*kenpō kondankai*), the notion of joint rule by the people and the emperor originated in Inada's draft. Announcing in large headlines "The Emperor as Ceremonial Representative," *Asahi Shinbun,* which reported the Socialist Party draft, was very wide of the mark. But judging by the debate within the Socialist Party, it was perhaps not altogether wrong.

Toward the end of 1945 a newspaper called *Minpō* began publishing under the direction of Matsumoto Shigeharu, a former chief editor of Dōmei Tsūshin news service. *Minpō* played quite a significant role in constitutional reform, and its editorials were carefully read in MacArthur's headquarters. *Minpō* made the following prediction in an article on the Socialist Party's draft constitution even before it was made public:

> As General Secretary Katayama and Hara Hyō, a central figure of the committee, appear to prefer to assign to the power of the Diet all basic provisions which regulate the people's lives, and to assign to a symbolic and ceremonial Emperor the prerogatives to grant honors and amnesties as well as to represent the State in diplomatic relations, it appears that the outline will be formulated along these lines.[39]

In other words, at this stage of debate on the outline, it appeared that the Socialist Party's draft would retain the ceremonial position of the emperor as a "symbol," which was very close to the idea expressed in the Constitutional Research Association's draft. How this "symbolic" position and the terminology were produced by the party's drafting committee is not certain. But it is important to note that Katō Kanjū—known as a polemicist in the party, though not a member of the drafting committee— published a short piece at this time with the title "Constitutional Debate as Political Debate." In it he argued:

> In view of its historical development, the imperial institution should always exist as a ceremonial and ritual symbol of the harmony of the Japanese. The emperor system is a product of history; the fact that it is not absolute is something to which history truly attests. That is to say, as one can see from history, the imperial institution was frequently exposed to crises. The reason why the emperor's position was preserved in such cases was not because he was absolute. Rather, it was the common feeling of the Japanese, in various periods of their history, that it was in their mutual interest to avoid the disorder that would arise from the abolition of the emperor as an historical institution, and they thought that by protecting the emperor they could maintain the unity of the country.[40]

This short article appeared in the small journal *Jiron* (Commentary on Current Events), which ceased publication a few years later. The piece received little attention, but we should note when and where Katō wrote the article—"November 10 (1945), in my rural home"—and that it defined the emperor as a "ritual symbol" before the association's draft constitution was even published. Moreover, Katō's proposal of a "symbol of national harmony"—extremely close to the "symbol of the unity of the people" written in the Japanese Constitution—was very significant when we consider the fact that Katō was greatly appreciated in MacArthur's headquarters, as we shall see in detail later.

There is a strong tendency even today, almost fifty years after the constitution took effect, to attribute to SCAP the idea of the emperor's "status as a *shōchō*" (symbol). There is even a tendency to view the Japanese word as a direct translation of the English word "symbol." In fact, however, well before SCAP thought of the word "symbol," there existed in the Socialist Party a draft that used the Japanese equivalent, *shōchō*. At the same time, we must not forget that Katō perceived the idea of *shōchō* as being a distinctive "product of Japanese history" and as an institution that transcended an "act of State" as described in the present constitution.

The Communist Party's Draft Constitution

We turn next to the Communist Party's draft constitution. The situation of the Communist Party's draft was quite different from that of other political parties. The Communist Party, which became a legal political party as a result of Japan's defeat, formulated the party's "Key Points of a New Constitution" during its first national council on November 9, 1945. The outline contained the following six points:

1. Sovereignty shall reside in the people.
2. A democratic Diet shall administer sovereignty. The democratic Diet shall be based on the right of men and women over eighteen years of age to vote and to stand for election, and the democratic Diet shall elect the individuals who shall form the Government.
3. The Government shall be responsible to the democratic Diet. When it does not carry out the decisions of the Diet, when its execution of them is inadequate, when it perverts them, or when it acts improperly in other ways, the Government shall immediately be dismissed from office.
4. The people shall be free politically, economically, and socially, and their right to supervise and criticize the Government shall be guaranteed.
5. The people's right to live, right to work, and right to be educated shall be assured with concrete facilities.
6. Fundamental abolition of class and racial distinctions.[41]

This outline was published on November 10 in *Asahi Shinbun* and elsewhere. As luck would have it, the outline appeared at the very time that the government was setting up the Committee to Study Constitutional Problems and that the Constitutional Research Association was preparing its own draft. The six key points were literally points and nothing more, not even an outline, and their contents—reflecting the party's typical views—were not at all surprising. In any case, as only the Communists had at this time made public their conception of a constitution, it is undeniable that their outline had some influence on Takano and Suzuki, if not also on the government.

However, the Communist Party did not produce a full draft based on these key points during the period January to March of 1946, when other political parties and individuals were publishing drafts one after another. The Communists thought that a decision should first be made on carrying out a "democratic revolution," and a constitution should then be written to accord with the form of government that emerged.

In the meantime, the Japanese government issued in March 1946 its "outline" draft constitution, modeled closely on SCAP's draft, and published the complete draft in April. The special Diet elected to deliberate on the government's draft constitution began meeting on June 20. In short, the "revolution from above" began to move forward with great speed.

The Communist Party very belatedly finished its draft and published it on June 28, 1946. A declaration "On Publishing a Draft for a New Constitution" from the Central Committee's constitution committee was issued along with the "New Constitution [draft]." The original is handwritten and reproduced in mimeograph form; copies have been preserved in both the Japanese Foreign Ministry Archives[42] and in the United States National Archives.[43] The original conveys strongly the energy of the masses in the early postwar years.

The draft constitution of the Communist Party had the character of an alternative draft to that of the government. Both the Communist Party and government versions consisted of a preamble and one hundred articles. However, instead of the first chapter of the government's draft on "The Emperor," the Communist Party's draft had as its first chapter "Constitution of the People's Republic of Japan," which established the basic structure of the state. The draft contained no clause renouncing war but did say that "the People's Republic of Japan shall not support or participate in aggressive war." However, there were no provisions on the military, the right to engage in war, the right to organize a military force, or the obligation of military service. This is not surprising given the generally strong influence of Stalin's constitution. For example, Article 9 provided:

> The people shall have all freedoms of expression, publication, assembly and association, and the complete freedom of labor to protest and march in demonstrations shall be recognized.
>
> To guarantee this right the necessary material conditions for exercising it, such as access to printing, paper, the use of public buildings and communication facilities, shall be provided to democratic political parties and mass organizations.

This was different from the "bourgeois rights of freedom," which merely guaranteed "the right of expression" in the sense that the state would not interfere. Only in the Communist Party's draft constitution and in the earlier "key points" do we see a pledge "to provide the necessary material conditions" for *realizing the right of freedom*. This resembles Article 125 of Stalin's constitution:

> Compatible with the interests of the workers and for the purpose of strengthening the socialist system, the following are guaranteed by law to the citizens of the Soviet Union: the freedom of expression, the freedom of publication, the freedom of assembly and mass assembly, and freedom of street demonstrations and demonstration marches.
>
> These rights of citizens are guaranteed by providing to the workers and their organizations access to printing, paper, public buildings, streets, means of communication and other essential material conditions for exercising these rights.[44]

In addition, such guarantees as the right to rest, protection of working women, establishing day nurseries, and the right of persons over eighteen years old to vote reflect the influence of Stalin's constitution. Not all of the rights included in the Communist Party's version, however, came from the Soviet constitution. For example, the guarantee of housing and "liberating the great mansions and protecting debtors" and other provisions show the influence of the Weimar Constitution (Article 155), while abolishing capital punishment and introducing the jury system were either original ideas or originated in Anglo-American law.

Drafts of the Conservative Parties

We have introduced several private draft constitutions that relate to the "New Constitution," but these were only minority views being expressed by certain organizations and individuals. Let us look next at drafts produced by the ruling Liberal and Progressive Parties.

The Liberal Party, that is, the Japan Liberal Party, was formed in November 1945 as a successor of the prewar Seiyūkai, with Hatoyama Ichirō as president. Immediately after its founding the party set up a Special Committee to Investigate Constitutional Revision and began working on a draft. At a general meeting of the party on January 21, 1946, the committee adopted the so-called Liberal Party draft, the "Outline of a Revised Constitution."

The full text of this draft was published the following day in the newspapers. The clause on the emperor read as follows:

The possessor [shutai] of sovereignty shall be the Japanese State.
The Emperor shall be the superintendent of sovereignty.
The Emperor shall be of a line unbroken for ages eternal.
The Emperor shall have no responsibility either legally or politically.[45]

We see at a glance that the draft is not very different from the provisions on the emperor in the Meiji Constitution. It is true that these provisions and other provisions of the draft provide for the abolition of the emperor's prerogatives. And there are other passages in which the wording differs from the provisions of the Meiji Constitution, for instance, in "the freedom of thought, expression, religious belief, scholarship and practice of arts shall not be limited arbitrarily by law." On the whole, however, in fundamental ways the Meiji Constitution was the model for the draft.

Mainichi Shinbun commented on this in an editorial on January 23. After noting that "the Liberal party's proposal for constitutional revision, in a word, accepts the status quo," it said that "even if a constitution cannot be forever immutable, at the very least we must be most cautious about using only the present single period of history as a model or as a standard for constitutional revision."[46]

In his book *Nihonkoku kenpō seiritsu shi* (History of the Making of the Japanese Constitution), Satō Tatsuo provided a detailed analysis of the process by which this proposal for revision was written. It is significant that the members of the Special Committee to Investigate Constitutional Revision were Andō Masazumi, Kanamori Tokujirō, Asai Kiyoshi, Yoshida Hisashi, Higai Senzō, Kure Bunpei, and Hasegawa Nyozekan. Neither Chairman Higai, who was preparing for his campaign for election to the House of Representatives, nor Kure, who was president of Nihon University, ever attended the committee's meetings. Andō served as chairman; Hasegawa expressed his views in a very general way; and Yoshida, a former director general of the Supreme Court, had a special interest in the judiciary. Asai (dean of the faculty of law of Keiō University) and Kanamori (former director general of the Cabinet Legislation Bureau) were generally the ones who had a deep interest in preparing the outline.[47] This is a fact of great interest, as just half a year later Kanamori became the state minister in the Yoshida cabinet in charge of constitutional revision. Through his responses to questions in the Diet Kanamori became the most ardent protector and foremost interpreter of the "New Constitution," which resembled in some respects the Liberal Party's draft.

Next, the Progressive Party's draft was adopted at a general meeting of the party on February 14 and was published in the newspapers the following day.[48] It was called an "outline"; the word "draft" was not used. However, the contents of the outline, like other policies of this party, were quite the reverse of "progressive" and contained virtually nothing that was different from the Meiji Constitution. The outline stipulated that the prerogatives of the emperor, for example, had to be submitted to the deliberation of the Diet. Concerning the "rights of subjects," such as freedom of expression, the draft provided that "laws limiting freedom may not be enacted except in cases where necessary to preserve public peace and order." The rights section of the draft was, in short, much like that of the Meiji Constitution and ironically contained little that was "progressive."

Draft of the Constitution Discussion Society

Following the publication of the draft constitutions of the two conservative parties, a draft constitution by the Constitution Discussion Society was published. Generally, constitutional scholars had little to do with preparing the earlier unofficial draft constitutions. The exception, as we have already noted, was Suzuki Yasuzō, a specialist in constitutional history who was involved in preparing the Constitutional Research Association's draft. The principal figure of the Constitution Discussion Society was Inada Masatsugu, who, like Suzuki, was a scholar of the history of the framing of the Meiji Constitution and a professor of science and literature at Tokyo University. Inada was already giving thought to the need to revise the constitution when the war ended. In May 1945, when Japan's defeat was certain, he wrote a memorandum in his diary titled "Political Reforms That Must Be Carried Out After the War" and listed revision of the Meiji Constitution as one such reform.[49] With this in mind, Inada wrote to his friend Ozaki Yukio, urging the necessity of constitutional reform, but Ozaki replied that "I don't think it is necessary to revise the Constitution." Nevertheless, Inada proceeded to prepare his own personal draft and on February 24, 1946, submitted it to the Shidehara government's Committee to Study Constitutional Problems, which had been organized the previous October.

Inada's draft generally took as its model the British Constitution and followed the articles of the American Constitution. It left the Meiji Constitution's chapters as they were and only indicated points that should be amended. The result was that, much like the Socialist Party's draft, "joint sovereignty by the Emperor and the people" formed the foundation. The guarantee of human rights was also expanded. Inada then enticed Unno Kyukichi, an attorney, to help him strengthen and polish his draft. This was at the end of January 1946, and Unno was already a member of the committee that was working on the Socialist Party's draft constitution. As we have seen already, it was at this point that the concept of "joint sovereignty of the Emperor and the people" was incorporated into the Socialist Party's draft. Thus it seems safe to say that Unno played a large role in the formulation of the Constitution Discussion Society's draft. When the draft was in its final stage Inada took it to Ozaki Yukio, who was staying at the villa of Iwanami Shigeo; both Ozaki and Iwanami expressed their approval and signed it.

The society's draft constitution was thus submitted to the Japanese government on March 4, 1946. Along with this "Draft Constitution of Japan," complete with fifty articles, was an "explanation" of the document. The final draft was generally not very different from the draft that Inada had written, although the way it was organized deserves further attention. Chapter 1 contained "Principles," including the provision of "joint sovereignty of the Emperor and the people," and was followed by Chapter 2, "The Rights and Duties of the People," and Chapter 3, "The Emperor." But when writing the "Principles" in the first chapter, Unno proposed inserting the following: "Article 5. Japan shall be a civilized country not possessing military armaments."

Although in the end it was eliminated from the draft, the article and events surrounding it are recalled by Inada.

> This article five was an independent proposal from Unno, who emphasized disarmament and pacifism if Japan was to be a cultured nation without armaments. When he and I discussed it, I expressed my belief that the article should be deleted and instead a statement emphasizing pacifism placed in the preamble. Without defending his position, Unno simply agreed. When I think about it now, we ought to have kept Unno's article pledging that Japan would not have armaments. I deeply regret that we deleted it.[50]

Thus even the "renunciation of war" in the present constitution, which is said to have been imposed on Japan by MacArthur, existed—though in an incomplete form—as a proposal in a Japanese private draft constitution.

Finally, let us mention the Constitutional Research Committee of Tokyo University. This committee was first proposed by the university's president, Nanbara Shigeru. The committee had a chairman, Miyazawa Toshiyoshi, and six special members, including Takagi Yasaka, Suehiro Gentarō, and Watsuji Tetsurō. The committee began its activities with twenty regular members, seven from the faculty of law, three from letters, and three from economics.[51] The committee, with its many luminaries as members, got off to an auspicious start, but it was already too late. The committee began meeting on February 4, 1946, and only twenty days later the government published an outline of its draft constitution. The Tokyo University committee, which from the outset was intent on studying the Meiji Constitution, essentially ended up concentrating its efforts on the government's draft, as it appeared before the committee could prepare its own.

After investigating these private draft constitutions, we have come to see that some of them were quite close to the MacArthur draft constitution that would come later. It is true, of course, that these private drafts were always written by only a small group of men. However, in periods of radical change it is often the case that the minority overthrows the majority. Not everything is determined by numbers and quantity. Of the drafts we have examined, the one most like the SCAP draft—and as we shall see later, the one most appreciated by SCAP—was the draft prepared by the Constitutional Research Association. Takano Iwasaburō and Suzuki Yasuzō were the heart of this group. Takano grew up breathing the ideas of the People's Rights Movement of the Meiji period. During the war Suzuki studied the movement's constitutional ideas. When we contemplate these two men and their backgrounds, we might say that— through these two historical successors of the constitutional ideas of the

People's Rights Movement—the Constitutional Research Association's draft signified the movement's revival after the agony of half of a century of suppression.

Notes

1. Irokawa Daikichi, "Jiyū minken undō to Suzuki Yasuzō," in *Nihon kenpō kagaku no shokō* (Tokyo: Keisō Shobō, 1987), p. 21. Irokawa's *Jiyū minken* (Tokyo: Iwanami Shoten, 1981), p. 105, lists forty varieties.
2. Samukawa Michio, *Ningen kyōshi to shite ikuru* (Tokyo: Shin Hyōron, 1978), p. 290.
3. Ōshima Kiyoshi, *Takano Iwasaburō den* (Tokyo: Iwanami Shoten, 1968).
4. *Asahi Shinbun*, October 26, 1945.
5. Suzuki Yasuzō, *Kenpōgaku sanjūnen* (Tokyo: Hyōronsha, 1967), p. 214.
6. Kenpō chōsakai, *Kenpō seitei*, p. 3.
7. The word *shin* (new) was used in the titles of many books and journals at the time, even "New Police." See Okuizumi Eisaburō, ed., *Senryōgun ken'etsu zasshi mokuroku* (Tokyo: Ōshōdō Shoten, 1982).
8. Suzuki Yasuzō, "Kenpō kaisei no konpon ronten," *Shinsei* 1, no. 2 (December 1945): 23.
9. Interview with Professor Suzuki at his home in Tokyo, July 20, 1981. He consulted his diary during the interview.
10. Suzuki, "Kenpō kaisei," p. 24.
11. Ibid.
12. Suzuki Yasuzō, *Kenpō seitei zengo* (Tokyo: Aoki Shoten, 1977), p. 73.
13. Nagai Ken'ichi, comp., "Professor Suzuki Yasuzo's Career and Publications," in *Kenpō chōsakai sōhihan*, ed. Arikura Ryōkichi (Tokyo: Nihon Hyōronsha, 1964), pp. 361 ff. Also, Kaneko Katsushi, "Suzuki Yasuzō sensei no shisō to gakumon," *Hō to minshushugi*, no. 187 (May 1984): 18–19.
14. Yamaryō Kenji, "Journalist no tenkō," *Shisō no kagaku* (July 1962).
15. "Zadankai: Kenpō wa nishūkan de dekitaka," *Kaizō* (April 1952): 16.
16. Ii Gentarō, "Sugimori Kōjirō to Nihon bunka no kindaika e no kōken," *Waseda daigaku seiji keizaigaku zasshi*, no. 177 (October 1962): 162.
17. Sugimori Kōjirō, *Sekai jinken no gensoku* (Tokyo: Kenshinsha, 1947), pp. 68 ff.
18. Suzuki, *Kenpō seitei zengo*, p. 77.
19. Suzuki, "Kenpō kaisei," p. 25. The Risshisha was a political organization founded by Itagaki Taisuke in the 1870s.
20. Miyamoto Saburō, *Baishin saiban* (Tokyo: Equality, 1987), p. 46.
21. Suzuki, *Kenpō seitei zengo*, p. 85.
22. Kenpō chōsakai, *Kenpō seitei*, p. 15.
23. Suzuki, *Kenpō seitei zengo*, pp. 101–102.
24. Suzuki, *Kenpōgaku sanjūnen*, p. 259.
25. For example, both the first (1968) and second (1984) editions of *Nihon kindai sōgō nenpyō* (Iwanami Shoten) give the date as December 27.
26. Hussey Papers, reel no. 6, kokkai toshokan shozō.
27. Ibid., reel no. 5.

28. Takayanagi Kenzō and others, *Nihonkoku kenpō seitei no katei* (Tokyo: Yūhikaku, 1972), 1:27 ff.

29. Suzuki, *Kenpōgaku sanjūnen,* pp. 264–265.

30. Iwasa Sakutarō, "Kokka no seimei to shakai kakumei," *Kakumei danso* (1958), pp. 118–119.

31. Suzuki, *Kenpō seitei zengo,* p. 90.

32. This reference was omitted when the draft was published in the February 1946 issue of *Shinsei.*

33. Takano Iwasaburō, "Torawaretaru minshū," *Shinsei* 2, no. 2 (February 1946): 2.

34. Ibid.

35. Suzuki, *Kenpō seitei zengo,* p. 93.

36. Takano, "Torawaretaru minshū," p. 6.

37. *Mainichi Shinbun,* January 19, 1946.

38. *Asahi Shinbun,* February 24, 1946.

39. *Minpō,* February 16, 1946.

40. Katō Kanjū, "Seijiron to shite no kenpōron," *Jiron* (January 1946): 37.

41. *Asahi Shinbun,* November 12, 1945.

42. Gaimushō gaikō bunsho, microfilm reel no. A'0091.

43. Draft Constitution Proposed by the Japan Communist Party, July 9, 1946, U.S. National Archives, 894.011/7–946.

44. Takagi Yasaki and others, *Jinken sengenshū* (Tokyo: Iwanami Shoten, 1957), pp. 294–295.

45. *Mainichi Shinbun,* January 22, 1946.

46. *Mainichi Shinbun,* January 23, 1946.

47. Kenpō chōsakai jimukyoku, *Asai Kiyoshi shi ni kiku* (July 1961), p. 2.

48. *Asahi Shinbun,* February 15, 1946.

49. Inada Masaji, "Sengo kenpō shian kisō no keika," *Fuji ronsō* 24, no. 2 (November 1979): 1–2.

50. Ibid., p. 19.

51. Wagatsuma Sakae, "Shirarezaru kenpō tōgi: seiteiji ni okeru Tokyo teikoku daigaku kenpō kenkyū iinkai hōkokusho o megutte," *Sekai,* no. 200 (August 1962): 50 ff. Although the discussion had absolutely no influence on the framing of the constitution, Wagatsuma's short paper apparently received some attention at the Constitutional Problem Research Society (Kenpō mondai kenkyūkai), for it is included as a chapter in a book published by the group, *Kenpō to watakushitachi* (Tokyo: Iwanami Shoten, 1963).

3

Captive Legal Scholars:
The Committee to Study
Constitutional Problems

Establishing the Committee

The Committee to Study Constitutional Problems (often referred to as the "Matsumoto Committee") was created by the Shidehara cabinet on October 25, 1945. The purpose was not to initiate the process of revising the constitution, for the work of constitutional reform had, as we have seen, started in earnest in the Office of the Privy Seal. Moreover, that this cabinet committee did not have constitutional reform as its purpose may be gathered from its name. The committee chairman himself, State Minister Matsumoto Jōji, explained the nature of the committee in this way: "Since the main purpose of this committee is to undertake a scholarly study, we are not thinking of preparing a draft even if we reach the conclusion that it is necessary to revise the Constitution."[1] In addition, the committee was, according to an understanding reached at a cabinet meeting, an unofficial body.[2]

The committee members, nevertheless, were indeed men of distinction. While there were some changes in membership along the way, the principal members did not change. At the outset they were:

Chairman: Matsumoto Jōji, state minister and former professor of Tokyo University;

Advisers: Shimizu Tōru, vice-president of the Privy Council and member of the Imperial Academy; Minobe Tatsukichi, member of the Imperial Academy and professor emeritus of Tokyo University; Nomura Junji, professor emeritus of Tokyo University;

Members: Miyazawa Toshiyoshi, professor of Tokyo University; Kiyomiya Shirō, professor of Tōhoku University; Kawamura Mata-

suke, professor of Kyushu University; Ishiguro Takeshige, chief
secretary of the Privy Council; Narahashi Wataru, director general
of the Legislation Bureau; Irie Toshio, deputy director general of
the Legislative Bureau; Satō Tatsuo, councillor in the Legislation
Bureau;
Assistants: Osakabe Tsuyoshi, associate professor of Tokyo University; and Satō Isao, instructor of Tokyo University.

No one from Kyoto University was involved, although initially Sasaki
Sōichi was invited to participate. Because he had served as a special assistant to the Office of the Privy Seal to help with Konoe's work on constitutional reform, Sasaki declined the appointment to the cabinet committee.[3] The original intention, it seems, was to make use of leading
scholars of constitutional law at the imperial universities. If that is the
case, however, why was Matsumoto, who had almost no previous connection with the constitution, appointed committee chairman? Before the
war Matsumoto was well known as a scholar of commercial law, but had
published nothing on the state or in the fields of political science or constitutional law. In later years Matsumoto explained the circumstances of
his appointment in this way:

> Concerning my relation with the work of constitutional reform, I had no de-
> sire to be involved and had no idea that I would have anything to do with it.
> One night in early October, 1945, Foreign Minister Yoshida [Shigeru] came
> to my house. He told me that the cabinet had changed and that a cabinet
> with Shidehara as its head had been formed. And he asked me if I would ac-
> cept appointment as head of two ministries with extremely important re-
> sponsibilities. I declined, saying that I could by no means do such important
> work. He then asked if I wouldn't in any case join the cabinet in some capac-
> ity. As it happened, at that time the position of Minister without Portfolio ex-
> isted. With the country in such a crisis, I couldn't just remain idle, and so I
> promptly consented to serve if it were as a Minister without Portfolio. . . . In
> the cabinet there were jurists such as Iwata Chūzō as Minister of Justice, my-
> self as Minister without Portfolio, and others as well; but in point of fact nei-
> ther of us were constitutional specialists. I, especially, knew little about the
> Constitution. But as a result of having proposed so many things, and be-
> cause Iwata had a great deal of work at the Ministry of Justice, it happened
> that I was put in charge. I accepted the appointment at a cabinet meeting in
> mid-October.[4]

We see from this quote that Matsumoto was appointed chairman of the
cabinet committee by a process of elimination rather than on his merits,
and that Yoshida's strong insistence was behind his becoming a cabinet

member. In short, Matsumoto was a politician-scholar (or more of a politician than a scholar) whom Yoshida favored. Matsumoto's greater political bent becomes clear as we review his career.

A Profile of Chairman Matsumoto

Matsumoto was one year older than Yoshida Shigeru. Born in 1877 after his father returned from a period of study in the United States, Matsumoto is said to have been named Jōji after the first U.S. president, George Washington. He became a professor of Tokyo University in 1909, specializing in commercial law. In 1913 he assumed the additional duty of councillor in the cabinet's Legislation Bureau. Subsequently, he resigned from Tokyo University when he was appointed a director of the Manchurian Railway Company, and later became vice president of the company. In 1922 he became director general of the Legislation Bureau in the Yamamoto cabinet and minister of commerce in the Saitō cabinet ten years later. Matsumoto was also a lawyer. Active in commercial law, he earned a reputation "for his work as an auditor and consultant of numerous corporations, and as the leading legal spokesman of the financial world."[5]

On the other hand, Matsumoto excelled at nepotism; his father was a director general of the National Railway Bureau. Koizumi Shinzō (president of Keiō Gijuku University) was his brother-in-law, and Tanaka Kōtarō (minister of education in the Yoshida cabinet, and later chief justice of the Supreme Court and justice of the World Court) was his son-in-law. Judgments of Matsumoto's character vary, but all agree that he possessed a sharp mind and an abundance of confidence in himself. One of Matsumoto's students, Suzuki Takeo, a scholar of commercial law and Tokyo university professor who in 1938 assisted in revising the Commercial Code, recalls: "Our meetings had the feeling of a one-man stage for Professor Matsumoto. Such brilliance—advancing his own opinion, demolishing opposing arguments, drafting provisions. He has been described as having the finest mind of his generation, and I think that is fully justified. We were always in awe of him."[6]

The constitutional scholar, Satō Isao, who worked with Matsumoto as an assistant in the cabinet committee, also recalls Matsumoto's way of managing the committee:

> Matsumoto sensei literally presided over the committee. I marveled at his erudite and minute arguments, just as though he were indeed a scholar of constitutional law, even though this was outside his area of expertise. I felt that he provided proof of the fact that a prominent scholar can excel in any

field. Another thing I felt as I observed his style of presiding over the committee was that he was a man brimming with self-confidence. That is, whatever the issue was, he had his own strongly held views.[7]

Both Suzuki and Satō were many years younger than Matsumoto; moreover, since they were paying tribute to him at a memorial service, their comments were quite reverent. Yet they do convey to us something of Matsumoto's personality. Indeed, in the committee sessions only Minobe and young Miyazawa regularly opposed the "brilliant" and "confident" Matsumoto.

Late in October 1945 Minobe published in the pages of *Asahi Shinbun* three articles on the problem of constitutional reform, in which he said, "I urgently hope that under the present critical conditions revision of the Constitution can be avoided."[8] He opposed reform for the moment, but he then proposed in a *Mainichi Shinbun* article reform of the Imperial Diet, not by amending the constitution but within the limits set by it.[9]

Like Minobe, Miyazawa was also opposed to revising the constitution. On September 28, 1945, he lectured at the Japanese foreign ministry on Japan's acceptance of the Potsdam Declaration and revision of laws and the constitution. He touched on three points contained in the Potsdam Declaration: territorial change, the dissolution of the military, and the promotion of democratic tendencies, finding objections to all of them. With respect to territorial change, since the constitution already contained provisions on territory, no revision was required. Concerning abolition of the military, laws and constitutional provisions that provided for obligations of military service, martial law, and emergency powers would "lose their reason for being." And concerning the encouragement of democratic tendencies, he said that "the Imperial Constitution does not deny democracy," listing the provisions on the emperor's powers and the parliamentary and judicial systems as three points that ought to be amended "in order to encourage more development of democracy."

Finally, he indicated a very cautious attitude toward revision by saying that while one "may consider the existence of a provisional Constitution, one should not act hastily in undertaking revisions of the Constitution."[10] It is doubtful that this lecture was generally known outside the foreign ministry, but Miyazawa did express very similar views in the pages of the *Mainichi Shinbun*.[11]

In short, it seems accurate to say that the Committee to Study Constitutional Problems, whose principal members held almost identical views on the issue of revising the constitution, proceeded ahead under the leadership of the "brilliant" and "confident" Matsumoto.

From Investigation to Reform

The committee held general meetings in which all members and advisers participated, and investigation or study sessions in which only the members participated. From October 27, 1945, to February 2, 1946, seven general meetings were held, and from October 30, 1945, to January 2, 1946, fifteen study sessions were held. At the committee's general meetings broad policy and research topics were discussed and decided. Based on the committee's decisions, the research subcommittee then proceeded to do its work.[12]

At the first general meeting of the committee on October 27, 1945, some debate on fundamental questions did take place. To begin with, Matsumoto repeated his view about the committee's objectives that he had expressed when the committee was first created: "It is unnecessary at this time to debate the pros and cons of constitutional revision." But one of the advisers, Nomura Junji, asked whether in connection with the Potsdam Declaration's statement about "revising and strengthening democratic tendencies," would "the committee . . . have also to touch on articles one and four to complete democratization? The United States will certainly mention them." Article 1 of the Meiji Constitution provided for continuity of imperial rule: "The Empire of Japan shall be ruled over and governed by a line of Emperors unbroken for ages eternal." Article 4 provided for imperial sovereignty: "The Emperor is the head of the Empire, combining in Himself the rights of sovereignty, and exercises them according to the provisions of the present Constitution."

In other words, revising these two articles would necessarily change the very foundations of the Meiji Constitution. Matsumoto responded that "since the Potsdam Declaration says that this issue shall be determined by the free will of the Japanese people, even America cannot forcefully order it. The general will of the Japanese people is as unmovable as a mountain. Therefore, there is no need to mention articles one and four. It is simply not the case that Japan cannot be democratic without revising articles one and four. Although there are many things that should be revised, I consider this part of the constitution permanent."[13] The statement reveals "Matsumoto the Confident," and since Minobe agreed with him, the committee, guided by Matsumoto's decision, moved on to other issues.

Taking the statement to represent a consensus of the whole committee, the research subcommittee convened its first meeting and, in addition to omitting Article 1 and 4 as irrelevant, decided to study all other articles of the Meiji Constitution. Miyazawa set the meeting's agenda with this as the "research theme." It is important to note at this point that the whole investigation took the Meiji Constitution as the point of departure. It undertook no fundamental spadework, such as comparing the Meiji Constitution with foreign constitutions. "Research" was defined from a narrow perspective. A study was done of the constitutional provisions and legal precedents of foreign countries, but only at the final stage of the investigation. Further, one can see in their research little indication of the use of reference works.

The research subcommittee had begun its work on the premise that the constitution would not be revised. At the second general meeting, however—a dinner meeting that convened immediately after MacArthur's repudiation of Konoe and included Prime Minister Shidehara in attendance—chairman Matsumoto redefined the committee's objective in the following comments:

> The circumstances both foreign and domestic in which Japan finds itself today are most urgent. Politically, nothing is likely to go smoothly. Consequently, we must obviously expect that something definite will have to be done in the very near future about the problem of constitutional reform. We must make preparations for that eventuality without being confused or bewildered. In short, we must be prepared to respond to demands for constitutional revision from the outside as well as from within. For the time being, we must be content to investigate the large issues of constitutional reform and urgently examine those articles which we cannot avoid revising.[14]

Driven now by Matsumoto's decisive about-face, the committee had to "examine carefully the large issues and the urgent articles." During the next two general meetings and three subcommittee meetings, the committee completed an examination of almost the entire Meiji Constitution and on November 24 distributed a printed copy of its members' collective views on revision.[15] It is clear from this early committee report that a consensus had been reached on Article 1 and 4, the general opinion being—as Matsumoto had already told Nomura—that they "require no revision."

Two major issues were debated in the report. The first had to do with provisions limiting the powers of the emperor. For example, Article 8 of the Meiji Constitution provided that the emperor "in consequence of an urgent necessity when the Imperial Diet is not sitting" had the power to issue Imperial ordinances "in the place of law." A majority of the committee members agreed to change this to "urgent Imperial ordinances shall be referred to a permanent committee of the Imperial Diet." Likewise, a proposal was made to revise Article 11 on the emperor's right of supreme command over the army and navy, and Article 12, the emperor's authority to determine "the organization of the different branches of the administration and salaries of all military officers." The words "army and navy" would be changed to "armed forces," and the administration and salaries of the armed forces would be "determined by law." It was also decided that Article 31, on the authority of the emperor in times of war or national emergency, "shall be deleted."

The second issue was the revision of constitutional provisions regarding the rights of the Japanese people. No significant amendments to these provisions were proposed, however. For example, on freedom of religion, Article 28 read: "Japanese subjects shall, within limits not prejudicial to peace and order, and not antagonistic to their duties as subjects, enjoy freedom of religious belief." The committee proposed to change this to "freedom of religious belief shall be enjoyed within the limits of the law." Because of its relation to the later government draft, the part of the discussion that deserves attention was the following statement, supported by a majority of the committee: "There shall be no compromise in providing as a matter of principle that foreigners shall be accorded the same treatment as Japanese subjects."

With the controversial issues resolved and the closing of the 89th Imperial Diet at hand, Matsumoto, in response to a question in the Diet on December 8, made public for the first time the general direction of constitutional revision. Ironically, this day was the fourth anniversary of the outbreak of the war between the United States and Japan, a fact that most likely eluded Matsumoto at the time. Following is a summary of what later became known as "Matsumoto's Four Principles."[16]

1. No change shall be made in the basic principle that the Emperor shall exercise the right of sovereignty.
2. Expand the number of issues which require decisions by the Diet, and as a result, restrict to some extent those which in the past have been called matters of Imperial sovereignty.
3. Extend the ministers of state's responsibility to all matters of State, and reduce the scope for those others than ministers of state to interfere in State affairs. And, at the same time, make the ministers of state responsible to the Diet.
4. Strengthen guarantees of the people's rights and freedoms. That is, the people shall not be restricted by laws and regulations that are not made by the Diet. And, on the other hand, measures shall be adopted to prevent violations of their rights and freedoms.

Matsumoto later said of this speech: "It might have been better if I had said nothing. . . . I thought I would make a very vague statement. . . . I didn't discuss it with anyone else. And I didn't have anything written out."[17] He claims to have spoken in an extemporaneous, offhanded manner. But if we look at the details contained in his statement, we cannot accept this. At the committee's dinner meeting with Prime Minister Shide-hara, the general direction of revision had already been mentioned. Moreover, the committee later conducted an examination of the entire Meiji Constitution, and the majority opinion was expressed in the form of questions and answers, not in heated debates. At the very least, there-fore, we have to believe that Matsumoto's speech reflected the majority view of the committee that had formed around him. Except for one or two incidents, no serious objection to Matsumoto's remarks was heard from members of the Diet, who had been elected in a nonpartisan elec-tion during the war. Nor, with rare exceptions, did the news media offer any serious critical comments.

The committee opened its sixth and last general meeting of the year on December 26, 1945. At this meeting, committee adviser Nomura Junji presented a 130-page "Opinion on Constitutional Revision."[18] The "No-mura opinion," however, had no appreciable influence on the commit-tee's deliberations; in fact, it was ignored.[19] Matsumoto, thinking that "there was no alternative but to draft it myself," went by car on Decem-ber 31 to his Kamakura villa, secluded himself there, and wrote the draft between January 1 and the night of January 3.[20] Known as the "Personal Draft of a Revised Constitution," Matsumoto completed it on January 4. Miyazawa then reorganized it in the form of an outline, and Matsumoto himself made some changes, producing a "Summary Revised Constitu-tion" that later became known as Matsumoto's draft "A."

In the meantime, after three days of New Year's celebration, three com-mittee members—Miyazawa, Irie, and Satō—convened the research sub-committee on January 4 and began discussion of two drafts of a revised constitution that Miyazawa had written. Matsumoto's draft "A" was pre-sented to the subcommittee at this time. One of the assistants, Satō Isao, has described the atmosphere of the group at the time.

> Some in the subcommittee were critical, saying this (such narrow revisions in the Matsumoto Personal Draft) is no good. It was suggested that a sub-stantial revised draft with many amendments should also be prepared. That was (Matsumoto) Draft "B" of the often cited (Matsumoto) Drafts "A" and "B"; it was in fact Professor Miyazawa's draft.[21]

Following is a comparison of the Meiji Constitution and Miyazawa's draft.

Meiji. Article 1. The Empire of Japan shall be reigned over and gov-erned by a line of Emperors unbroken for ages eternal.
Miyazawa. Article 1. Japan is a Monarchy.

Meiji. Article 2. The Imperial Throne shall be succeeded to by Imperial male descendants, according to the provisions of the Imperial House Law.

Miyazawa. Article 2. The Emperor is the monarch and exercises the rights of sovereignty according to the provisions of the present Constitution.

Meiji. Article 3. The Emperor is sacred and inviolable.

Miyazawa. Article 3. The Imperial Throne shall be succeeded to by Imperial male descendants unbroken for ages eternal according to the provisions of the Imperial House Law.

Meiji. Article 4. The Emperor is the head of the Empire, combining in Himself the rights of sovereignty, and exercises them according to the provisions of the present Constitution.

Miyazawa. Article 4. The Emperor assumes no responsibility for his actions. (Different draft) No one shall profane the Emperor's dignity.

Meiji. Article 8. The Emperor, in consequence of an urgent necessity to maintain public safety or to avert public calamities, issues, when the Imperial Diet is not sitting, Imperial Ordinances in the place of law.

Miyazawa. Article 8. The Emperor in consequence of the need for the maintenance of public safety or to avoid public calamities, issues, when the Imperial Diet is not sitting, with the approval of the Diet Deliberation Committee, Imperial Ordinances in place of law. Such Imperial Ordinances shall be laid before the Imperial Diet at its next session, and when the Diet does not approve the said Ordinances, the Government shall declare them to be invalid for the future.

Meiji. Article 11. The Emperor has the supreme command of the Army and Navy.

Miyazawa. Article 11. Delete.

Meiji. Article 12. The Emperor determines the organization and peace standing of the Army and Navy.

Miyazawa. Article 12. Delete.

Meiji. Article 28. Japanese subjects shall, within limits not prejudicial to peace and order, and not antagonistic to their duties as subjects, enjoy freedom of religious belief.

Miyazawa. Article 28. Japanese subjects shall enjoy freedom of religious belief. The restrictions necessary to maintain peace and order shall be determined by law. The special privileges of shrines shall be abolished. (Alternate draft, item three) No state religion shall exist.

Meiji. Article 31. The provisions contained in the present Chapter shall not affect the exercise of the powers appertaining to the Emperor, in times of war or in cases of a national emergency.
Miyazawa. Article 31. Delete.

Matsumoto's several drafts can best be compared by looking at key articles.

I. Matsumoto Draft "B" Article 1.
    (First draft) The Emperor of a line unbroken for ages eternal combines in Himself the rights of sovereignty, which he exercises according to the provisions of this Constitution.
    (Second draft) The sovereignty rights of Japan are combined in the Emperor of a line unbroken for ages eternal, who exercises them in accordance with the provisions of this Constitution.
    (Third draft) Japan shall be a monarchy headed by the Emperor of a line unbroken for ages eternal. Add Article: The Emperor combines in Himself the rights of sovereignty, and he exercises them according to the provisions of this Constitution.
    (Fourth draft) Japan shall be reigned over by the Emperor of a line unbroken for ages eternal.

II. Draft "A" Article 3. "The Emperor is sacred and inviolable" change to "The Emperor is exalted and inviolable."

III. Draft "B" Article 3.
    (First draft) The Emperor is responsible to no one in exercising the rights of sovereignty. Add paragraph 2: The Person of the Emperor is inviolable.
    (Second draft) The Emperor is the head of the State, and is inviolable.
    (Third draft) The person of the Emperor is inviolable.

IV. Draft "A" Article 8. In issuing emergency Imperial Ordinances, the Emperor shall consult the Diet Standing Committee, according to the provisions of the Diet Law.

V. Draft "B" Article 8. The Emperor, in case of urgent necessity to maintain public safety or to avert public calamities, issues, when the National Diet is not sitting, Imperial Ordinances in the place of law by consulting with the Diet Standing Committee.
    Such Imperial Ordinances shall be laid before the National Diet at its next session; and when the Diet does not approve them, the Government shall declare them to be invalid for the future.

VI. Draft "A" Article 11. "Army and Navy" to be changed to "armed forces."

VII. Draft "B" Article 11. Delete.
VIII. Draft "A" Article 12. The organization and peace standing of the armed forces shall be determined by law. (See 21 of the Summary.)
IX.   Draft "B" Article 12. Delete.
X.   Draft "A" Article 28. Japanese subjects shall, within limits not prejudicial to peace and order, enjoy freedom of religious belief. (Enact provisions which say that, except for the cases mentioned in the Articles of this Chapter, Japanese subjects shall not have their rights and liberties impaired without recourse to law.)
XI.   Draft "B" Article 28. All Japanese shall enjoy the right of religious belief. Such restrictions that are necessary to maintain public order shall be fixed by law.
XII. Draft "A" Article 31. Delete.
XIII. Draft "B" Article 31. Delete.

Thus at its fifteenth meeting on January 26, the research subcommittee completed work on drafts "A" and "B" and decided to submit a proposal for revising the constitution to the cabinet. Matsumoto presented the draft revision on January 29, and the cabinet met in special session for three consecutive days, January 30–February 1, to discuss the draft. The first meeting began with an examination of the articles about the emperor. Ministers offered various views on whether it was better when describing the emperor to say "exalted" or "dignified." But, generally speaking, no one expressed opposition to or proposed major revisions of Articles 1 through 4. On the supreme command of the military, however, the minister of health and welfare, Ashida Hitoshi, advanced the view that the military ought to be subordinate to the representatives of the people; and the minister of justice, Iwata Chūzō, suggested that the military ought to be completely eliminated.[22]

Mainichi Shinbun Breaks the Story

On the morning of February 1, when the cabinet was engaged in this examination of drafts, *Mainichi Shinbun* published on its front page the full text of the "Provisional Draft of the Committee to Study Constitutional Problems." In response to this shocking report, Matsumoto quickly denied at the special cabinet meeting that day that this was the committee's draft. "What the newspaper has published," he said, "is nothing more than one draft made in the course of our research." The government anxiously denied that it was a government draft, directing the cabinet secretary, Naruhashi, to issue a statement that "this draft has absolutely no connection with the Committee's draft."

The "provisional draft" that *Mainichi* had published was actually Miyazawa's draft "A." The *Mainichi* document, when examined in detail, appears to be slightly different from Miyazawa's draft, but the differences are, I think, due to minor errors made when the reporter hurriedly copied it. If these errors are removed, it matches exactly Miyazawa's draft. Strictly speaking, it is true that the *Mainichi* document was neither Matsumoto's draft "A" nor draft "B." But a careful comparison reveals that there is virtually no difference in the basic provisions of the three drafts. In short, each of them is based on the Meiji Constitution, with nothing more than a few modifications. Consequently, publication of the Miyazawa draft was hardly different from publication of the so-called government draft.

The reaction to the "provisional draft" was extremely unfavorable. *Mainichi* itself offered this assessment: "We think that most people will feel disappointed that it is so conservative and does nothing more than preserve the status quo."[23] SCAP's appraisal was even less favorable. Because SCAP became aware of this "provisional draft" through the *Mainichi* publication, its attitude toward constitutional reform underwent a fundamental change. Before discussing SCAP's reaction, however, let us explore the background of how this draft came to be.

First, above all else, it is clear that members of the Matsumoto committee failed to understand fully the implications of Japan's acceptance of the Potsdam Declaration, the meaning of defeat in the war, and, especially, the significance of a policy of democratization. Recall that immediately after the formation of the Shidehara cabinet, MacArthur had issued to Shidehara the so-called five great reforms directive, consisting of emancipation of women, encouragement of labor unions, democratization of education, abolition of repressive organizations, and democratization of economic organizations. Indeed, the Shidehara cabinet had accepted these reforms and, as of late January 1946, had already revised laws in order to achieve some of them. For example, in December 1945 it enacted laws on labor unions and female suffrage and revised the House of Representatives Election Law. In none of the three subcommittee drafts, however, do we find provisions for such rights. With respect to the emperor system, since the emperor himself had issued a denial of his divinity on January 1, 1946, there was no reason to preserve the first four articles of the Meiji Constitution, or to make only slight changes in them. In this regard, Takagi and others who worked with Konoe were much more conscious of being "under the Allied occupation."

On January 26, 1946, the very day that the two Matsumoto drafts were presented to the full committee, Takagi called on Matsumoto at the prime minister's official residence and recommended that Matsumoto attempt to solicit SCAP's views on constitutional revision. But Matsumoto countered forcefully that "I don't think there is any need to negotiate with the Americans or to seek their views any further, because constitutional revision is something that we are determined to do voluntarily and independently."[24] This scene reveals Matsumoto's tendency to be "overconfident," but in this case it probably accurately reflected his views. Takagi later gently criticized the Matsumoto group:

> Because the [Matsumoto] committee did not attempt to learn the views of the American side concerning constitutional reform, it was destined to fail. The Government's Committee to Study the Constitution worked for three months on constitutional revision, but during that time did not once have contact with the Americans, and did not once try to inform the Japanese people about the work of the committee.[25]

Furthermore, as we have mentioned earlier, the research subcommittee's draft completely ignored the draft constitutions drawn up by private citizens. Among the private drafts, at least the Constitutional Research Association's draft and Inada Masaji's draft were sent to the government at the end of December 1945. The subcommittee was thus in a position to know about them. Moreover, of the various private drafts, the subcommittee had direct contact with the members of the Constitutional Research Association, with Takano, and with the Socialist Party. Takano Iwasaburō, who played a leading role in preparing the drafts, and Prime Minister Shidehara graduated in 1896 (Meiji 28) in the same class at Tokyo University. The alumni of that year organized the "Twenty-Eight Club" and kept in touch through their meetings on the twenty-eighth of each month. Both Takano and Shidehara were members.[26] Although it is true that they represented different ideological extremes, when we consider that Takano was appointed chairman of NHK (Japan Broadcasting Corporation) during the Shidehara administration, it would appear that relations between the two were hardly strained. Consequently, if Shidehara had wanted to hear views on the various private drafts, he was in a position to do so at any time.

All the authors of the private drafts expressed interest in examining foreign constitutions—especially those of the United States, the Soviet Union, and Germany (the Weimar Republic)—and referred to them when working on their own drafts, in marked contrast to Matsumoto. Matsumoto used the Meiji Constitution as his only source when formulating his constitutional revisions. Moreover, when he did refer to foreign constitutions, it was for no other reason than to attack the private drafts. When his committee was nearing completion of its work, Matsumoto ordered a committee member to study the Weimar Constitution; it was necessary, he said, to show that although the private drafts "were incorporating provisions of the Weimar Constitution uncritically," that constitution had done nothing less than "harm German democracy and help the Nazi movement."[27]

Although it is true that the Nazis used the Weimar Constitution's national emergency powers provision, it is difficult to deny the epochal significance of the constitution's social rights provisions, which "guaranteed the value of life as human being" to workers and others who were poor and weak. Moreover, considering the similarities between a defeated Germany after World War I and a defeated Japan after World War II, such provisions could have been highly beneficial for Japan. But for Matsumoto, who reveled in the court ranks and honors of the "incomparable" Great Empire of Japan, the inclusion of such provisions was beyond his comprehension.

The Organization That Could Not Be Revived

Even among members of the Matsumoto committee, there were objections to his drafts "A" and "B," prepared by the young Miyazawa Toshiyoshi, Irie Toshio, Satō Tatsuo, and other Matsumoto followers. The most important of these was the "Nomura statement of views," touched on earlier. In this sixty-thousand-word statement, Nomura offered these direct criticisms of the drafts by Matsumoto and his followers:

> There are not a few optimists who conclude that if by the freely expressed will of the Japanese people Japan's constitutional monarchy is continued as in the past, without radically revising the present Japanese constitutional system, the four powers—the United States, Britain, the Soviet Union and China—will raise no objections. However, the allied powers will not leave the issue of what the ultimate form of the Japanese government should be to the free will of the Japanese people to decide. The absolutely necessary condition of the final decision to be made based on the free will of the Japanese people is that it must abide by the Potsdam Declaration. Examining the provisions of the Declaration, with regard to determining the final form of the Japanese government, the Japanese people do not have complete free will. Rather, concerning the Japanese people's having freedom of will in this matter, a serious responsibility accompanies this. What is this serious responsibility? It is nothing less than the requirement that the Japanese people put democratic government into practice.[28]

Nomura then proposed the following very important reforms: abolish the first four articles of the Meiji Constitution and introduce a presidential system of government; reform the judicial system, adding a councillor court system; adopt the jury system, including an appeals jury (grand jury); abolish the administrative court system; in addition to nationalizing land, carry out a nationalization of major industries; and expand the rights of "subjects" and add rights of labor, recreation, existence, and education. It appears that no serious attempt was made to incorporate these ideas into the draft revision. Quoting from a popular prewar guide to Marxism known as *The ABC's of Communism* by Bukharin, Nomura resisted Matsumoto's "technical expertise" and made an ardent effort to counter Matsumoto with a ponderous "statement of opinion" from a broad historical perspective.

In addition to Nomura the elder statesman, the young assistant Satō Isao had ideas early on about constitutional reform that differed from those of Matsumoto and his followers. Unlike Nomura, however, Satō did not present a statement of his views, nor did he occupy a conspicuous position on the committee. Yet he did begin to write on the issue immediately after he was appointed to the research subcommittee.

In an article published in a small journal, Satō criticized the "thesis that it was unnecessary to hasten revision" of the constitution.[29] Needless to say, this implied criticism of Minobe, Matsumoto, and Miyazawa. Satō also saw in the conditions of Japan's defeat in the war the urgent need to revise the constitution. His argument was vigorous and explicit.

> The present task of constitutional reform is the result of Japan's defeat in the Greater East Asian War. One should never forget the grim reality that this is something that is demanded by the Allied powers. . . . Essentially, for the present Japan does not have the right even to choose whether the new Constitution will be temporary or whether it will be permanent. The only thing that Japan can do is to write a Constitution based on the reality of Japan as it exists today.

Satō offered the following examples of his ideas for a new constitution. First, modify the legal system to accompany territorial changes; second, eliminate the military provisions stipulated in the Meiji Constitution to accommodate demilitarization; and third, "strengthen democratic elements," which is the "central issue of constitutional revision." Satō believed, however, that abolishing the emperor system would "not be permitted" and envisioned "a political structure, assuming the sovereignty of the Emperor, which is based on the people's will to the maximum extent possible under Imperial rule, without threatening the position of the Emperor as the superintendent of legislative, administrative and judicial powers." Consequently, Satō's proposals were directed toward such things as limiting the imperial sovereignty provision, reform of the Diet, and establishing a cabinet system responsible to the Diet—in substance, not necessarily "a new Constitution."

Had the committee under the direction of Matsumoto been inclined even in a modest way to include views from inside and outside the committee, there would have been an abundance of such ideas as these. That they were ignored was due in part to Matsumoto's idiosyncratic "self-confidence." More than anything else, however, the major cause was that Matsumoto and his followers were clinging to the Meiji Constitution on the backs of "the masses imprisoned" in the emperor system.

When one observes the operating style of the Committee to Study Constitutional Problems, the political structure of the emperor system emerges very sharply. Without anyone bearing clear responsibility, the process moved forward in a "private world." The research subcommittee itself was set up not by statute or government regulation, but as we have already seen, by an informal understanding at a cabinet meeting. Moreover, the committee conducted no "research or investigation," proceeding in this fashion even after the first step toward "reform" that occurred in November 1945. And even though a government draft was produced in the middle of January 1946, the committee ended its work without the draft ever having been officially announced.[30]

Furthermore, the committee was run as a private entity rather than as an official body. As symbolized by the name, "Matsumoto draft," draft "A" was put in final form while Matsumoto was secluded in his Kamakura residence. In this respect it was similar to Konoe's working on his draft while secluded at Hakone, and reminiscent of Itō Hirobumi, in the 1880s, secluding himself in his Natsushima villa in Yokohama as he prepared the draft of the Meiji Constitution. On the other hand, the Matsumoto draft "B" was in fact Miyazawa's draft, written for the most part by Miyazawa, Satō Tatsuo, and Irie Toshio. This is in striking contrast to the drafting process used by MacArthur and his staff, which we shall examine later. The American draft was prepared by several subcommittees, one for each chapter of the constitution, and the preliminary drafts written by these subcommittees were consolidated by a coordinating committee.

The event that exposed the most shameful practice of substituting the "private world" for the "public world" occurred after *Mainichi Shinbun* published the "provisional draft." Because MacArthur's Government Section demanded that the Japanese government submit its draft revision, following its publication on February 1, 1946, the cabinet decided that Matsumoto would enter into negotiations with SCAP. Matsumoto therefore presented an "explanatory statement" to General Courtney Whitney, chief of Government Section, that began with this sentence: "General Explanation of the Constitutional Revision Drafted by the Government." However, the draft was not approved at the cabinet meeting of February 4.[31] Indeed, Matsumoto's "Government draft" never received formal cabinet approval; it was nothing more than a draft prepared by the Matsumoto committee. Furthermore, in the sense that it was the committee's work and not based on government regulation or statute, it was not even a public document. Because the authors of this private draft had not followed proper legal procedures, the framing process of the constitution, the nation's highest law, was about to take a fateful turn.

Notes

1. *Mainichi Shinbun*, October 26, 1945.

2. Satō Tatsuo, *Nihonkoku kenpō seiritsushi* (Tokyo: Yūhikaku, 1964), 2:252. Satō says on p. 253 that "no Cabinet document establishing the committee was found."

3. Tabata Shinobu, *Sasaki hakase no kenpōgaku* (Kyoto: Ichiryusha, 1964), p. 124.

4. Matsumoto Jōji kōjutsu, "Nihonkoku kenpō no sōan ni tsuite," Kenpō chōsakai jimukyoku, *Kenshi, sō dai nijūhachi gō* (October 1958): 2–4.

5. Abe Shinnosuke, *Gendai Nihon jinbutsuron* (Tokyo: Kawade Shobō, 1952), p. 164.

6. Suzuki Takeo, "Matsumoto Jōji sensei no omoide," *Hōritsu jihō* 26, no. 11 (November 1954): 80.

7. Satō Isao, "Matsumoto sensei to Nihonkoku kenpō," *Toki no hōrei*, no. 151 (November 1954): 16–17.

8. *Asahi Shinbun*, October 20, 1945.

9. *Mainichi Shinbun*, October 25, 1945.

10. Gaimushō gaikō bunsho, microfilm reel no. A'0092.

11. *Mainichi Shinbun*, October 19, 1945.

12. This discussion of the committee's activities and records of its meetings draws on Satō Tatsuo, *Nihonkoku kenpō seiritsushi*, vol. 1 (Tokyo: Yūhikaku, 1962) and vol. 2 (Tokyo: Yūhikaku, 1964).

13. Satō Tatsuo, *Nihonkoku kenpō seiritsushi*, 1:264.

14. Ibid., p. 296.

15. Ibid., pp. 335 ff. gives the complete text.

16. Ibid., pp. 423–424.

17. Kenpō chōsakai jimukyoku, *Matsumoto Jōji shi ni kiku* (October 1958): 12.

18. The complete document appears in Irie Toshio, *Kenpō seiritsu no keii to kenpōjō no shomondai* (Tokyo: Daiichi Hōki Shuppan, 1976). A summary is included in Tanaka Sei, "'Nomura Ikensho' no sonzai igi o megutte," in *Gendai kokka to kenpō no genri*, ed. Gendai rekishigaku kenkyūkai (Tokyo: Yūhikaku, 1983).

19. Satō Tatsuo, *Nihonkoku kenpō seiritsushi*, 1:326.

20. Matsumoto Jōji kōjutsu.

21. Satō Isao's words appear in "Zadankai: Miyazawa Toshiyoshi sensei no hito to gakumon," *Jurist*, no. 634 (March 26, 1977).

22. Satō Tatsuo, *Nihonkoku kenpō seiritsushi*, 2:629.

23. *Mainichi Shinbun*, February 1, 1946.

24. Kenpō chōsakai jimukyoku, "Takagi Yasaki meiyō kyōju danwaroku," *Kenshi, sō dai nijūgo gō* (July 1958): 8.

25. Takagi Yasaka, "Nihon no kenpō kaisei ni taishite 1945 nen ni Konoe kō ga nashita kiyo ni kansuru oboegaki" (Kenpō chōsakai jimukyoku *Kenshi, sō dai sanjūroku gō*) (1958), p. 9.

26. Ōshima Kiyoshi, *Takano Iwasaburō den* (Tokyo: Iwanami Shoten, 1968), p. 424.

27. Satō Tatsuo, *Nihonkoku kenpō seiritsushi*, 2:523.

28. Irie Toshio, *Kenpō seiritsu*, pp. 119–190.

29. Satō Isao, "Furuki kenpō to atarashiki kenpō," *Jiron* (January 1946). The date Satō wrote the article, November 10, is noted at the article's conclusion.

30. The completed draft is dated January 19. The whole document is in Satō Tatsuo, *Nihonkoku kenpō seiritsushi*, 2:590.

31. Ibid., p. 644, and Irie Toshio, *Kenpō seiritsu*, p. 85.

4

A Week in a Secret Room: Writing the SCAP Draft

Establishing the Far Eastern Commission

When did General MacArthur's staff begin preparations for writing a draft constitution for Japan? As we have seen, in the fall of 1945 MacArthur had suggested to Konoe and had told Shidehara that the constitution ought to be revised. At the time he was contemplating a revision that would be done entirely by the Japanese government. The creation of the Far Eastern Commission (FEC) in late 1945 changed his mind.

The year 1945 was indeed a time worthy of the "blue-eyed shogun," MacArthur's Japanese nickname. He was directly responsible only to the Joint Chiefs of Staff (JCS) in the U.S. government. His former subordinate, General Dwight Eisenhower, occupied the position of army chief of staff of the Joint Chiefs. Given his seniority, it is understandable why MacArthur was indeed the "shogun in Tokyo."

Despite MacArthur's official title—Supreme Commander for the Allied Powers (SCAP)—the Allied nations were totally powerless to control him. In the confrontation between the United States and the Soviet Union over control of Japan that arose soon after the war, the Soviet Union boycotted meetings of the Far Eastern Advisory Commission (FEAC), an organization that the United States had proposed to satisfy demands for Allied participation in the occupation of Japan. Established on October 2, 1945, the FEAC had "responsibility for making recommendations to the participating governments" on the "formulation of policies, principles and standards" for the occupation of Japan. In fact, however, it exercised no control whatsoever over the operation of the occupation.[1] Consequently, when MacArthur heard from Washington at the end of November 1945 that members of the FEAC planned to visit Japan early the next year, he replied that he would be "delighted to welcome the visit," knowing they could only "advise" on the operation of the occupation; moreover, the Soviet Union would not be participating.[2]

Immediately after this, however, the international machinery for controlling Japan began to undergo major change. The American, British, and Soviet three-power Foreign Minister's Conference met in Moscow on December 16 to discuss the organization of the occupation for all the former Axis powers. The control mechanism for Japan was reorganized. The FEC was set up to replace the FEAC, and an agreement on the "Terms of Reference of the Far Eastern Commission and the Allied Council for Japan" was signed on December 27, 1945.

According to that agreement, the members of the commission were to include eleven countries: the United States, the United Kingdom, China, the Soviet Union, France, India, the Netherlands, Canada, Australia, New Zealand, and the Philippines. The functions of the commission were "to formulate the policies, principles, and standards" of the occupation government, and "to review . . . any directive issued to the Supreme Commander . . . and action [taken by him]." For this purpose the U.S. government "shall transmit this directive to the Supreme Commander, and the Supreme Commander shall be responsible for implementing any directive which expresses a policy decision by the Commission."[3]

In brief, MacArthur was made subordinate to the FEC and was ordered to follow its directives, a decision which—needless to say—MacArthur strongly opposed. The FEC, initially located in Tokyo, was later relocated to Washington. Replacing the commission in Tokyo was its representative organ, the Allied Council for Japan (ACJ). In return for this concession to the Soviet Union, the United States retained for itself the right to issue interim directives "on all urgent matters" and—along with the United Kingdom, China, and the Soviet Union—the right to veto decisions of the commission.

The one notable exception to this rule was that the United States could not issue an interim directive on constitutional reform. The FEC's terms of reference specified: "Directives which prescribe fundamental changes in Japan's constitutional structure . . . or changes in the Japanese Government as a whole shall be issued only after consultation and agreement has been reached in the Far Eastern Commission." Accordingly, MacArthur was prohibited from arbitrarily undertaking reform that involved "fundamental changes in the Japanese constitutional structure."[4] He could carry out such changes only in accordance with an FEC decision and based on a directive from that body.

Preparatory Work Proceeds in Secret

At the end of 1945, as control of Japan by the Allied powers underwent significant change, the movement for constitutional revision within Japan was approaching a serious impasse. First of all, there was the activ-

ity of the Konoe group. The so-called Konoe draft was presented to the
emperor on November 22, following MacArthur's November 1 declaration [disavowing Konoe]. At MacArthur's headquarters, concern about
the direction of constitutional reform mounted. Army Lieutenant Colonel
Milo E. Rowell, later to play a key role in revising the constitution as a
member of the public administration branch of Government Section,
summoned to his office the director of the political section of the Central
Liaison Office (CLO), Sone Eki, who confirmed that the Konoe draft had
not been formally submitted to the Japanese government.[5]

Second were the activities of Matsumoto's Committee to Study Constitutional Problems. As we have seen, the committee's activities were followed closely by the press, enabling SCAP to stay well informed from a
fairly early stage about Matsumoto's draft. For example, George Atcheson, SCAP's politic adviser, sent a cable to the secretary of state on November 29 reporting quite accurately that the Matsumoto committee had
reached the summary stage of constitutional revision, that the draft was
expected to be published in the middle of January 1946, and that the first
four articles of the Meiji Constitution would probably not be changed.[6]

Toward the end of December drafts from civilian organizations began
to appear one by one. Of these, SCAP gave the most attention to the one
by the Constitutional Research Association. This draft was first published in the press on December 28, 1945, and it was quickly translated
on December 31 by the Allied Translation and Interpreter Service (ATIS).[7]
But Government Section apparently was dissatisfied with the ATIS translation and had the political adviser's office retranslate the draft. On January 11, 1946, Lieutenant Colonel Rowell prepared detailed "comments"
on the draft in a memorandum for the chief of staff.[8] Since Brigadier General Courtney Whitney, Chief of Government Section, also signed the
memorandum, we know that Government Section took a serious view of
the draft and that, therefore, Rowell's comments also reflect the views of
Government Section.

Following an analysis of each article, Rowell listed as "outstanding liberal provisions" of the draft such things as sovereignty of the people,
protection of workers, a system of popular referendum, annual budgets
approved by the Diet, an audit bureau, limits on the right to possess
property, and the proposal for a temporary constitution with a ten-year
limit. Rowell said of the draft: "The provisions included in the proposed
constitution are democratic and acceptable." He then listed provisions
that ought to be added: a statement that the constitution is the supreme
law of the land and provisions on the rights of the people, including
among others a writ of habeas corpus. That Rowell was able to make a
rather quick, though not immediate, positive judgment on the association's proposed constitution is explained by the fact that he himself had

prepared a "Report on Preliminary Studies and Recommendations of Japanese Constitution" just a month before.[9]

As the date approached for the publication of the government's own plan for constitutional revision, proposals began to appear from private organizations. In Washington, meanwhile, the State, War, Navy Coordinating Committee (SWNCC) approved on January 7, 1946, its own proposals for "Reform of the Japanese Governmental System" (SWNCC 228) and sent them on the January 11 to MacArthur for his "information."[10] Created in late 1944, SWNCC was a U.S. foreign policy making committee composed of assistant secretaries of three departments. SWNCC 228 had an enormous influence on SCAP's draft constitution. At Government Section's meeting on February 6, during which the writing of the SCAP draft began, General Whitney confirmed that "SWNCC 228 must be used as a control document."[11] One historian has called it the "original source of the Japanese Constitution."[12]

SWNCC 228 is a very long document, but can be summarized as follows: all rights of rule shall reflect the will of the people; fundamental human rights shall be guaranteed; and, therefore, the abolition or revision of the emperor system is essential. At the end of the document a statement was added that contained a clear warning to MacArthur, one that MacArthur himself later used many times when he and his staff "imposed" their draft constitution on the Japanese government.

> Only as a last resort should the Supreme Commander order the Japanese Government to effect the above listed reforms, as the knowledge that they had been imposed by the Allies would materially reduce the possibility of their acceptance and support by the Japanese people for the future.[13]

This was indeed a statement with profound implications.

MacArthur's first important decision after receiving SWNCC 228 was to exclude the emperor from trial as a war criminal. The issue of the emperor's war guilt had to be dealt with before the FEC began its operations, for countries that had long called him a war criminal—the Soviet Union, Australia, New Zealand, the Philippines, among others—were members of the FEC. On November 29, 1945, MacArthur had received a message from the Joint Chiefs of Staff [sent at SWNCC's request] directing him to gather information and evidence to determine whether the emperor should be tried as a war criminal.[14] On January 25, 1946, MacArthur responded by telegram to Army Chief of Staff Eisenhower that no evidence had been found connecting the emperor to war crimes.

> Since receipt of [your directive] investigation has been conducted here under the limitations set forth with reference to possible criminal actions

against the Emperor. No specific and tangible evidence has been uncovered with regard to his exact activities which might connect him in varying degrees with the political decisions of the Japanese Empire during the last decade. . . . His indictment will undoubtedly cause a tremendous convulsion among the Japanese people, the repercussions of which cannot be overestimated.

It would be absolutely essential to greatly increase the occupational forces. It is quite possible that a minimum of a million troops would be required which would have to be maintained for an indefinite number of years.[15]

By excluding Emperor Hirohito from trial as a war criminal, MacArthur effectively made the decision to retain the emperor system itself, at the same time determining much about the future of Japan's state system.

Only four months had passed since the occupation began. SCAP was facing a period of transition in the occupation government, which was shifting from military to civilian rule, and deep divisions were beginning to surface between the military and civilians in MacArthur's headquarters. The military tasks of demobilizing and disbanding the Japanese military were finished. It was now necessary to employ specialists—that is, civilians—in other areas to strengthen democracy, guarantee human rights, and encourage the establishment of a peacefully inclined government, which were other objectives of the occupation mentioned in the Potsdam Declaration. From the early days of the occupation, Government Section had been considering these needs, which arose from the U.S. government's broad occupation policy for Japan.

Brigadier General William E. Crist, the first chief of Government Section, proposed in a memorandum of November 1, 1945, that the public administration branch of his section, headed by Colonel Charles L. Kades, be reorganized and divided into operations and planning groups.[16] On the same day the Joint Chiefs of Staff in Washington approved their directive for the occupation, JCS 1389/15, "Basic Initial Post-Surrender Directive to Supreme Commander for the Allied Powers for the Occupation and Control of Japan."[17] Crist's reorganization plan made Lieutenant Colonel Erickson director of the operations group and set up units for judicial affairs, internal affairs, and external affairs. Crist placed the planning group under the jurisdiction of Lieutenant Colonel Frank E. Hays, but made Mr. Bowen Smith, a civilian, its director. Under Smith's direction were twenty civilian experts who were to prepare legislation for demilitarization and decentralization of government, elimination of feudal and totalitarian practices, elimination of "relationships contributive to Japanese war potential," and strengthening of democratic tendencies in governmental, economic, and social institutions.

Based on this reorganization plan, Hays prepared a concrete operational plan for his group, assigning personnel to seventeen different projects to implement the policies set forth in the JCS directive of November 1.[18] Constitutional revision came under the third project, which included an important description suggesting SCAP's schedule for revising the constitution.

> Project: Study of constitution and changes required to establish government on democratic basis. Personnel: Col[onel] Rowell has made preliminary study. Further study to be made by [John] Masland and/or [Kenneth] Colegrove. Time and Priority: Length of time to be devoted to this project should be determined by rate with which Japanese proceed with their own revision so as to be in position to criticize draft proposals submitted by Japanese government. Liaison: Col[onel] Rowell. No consultations to be held with Japanese on subject until further notice.

In other words, the public administration branch, which subsequently took charge of revising the constitution, had planned from the end of 1945 to carry out democratic reform in Japan by reorganizing and increasing the number of personnel. By the middle of January 1946, the branch was also beginning to prepare for the Japanese government's submission of its draft constitution. Furthermore, the Hays plan makes clear that Government Section was already prepared at this stage to reject the Japanese government's plan, anticipating that an unacceptable rival proposal would be forthcoming from the Japanese people. Thus for the time being SCAP would also refrain from pressuring the Japanese government to produce a draft.

The Meeting with Visiting FEC Members

A meeting that occurred several days before Hays prepared his plan was apparently closely related to Government Section's preparations for writing its own draft constitution. Most senior members of Government Section attended this meeting on January 17, 1946, with a visiting delegation of FEAC members. Since the FEAC was reorganized a few days later as the FEC, the meeting was essentially with the FEC. Indeed, the occasion was recorded by SCAP as "A meeting between Government Section and the FEC."[19]

Members of MacArthur's staff attending the meeting included Courtney Whitney, the new chief of Government Section; Charles L. Kades, chief of the public administration branch; Hussey, Rowell, and eleven others. From the FEC were eleven members representing ten countries, including [Major General] Frank R. McCoy, chairman of the FEC and the U.S. representative, and Nelson T. Johnson, the secretary general of the FEC. Only the Soviet Union was not represented. During the meeting, Thomas Confessor, the Philippine representative, and Charles Kades had the following very significant exchange:

> *Confessor.* Are you considering revising the Constitution?
>
> *Kades.* No, we aren't. Government Section considers constitutional reform a long-term problem pertaining to fundamental change in government structure, and thought it was within the area of your Commission's authority.
>
> *Confessor.* We were given to understand by a headquarters spokesman that your section was studying the Constitution. Is that wrong?
>
> *Kades.* There must be some misunderstanding. Government Section advises the Supreme Commander on policies pertaining to the internal structure of civil government for the purpose of implementing the basic initial directive for the occupation of Japan which was issued by the U.S. Joint Chiefs of Staff. It has not considered the Constitution as part of this work. It has been thought that the Constitution was within the terms of reference of your Commission.[20]

It appears from a reading of this exchange that Kades was being very cautious. When asked, "are you considering . . . ," Kades just answered "no," which seems unusual. As we have seen, SCAP had urged Konoe and Shidehara to revise the constitution, had continued to show interest in the Japanese government's reform effort, and had initiated an internal revamping of Government Section. Yet Kades, without referring to these facts, merely said that "it was within the terms of reference of your Commission." His response to the question seems almost unnatural. Did Kades answer in this way to give the FEC representatives the impression that SCAP had absolutely no interest in constitutional reform, or was he trying to reassure them? Perhaps Kades, surprised at a question that he did not anticipate and knowing that the FEC was interested in the issue of constitutional reform, was trying to avoid delving more deeply into the matter?

The discussion between Government Section and the FEC contains one element that is especially puzzling—that is, the person who raised the important question about constitutional reform, Philippine representative Confessor, was in fact a Philippine patriot, mentioned in the memoirs of the three leading members of SCAP—MacArthur, Whitney, and Charles A. Willoughby.[21] Strangely enough, the accounts written about Confessor during the war agree completely in each of the three memoirs. Confessor is described as the governor of Panay Island (a medium-sized island in the middle of the archipelago), who resisted the Japanese occupation of the Philippines, and as a patriot who supported the anti-Japanese guerrilla forces. All three accounts describe his activities and quote his letters, but not one mentions having met him. Therefore, it seems odd to imagine that—when this Philippine patriot arrived in Tokyo—neither MacArthur nor his subordinates planned a special meeting with him, quite separate from meetings with other FEC representatives. That would have been the natural thing to do.

In any case, Confessor's questions served as a trigger for SCAP's first momentous step toward drafting a revised constitution for Japan. If a meeting did occur between SCAP officials and Confessor before the discussion with FEC, Confessor's questions about constitutional reform may have been prearranged to create an opportunity for SCAP to prepare its own draft, which it had been thinking about for some time. Whether the discussion with the FEC representatives—and especially Confessor's questions—were completely fortuitous, or whether they were planned, is a question that cannot easily be answered.

The FEC representatives met next with MacArthur on January 29, the day before they left Japan. In the two and one-half hour meeting, MacArthur was the center of attention, giving his views in detail and with complete candor.[22] Since Johnson's record of the meeting was a summary, it is not clear who broached the constitutional issue. But on that issue, which came up after a discussion of reparations, MacArthur said, unlike Kades, that he had issued no "orders or directives" to the Japanese government, but had made "suggestions."

With reference to the question of constitutional reform, the Supreme Commander stated that this matter had been taken out of his hands by the Moscow Agreement, and he did not know now just how that was going to be worked out. He pointed out that when he started out in Japan his original directive gave him jurisdiction in the matter, and stated that he had made certain suggestions and the Japanese had begun to work on these suggestions. A committee had been formed for the purpose of carrying out certain constitutional reforms, but insofar as his own part in this work was concerned, the Supreme Commander had ceased to take any action whatever. He said that he had issued no orders or directives, and that he had limited himself merely to suggestions. . . . He stated that it was his belief, that it was his conviction, that a constitution, no matter how good, no matter how well written, forced upon the Japanese by bayonet would last just as long as bayonets were present, and that he was certain that the moment force was withdrawn and the Japanese were left to their own devices they would get rid of that constitution.[23]

What can we make of MacArthur's statement? Either he wanted to convey the message that SCAP had no intention of writing a constitution and forcing it on Japan, or he wished to let the FEC know that he had made "suggestions" to the Japanese government. Considering that Johnson, in his summary of the record of this long meeting, gave much space to MacArthur's comments on constitutional reform, we must conclude that he thought the comments were quite important. On the other hand, MacArthur's comments were not even mentioned by New Zealand's FEC representative, Carl Berendsen, in his report on the meeting to his foreign minister.[24]

On February 1, 1946, the very day that the FEC delegation sailed home from Yokohama, the *Mainichi Shinbun* published its scoop on the "Provisional Revised Constitution of the Constitutional Problem Investigation Committee." This "provisional draft" was translated into English on February 2. But Whitney, without waiting for an English translation of the draft, quickly prepared two documents on February 1. The first was titled "Memorandum for the Supreme Commander: Constitutional Reform." It was very long, but everything important was said in the first section.

> The question of constitutional reform of the Japanese governmental system is rapidly approaching a climax. Several proposed revisions of the Japanese constitution have been drafted by governmental and private committees. Constitutional reform may well be a cardinal issue in the coming election campaign.
>
> In these circumstances, I have considered the extent of your power as Supreme Commander to deal with fundamental changes in the Japanese constitutional structure, either by approving or disapproving proposals made by the Japanese government or by issuing orders or directives to that government. In my opinion, in the absence of any policy decision by the Far Eastern Commission on the subject (which would, of course, be controlling), you have the same authority with reference to constitutional reform as you have with reference to any other matter of substance in the occupation and control of Japan.[25]

In other words, on reading the "provisional draft," Whitney interpreted the FEC's "terms of reference" to mean that MacArthur had the authority to revise the constitution before the FEC made a policy decision on constitutional reform. This was an unwarranted interpretation that, as we shall see, became the source of a heated dispute within the FEC.

Next, Whitney turned his attention to reorganizing Government Section. First of all, on January 28 he rejected as "lacking in logic" the reform plan proposed by his predecessor, Crist, and implemented by Hays.[26] Second, on February 1 he had Kades announce, effective immediately, the reorganization of the public administration division into six branches: Legislative and Liaison Branch, Political Parties Branch, Government Powers Branch, Local Government Branch, Opinions Branch, and Review and Reports Branch.[27] In fact, as we shall see, this was the plan of reorganization that was officially announced on February 4 as the new branches and personnel of the public administration division when that division of Government Section became a "Constitutional Convention."

Whitney began preparing to draft a revised constitution as soon as the *Mainichi* scoop was published, as though he had been waiting for the article to appear. Although it is fruitless to ask "what if" questions about the past, it is interesting to consider how the situation might have developed for SCAP if the *Mainichi* had not published its story at this time.

No matter how much SCAP had pressed the Japanese government, gaining cabinet approval of a government draft and publishing it would have required quite a long time. It would have been difficult, moreover, to produce a draft that, according to the Hays plan, would have met with the approval of the Japanese people, not to mention one that would have satisfied the FEC. It follows, therefore, that SCAP had no option but to make a "suggestion," though there was quite a gap between a "suggestion" and producing a draft that could be accepted by the FEC. In addition, because the matter would have required a public airing, a great deal of time would have been necessary to produce a draft based only on SCAP's "suggestions." If time had been short, SCAP would have had to go beyond making "suggestions." Either course would have invited interference from the newly activated FEC.

The *Mainichi* scoop made it possible in one stroke to avoid such a situation. In a memorandum to MacArthur dated February 2, which was attached to the English translation of the *Mainichi* publication, Whitney expressed very well the significance of the report in the advice he offered:

> I thought it better strategy to orient them [the Japanese government] before the formal submission of a draft than to wait and force them to again start from scratch once an unacceptable draft had been submitted to which they were committed.[28]

Considered in this way, we see that the *Mainichi* scoop unofficially made public the government draft; informed not only SCAP but the Japanese public of its contents; persuaded the government that the draft had little public support; offered policy guidance, by way of the

MacArthur draft, before the government produced its own official draft; and created an excellent opportunity to turn quickly to the writing of a draft constitution. It is clear that the appearance of the Matsumoto draft was not inconvenient for SCAP, for if it had been, SCAP could have exercised censorship to prohibit its publication. It is not especially strange, therefore, that some observers have even suspected that the publication was too timely to be a *Mainichi* exclusive at all, and was instead a *Mainichi* exclusive arranged by SCAP. In 1973 Tanaka Hideo, a scholar specializing in English and U.S. law, elicited the following statement from the *Mainichi* correspondent, Nishiyama Ryūzō, who had scored the scoop in 1946.

> On January 31, 1946, I got an exclusive news story from the [Matsumoto] committee's secretariat. . . . Because I was at the secretariat at that time, I "received it." That's all there was to it. It was published in the morning edition on February 1 only because I gathered the information on January 31.[29]

It certainly appears that the incident was entirely fortuitous. In any case, there is no documentary evidence of a leak. Fortuitous or prearranged, the *Mainichi* revelation was, from SCAP's perspective, most desirable, both in its timing and in the form it took, as a leading newspaper's exclusive story.

The following day, February 3, having received advice from Whitney that, at least for the time being, he had the authority to revise the constitution, MacArthur indicated the principles—later called "MacArthur's Three Principles"—that should guide Government Section in drafting a new constitution for Japan. On February 4 Whitney called together the public administration division of Government Section and ordered the drafting to begin. We can thus conclude from these events that it was on February 1, at the very latest, that MacArthur made the decision to draft a new constitution for Japan.[30] However, Government Section did not change course suddenly because of the *Mainichi* story. In its continuing competition with the other general staff sections, Government Section had been striving to establish its hegemony within MacArthur's headquarters. In other words, Government Section, hoping to replace the hapless Japanese government and take charge of the "great task" of revising the constitution, was already making preparations in its own way. Ever since the subject of constitutional reform had surfaced, SCAP had shown constant concern about revising the constitution, even in the meeting with the visiting FEC delegation. One can say with confidence that the question of constitutional revision had become a burning issue within MacArthur's headquarters by the middle of January, and that the

Mainichi story of February 1 was the spark for the decision to proceed with the revision plans.

Presenting "MacArthur's Three Principles"

February 3, 1946, the day that marked an epochal turning point in Japan's constitutional history, was a beautiful Sunday. MacArthur sent to Whitney the essential requirements for constitutional reform, that is, a note containing his "Three Principles."

1. Emperor is at the head of state.
   His succession is dynastic.
   His duties and powers will be exercised in accordance with the Constitution and responsive to the basic will of the people as provided therein.
2. War as a sovereign right of the nation is abolished. Japan renounces it as an instrumentality for settling its disputes and even for preserving its own security. It relies upon the higher ideals which are now stirring the world for its defense and its protection.
   No Japanese Army, Navy or Air Force will ever be authorized and no rights of belligerency will ever be conferred upon any Japanese force.
3. The feudal system of Japan will cease.
   No rights of peerage except those of the Imperial family will extend beyond the lines of those now existent.
   No patent of nobility will from this time forth embody within itself any National or Civic power of government.
   Pattern budget after British system.[31]

Armed with these three principles from MacArthur, Whitney opened the meeting of all members of the public administration division of Government Section on February 4, and addressed them as follows:

> In the next week the Government Section will sit as a Constitutional Convention. General MacArthur has entrusted the Government Section with the historically significant task of drafting a new Constitution for the Japanese people. Three principles, outlined by General MacArthur, must be basic in the Government Section's draft.[32]

He then introduced the three principles. During the discussion that followed, Whitney confirmed that the draft was to clarify the people's sovereignty, limit the emperor's role to that of a social monarch, and keep in mind the United Nations Charter. Before ending the meeting, he told them that absolute secrecy must be maintained and that a tentative draft must be ready by the end of the week.

The actual work on the draft began the next day, but on this day, Sunday, February 4, the plan to divide the division into six branches, which Kades had already presented on February 1, was confirmed and the branch chiefs and personnel were announced. Small working subcommittees were created to prepare different parts of the draft.[33]

> *Steering Committee:* Colonel Charles L. Kades, Commander Alfred R. Hussey, Lieutenant Colonel Milo E. Rowell, and Miss Ruth Ellerman.
> *Legislative Committee:* Lieutenant Colonel Frank E. Hays, Commander Guy J. Swope, Lieutenant (JG) Osborne Hauge, and Miss Gertrude Norman.
> *Executive Committee:* Cyrus H. Peake, Jacob I. Miller, and First Lieutenant Milton J. Esman.
> *Civil Rights Committee:* Lieutenant Colonel Pieter K. Roest, Harry Emerson Wildes, and Miss Beate Sirota.
> *Judiciary Committee:* Lieutenant Colonel Milo E. Rowell, Commander Alfred R. Hussey, and Miss Margaret Stone.
> *Local Government Committee:* Major Cecil G. Tilton, Lieutenant Commander R. L. Malcolm, and Mr. Philip O. Keeney.
> *Finance Committee:* Captain Frank Rizzo.
> *Committee on the Emperor and Enabling Provisions:* First Lieutenant George A. Nelson and Ensign Richard A. Poole.
> *The Preamble:* Commander Alfred R. Hussey.

In brief, under the steering committee, which controlled the entire operation, eight subcommittees were organized. The difference between the Japanese and U.S. approaches to revising the constitution is clearly revealed here. The reader will recall how the Japanese draft was done. Konoe, asked by the emperor to produce the draft, sought Sasaki's help, took him to Hakone, and wrote the draft there in complete seclusion. Konoe did not, of course, share the work with Sasaki. The government's Committee to Study Constitutional Problems, a committee in name only, also operated in this way. Matsumoto's draft "A" was written almost entirely by Matsumoto himself while secluded in his home in Kamakura. Matsumoto's draft "B" was the product of some changes that Irie and Satō made to a draft that was originally written by Miyazawa.

In contrast to this, MacArthur ordered Whitney to write a model constitution based on three principles, and Whitney assigned the whole task to the public administration division of Government Section. The division set up a steering committee with Kades as chairman, appointed subcommittees, and divided the work of writing the draft between them. The conference room door was locked while the drafting was in progress, but Kades did not gather up his materials, isolate himself in a hotel room, and write the draft there. In other words, the Americans worked not as individuals but as part of an organization. Another point worth mentioning is that neither the emperor nor Prime Minister Shidehara, when ordering Konoe and Matsumoto to prepare drafts, provided principles to guide the work. Judging by the results, one might say that their only principle was the protection of the Tennō system. All guiding principles were, after all, contained in the Meiji Constitution. Revision was merely a matter of technique; technical skills were indeed what legal scholars were expected to demonstrate. This meant, therefore, that principles were not to be articulated in advance.

Members of the Steering Committee

Thus the work of drafting finally got underway in Government Section. The military ranks of subcommittee members give the [false] impression that "the constitution was drafted by military men." Allow me, then, to introduce the careers of the steering committee members. Their ages are as of January 1946.[34]

Charles L. Kades. Forty years old. Colonel in the infantry. Born in Newburgh, New York. Graduate of Cornell University and Harvard Law School. Employed by the law firm of Hawkins, Delafield and Longfellow (New York City), 1930–1933. Assistant general counsel to the Federal Public Works Administration, 1933–1937. Assistant general counsel in the U.S. Treasury Department, 1937–1942. From April 1942, Charles Kades [already an officer in the army reserve] went on active duty, graduated from the Infantry School and the Command and General Staff School. Following service with the Civil Affairs Division of the War Department, he served as assistant G-5 of the Seventh Army and the First Airborne Task Force in the invasion of southern France and in the Alpine and Rhineland campaigns. He was awarded the Legion of Merit.

Alfred R. Hussey, Jr. Forty-four years old. Commander, U.S. Navy. Born in Plymouth, Massachusetts. Graduated Phi Beta Kappa from Harvard University, department of government, and from the University of Virginia Law School. He practiced law from 1930 until he entered active duty in September 1942. He was auditor and special master in chancery for Massachusetts Superior Court, and held various local elective and appointive public offices. His military service included duty with the Amphibious Training Command, Pacific, as maintenance, transportation, and legal officer. He was a graduate of the Navy School of Military Government, Princeton University, and of the Civil Affairs Training School, Harvard University.

Milo E. Rowell. Forty-two years old. Lieutenant Colonel, U.S. Army. Born in Fresno, California. A graduate of Stanford University, he attended Harvard Law School and obtained his law degree from Stanford University Law School. From 1926 until he entered active military service in July 1943, Rowell practiced law in Fresno, specializing in representing business associations in their relationships with various governmental agencies. He was also assistant U.S. attorney, Los Angeles. His military service included graduation from the Provost Marshal General's School, the School of Military Government, and the Civil Affairs Training School, University of Chicago; instructor at the Chicago Civil Affairs Training School, at the Civil Affairs Detachment, Oro Bay; and service as commanding officer of the Pacific Command Army Unit No. 30. He was awarded the Bronze Star Medal and Military Merit Medal of the Philippine government.

As this indicates, while the three members of the steering committee had served in the military during the war, they were all graduates of law school and had experience as practicing lawyers. Moreover, it is important to note their ages. They were all in their early forties, in the prime of their careers, and they had been in their twenties during the 1930s, a time of such crises as the Great Depression and the New Deal, as well as a time of liberal thought.

On February 5, 1946, the public administration division set about their work. Since a draft of a model constitution had to be ready in just a week, the scene was indeed hectic. Ruth Ellerman, who served as secretary to the steering committee and later married Hussey, a member of the committee, remembered the experience well:

> There was a small snack bar on the top floor of the Daiichi Seimei Building. We ate sandwiches and donuts standing up, and worked every night until daybreak. People would return to their quarters at dawn, shower, sleep for about an hour, and then at 8:00 a.m. sharp everybody would gather again and continue working on the draft. As a woman, I did the same thing.[35]

The Author of Article 9, "Renunciation of War"

Perhaps the most distinctive feature of the SCAP draft—also known as the MacArthur draft—was the provision renouncing war, Article 9 of the present constitution. The process by which this article was written is the most controversial feature of the draft even today. The renunciation of war is clearly stated in "MacArthur's Three Principles"; there is no question about that. The theory that Shidehara was the author of the provision has been circulating since 1951, when MacArthur first testified to this effect before the Senate Military and Foreign Relations Committees a month after he had been dismissed from his post as Supreme Commander during the Korean War.

He testified to this during a series of congressional hearings, during which he also made the infamous statement that so shocked the Japanese—that "if we are 45-year olds, the Japanese are 12-year olds."[36] He did not stop here; in his *Reminiscences* as well, MacArthur repeated that Shidehara had proposed the no-war clause.[37] Even Japanese close to Shidehara began to advance the Shidehara thesis, and at one time this became the most widely accepted explanation of the origins of the provision. Later, as interviews with Kades, the Rowell papers, and the Hussey papers became public, some scholars suggested the "Kades theory,"[38] others the "Whitney-Kades theory."[39] Researchers left no stone unturned as they conducted careful archival research in hope of "discovering" proof. In this effort, Kades himself has recently begun to say that "at the time everybody was thinking much the same thing about renunciation of war and pacifism. It is difficult to determine whose idea this was or where it got started."[40]

But before we search for the mother lode by asking who initially proposed it, it is essential to find where the vein of gold is located. First, there is nothing in the committee organization that suggests that the committee that drafted the renunciation of war provision presented the idea during the drafting stage. In fact, at the outset there was no plan to put the no-war clause in the body of the constitution; it was placed in the preamble, which, as we see from the assignment of responsibilities, was drafted by Hussey. By contrast, at MacArthur's suggestion the following section was moved to the body of the main text and was then called Article 1.[41]

> Article One. 1. War as a sovereign right of the nation is abolished. 2. The threat or use of force as a means of settling disputes with any other nation is forever renounced. 3. The right to maintain land, sea and air forces as well as other war potential shall not be conferred, and right of belligerency shall not be conferred on the nation. (numbers 1, 2, and 3 inserted by the author)

If we give some thought to these details, we can see just how important MacArthur considered the "renunciation of war" provision. In the final SCAP draft, however, a separate chapter was devoted to this one article, and it followed "Chapter One, The Emperor" as "Chapter Two, Renunciation of War," changing Article 1 into Article 8. Whitney explained the reason for this reorganization:

We made it [the renunciation of war] Chapter 2 rather than Chapter 1 of the Constitution in deference to the Emperor and his place in the hearts of the Japanese people. For my part, and in terms of its decisive importance, I should prefer the Renunciation of War to be Chapter 1 of the new Constitution.[42]

"Renunciation of War" thus became chapter 2, and Whitney considered this as "having decisive importance." Whoever the originator of the provision, there is no doubt that the Americans—especially MacArthur and Whitney, the most powerful of them—viewed the provision as extremely important. It is often said that there is nothing like this provision to be found in any other constitution in the world. But, in fact, is it really unprecedented? The concept of nations "renouncing war" first made its appearance in law through the antiwar treaties following World War I (for example, the Kellogg-Briand Pact of 1928). Article 1 of that treaty read:

The High Contracting Parties solemnly declare in the names of their respective peoples that they condemn recourse to war for the solution of international controversies, and renounce it as an instrument of national policy in their relations with one another.

This corresponds to Article 1 of MacArthur's draft. But his draft also states: "[Japan] forever renounces the threat or use of force as a means of settling disputes with any other nation." In other words, the "renunciation of war" in the draft was expanded to the renunciation of "the threat or use of force," not only "war" as in the Kellogg Pact. This expanded provision can be considered an heir to the provision established in the United Nations Charter prohibiting not only war, but also the settlement of disputes by force in order to deal successfully with such evasions of law as the "Manchurian Incident" and the "China Incident" of the 1930s. As a signatory of the Kellogg antiwar pact, Japan had called these "incidents" rather than "wars" to avoid having to declare war, repeatedly sending troops into China and committing aggressive acts there.[43] The United Nations Charter defines member nations' principles of action in the following way:

All members shall refrain in their international relations from the threat or use of force against the territorial integrity or political independence of any state, or in any other manner inconsistent with the Purposes of the United Nations.[44]

When Government Section began working on the draft on February 4, General Whitney told the meeting: "No explicit mention need be made of the United Nations Charter, but the principles of the Charter should be implicit in our thinking as we draft the Constitution."[45] This idea is seen in Article 8 of the draft. Upon reflection, it seems only natural that Allied (United Nations) occupation forces would take the United Nations Charter seriously.

Let us return to the question of the no-war clause. Was the Japanese Constitution really the first in which a provision for the "renunciation of war" appeared? Nakagawa Tsuyoshi has asserted in his 1987 study that the world's first constitution to renounce war was actually the Philippine Constitution of 1935.[46]

> The Philippines renounces war as a means of implementing national policy, and adopts the principles of generally established international law as one part of its state law. (Article 2)

With the aid of the Philippine Constitution, on November 15, 1935, the American colony took its first step toward complete independence as the Republic of the Philippines. MacArthur was appointed military adviser to the Philippine national militia a few days before the transition to independence began.[47] It seems highly likely, therefore, that MacArthur had this 1935 constitution in mind when his staff began drafting a constitution for Japan in 1946.

Relating the origin of the Philippine Constitution to that of Japan in this way, we might also tend to regard Japan as a colony—like the Philippines—and Article 9 (renunciation of war) as simply a military measure. But that would be a distortion. We should not forget that Okinawa was already under direct U.S. military rule and, as we shall see, MacArthur proceeded to draft the new constitution on the assumption that Okinawa would be made into a fortress and that the Japanese mainland would be demilitarized. Nevertheless, the origin of the idea of Article 9 must be sought in the 1935 Philippine Constitution. Considering the following three facts, there seems to be little doubt that it was MacArthur who proposed Article 9, not Shidehara: MacArthur ordered the war-renouncing provision moved from the preamble to the body of the draft constitution; a very similar provision can be found in the Philippine Constitution; and at the Shidehara-MacArthur meeting of February 21, when Shidehara expressed apprehension about Japan being the only nation to renounce war, MacArthur replied, "even if there are no followers, Japan has nothing to lose."[48]

How do we explain MacArthur's action in this case? Was he a pacifist? Let us leave for later discussion the question of his pacifism, and instead ask why MacArthur claimed that Shidehara proposed Article 9 to him. Professor Sodei Rinjirō, a student of MacArthur, analyzed the matter in the following way:

It seems likely that it was painful for MacArthur himself to have to deny, due to the outbreak of the Korean War, the antiwar clause which was born of feelings deep in his heart in a brief moment following the war. It was a dishonor for a strategist only five years later to have been so wrong about his predictions of history. Perhaps by shifting to Shidehara the responsibility for proposing the antiwar provision, MacArthur was attempting to avoid historical responsibility himself.[49]

Drafting the Human Rights Provisions

The second major characteristic of the SCAP draft was its human rights provisions. The full draft was made up of ninety-two articles, and of these thirty-one pertained to human rights, accounting for a third of the whole. Those in charge of drafting the provisions were, needless to say, the three members of the "subcommittee on human rights." The backgrounds of the three, despite differences of age, were similarly rich in experience.[50]

Pieter K. Roest. The leader of the subcommittee. Forty-seven years old. Born in California. After graduating from Meiden University medical school in Holland, he studied anthropology and sociology at the University of Chicago and was awarded a Ph.D. He then studied international relations, law, and economics at the University of Southern California, and taught at colleges in India and the United States. After working in the U.S. Surplus Marketing Administration, he joined the navy in 1942 and served as liaison officer to the Dutch and Australian navies.

Harry Emerson Wildes. Fifty-five years old. Born in Delaware. Known in Japan as the author of *Typhoon in Tokyo* (1954). After graduating from Harvard, where he studied economics, he earned an M.A. and Ph.D. from the University of Pennsylvania and later earned another doctorate in humanities at Temple University. He had held various jobs at Bell Telephone and had worked as a newspaper reporter, a high school teacher, and an editor of a magazine. He was well informed about Japan, having lectured in economics at Keiō University in 1924–25 and authored the book *Social Currents in Japan* (1927).

Beate Sirota. Twenty-two years old. Born in Vienna, Austria. She had spent ten years in Japan after the age of five. Her father was a pianist and professor at Tokyo Academy of Music. After graduation from Mills College in California, making use of her ability in Japanese, she landed a job at the Japan section of *Time* magazine's foreign news division and later at the U.S. Foreign Economic Administration.

What the three had in common was that, despite their varied backgrounds, not one of them had ever been trained in or practiced law. But all three, especially Roest and Sirota, had traveled and lived in many countries during periods of international tension brought on by war. And probably this variety of training and experience better qualified them for writing the "rights of human life" that transcended race and nation than jurists equipped only with technical legal training. As Japan specialists, Wildes and Sirota had lived in Japan before the war and knew firsthand the condition of Japanese human rights under the Meiji Constitution.

The fact that the human rights provisions of the SCAP draft were, unlike those of the Meiji Constitution, unrelated to citizenship or race was probably due to the experiences of these three people. The following two articles were included in their draft:[51]

> Article. All natural persons are equal before the law. No discrimination shall be authorized or tolerated in political, economic, educational or domestic relations on account of race, creed, sex, social status, caste or national origin.
> Article. Aliens shall be entitled to the equal protection of the law. When charged with any offense they are entitled to the assistance of their diplomatic representatives and of interpreters of their own choosing.

These were provisions for "human rights" that transcended by far the "rights of the people." The authors understood that human rights are universal in nature and transcend nation states. If these two articles—as written in the SCAP draft—had been included in the present Japanese Constitution, the recent controversy over fingerprinting foreigners would probably not have arisen, and Japan would today have human rights provisions appropriate to its status as an "international state." As we shall see, the Japanese government excised the words "national origin" from the first article and eliminated the whole second article. Yet these two articles had not become much of an issue when consultation with the coordinating committee took place on February 8. With some changes, they were incorporated into SCAP's final draft in the following form:

> Article 13. All natural persons are equal before the law. No discrimination shall be authorized or tolerated in political, economic or social relations on account of race, creed, sex, social status, caste or national origin.
> Article 16. Aliens shall be entitled to the equal protection of law.

The subcommittee's draft also included a rather concrete provision concerning the "human rights of women," who had no rights under the Meiji Constitution.[52]

> Article. The family is the basis of human society and its traditions for good or evil permeate the nation. Hence marriage and the family are protected by

law, and it is hereby ordained that they shall rest upon the indisputable legal and social equality of both sexes, upon mutual consent instead of parental coercion, and upon cooperation instead of male domination. Laws contrary to these principles shall be abolished, and replaced by others viewing choice of spouse, property rights, inheritance, choice of domicile, divorce and other matters pertaining to marriage and the family from the standpoint of individual dignity and the essential equality of the sexes.

This long article expresses the subcommittee's determination to reform the male-centered Japanese family system. The third MacArthur principle included a sentence that said "the feudal system of Japan will cease," but it did not touch on the family system or women. The "human rights of women" provision certainly reflected the thinking of Wildes and Sirota, who knew the lowly status of women in the Japanese family system, and especially the thinking of Sirota, who had experienced that system in her youth. This article encountered no objections from the coordinating committee and with some changes became Article 23 of SCAP's final draft. The subcommittee next prepared a provision which protected women in the area of social welfare:

Article. In all spheres of life laws shall be designed for the protection and extension of social welfare, and of freedom, justice and democracy. . . . To this end the Diet shall enact legislation which shall: Protect and aid expectant and nursing mothers, promote infant and child welfare, and establish just rights for illegitimate and adopted children, and for the underprivileged.

Sirota remembers that when working on the draft, she found "the constitutions and laws of the Weimar Republic and Scandinavian countries were the best guides."[53] Certainly the social welfare provision closely resembles Article 161 of the Weimar Republic's constitution.[54] But this article ran into objections from members of the coordinating committee, who thought that "these provisions were the concern of statutory regulation and not constitutional law." Roest countered passionately that

It is peculiarly necessary to include them here since state responsibility for the welfare of its people is a new concept in Japan and demands constitutional approval to encourage its widespread acceptance. At present women are chattels here, bastards take precedence over legitimate sons on the mere whim of a father, and any peasant can sell his daughter if the rice crop is bad.[55]

One finds here perhaps "the clearest expression of the revolutionary zeal" of the members of the subcommittee on human rights, who knew well the Japan that had continuously ignored the human rights of women and children.[56]

The differences between the members of the human rights subcommittee and the coordinating committee, however, could not be easily reconciled. In the end, the two groups sought a ruling from the chief of Government Section, General Whitney, who decided that "the minutiae of social legislation should be omitted and a general statement should be made that social security shall be provided."[57] Following Whitney's decision, the final draft left almost untouched the general provisions of the subcommittee's earlier draft, but eliminated completely wording on protective legislation for expectant and nursing mothers, infants, children, and illegitimate and adopted children.

The Model for Local Autonomy

One last specific point in the SCAP draft that we must consider is local government. Until this time, Japan had no system of local government. As we have already seen, then, there was nothing in the several draft constitutions—with one exception—that dealt with local government. Surprisingly, that one exception was Sasaki Sōichi's draft, which included one chapter with three articles covering local government.[58] But Sasaki's concept was quite different from today's idea of local government, for it said nothing more than "when the nation recognizes the need" it can establish local organizations. Nevertheless, that was an epochal change.

The SCAP chapter on local government was prepared by a subcommittee of three: Tilton, Malcolm, and Keeney. Major Cecil G. Tilton, born in Arizona, was forty-four in 1946. He had been educated at the University of California (B.S. and M.S. degrees) and at Harvard Graduate School of Business Administration (M.B.A.). He had taught at the universities of Hawaii and Connecticut; he was an author, a consultant for United Aircraft Corporation, and a special administrator of the Office of Price Administration in Washington, D.C. He had done economic and political research on Japan, China, and Korea, and had traveled in these countries as well as in Manchuria.[59] Although experienced in many areas, Tilton had no expertise whatsoever in Japanese local government. But he had begun in October 1945 to study Japan's system of local government with the help of Professor Tanaka Jirō, a Tokyo University specialist in administrative law. Tanaka recalls that from late October 1945 to March 1946 he

went to [Tilton's office] once or twice, and sometimes three times, a week.[60] He had virtually no knowledge of the subject in the beginning, but asked questions and made certain of the actual facts and accumulated considerable knowledge. Therefore, by roughly January of the next year [1946] he had become something of an expert on the subject.[61]

The draft written by Tilton and others of the subcommittee included three articles in the "Local Government" chapter.[62] Although there is some confusion about how this term should be translated into Japanese, whether *chihō seiji* (local politics) or *chihō gyōsei* (local administration), the latter seems best; in any case, it was not *chihō jichi* (local self-government), as it was later called. Article 1 gave "prefectural, city, town and village governments" the power to levy and collect taxes, the power to establish and maintain a local police force, and so forth. Article 2 provided "the power to establish laws and ordinances in conformity with this constitution and the laws passed by the Diet." Article 3 provided that governors, mayors, headmen, and members of assemblies be elected by popular vote.[63] In a meeting with the coordinating committee, however, this subcommittee draft was "discarded as inadequate, and a new draft prepared by the Steering Committee."[64] Since the steering committee's draft was almost identical to SCAP's final draft, we produce below the latter.[65]

Article 86. The governors of prefectures, the mayors of cities and towns and the chief executive officers of all other subordinate bodies politic and corporate having taxing power, the members of prefectural and local legislative assemblies, and such other prefectural and local officials as the Diet may determine, shall be elected by direct popular vote within their several communities.

Article 87. The inhabitants of metropolitan areas, cities and towns shall be secure in their right to manage their property, affairs and government and to frame their own charters within such laws as the Diet may enact.

Article 88. The Diet shall pass no local or special act applicable to a metropolitan area, city or town where a general act can be made applicable, unless it be made subject to the acceptance of a majority of the electorate of such community.

First of all, SCAP's final draft provided for a system of popular elections of the chief executives of prefectures, cities, towns, and villages and of members of prefectural and local assemblies. This was not very different from Article 3 of the subcommittee's draft. Next, Article 87 gave metropolitan areas, cities, and towns the power to enact charters (usually translated in Japanese as *kenshō*). This was different from the subcommittee's provisions in that it guaranteed the right of self-government to metropolitan areas, cities, and towns, but not to prefectures (villages are not mentioned). Prefectures were not given the right to enact charters because "it was thought that Japan was too small to have states rights in any form and that the protection of local communities could be left to the Diet and the courts."[66] The charters mentioned in SCAP's draft served a similar function to charters in the United States, which are guaranteed in state counties under the American system of local government. But to what extent these charters ensured the right of local autonomy is unclear. Finally, Article 88 of the SCAP draft was revived in almost the same form in Article 95 (special law on local self-government) of the present constitution.

Subcommittee drafts were examined in meetings between the coordinating committee and each subcommittee. The SCAP draft included, in addition, the following article providing for state ownership of land and a unicameral legislature.

> Article 28. The ultimate fee to the land and to all natural resources reposes in the State as the collective representative of the people. Land and other natural resources are subject to the right of the State to take them, upon just compensation therefor, for the purpose of securing and promoting the conservation, development, utilization and control thereof.
>
> Article 41. The Diet shall consist of one House of elected representatives with a membership of not less than 300 nor more than 500.[67]

To be sure, the provision for a unicameral legislature was added because of Kades's judgment that "this issue might give us an effective bargaining lever."[68] He believed that "if we propose the unicameral legislature and the Japanese strongly oppose its adoption, we might well compromise on this issue in order to strengthen our position in insisting upon a more important issue."[69]

Special Features of the Constitution's Organization

The MacArthur draft thus differed fundamentally from both the Meiji Constitution and the Matsumoto draft that was made in the image of the Meiji Constitution. Still, MacArthur's organization of the whole and its chapters followed the organization of the Meiji Constitution very closely. To explain why this was so, Government Section took the official position that "it was fully understood that the organization of the whole and the subject of chapters and so forth was to follow the Meiji Constitution."[70] At the meeting of February 6, moreover, when Government Section began organizing sections of the draft, Kades stated that "the Section defining the position of the Emperor should immediately follow the Preamble."[71] It is by no means clear, however, why such organization was important. A comparison of the chapters of the two documents shows the similarities:

The Meiji Constitution
    Chapter 1. The Emperor
    Chapter 2. Rights and Duties of Subjects
    Chapter 3. The Imperial Diet
    Chapter 4. The Ministers of State and the Privy Council
    Chapter 5. The Judicature
    Chapter 6. Finance
    Chapter 7. Supplementary Rules
The SCAP Draft
    Chapter 1. The Emperor
    Chapter 2. Renunciation of War
    Chapter 3. Rights and Duties of the People
    Chapter 4. The Diet
    Chapter 5. The Cabinet
    Chapter 6. The Judiciary
    Chapter 7. Finance
    Chapter 8. Local Self-Government
    Chapter 9. Amendments
    Chapter 10. Supreme Law
    Chapter 11. Ratification

It is true that the first chapter of the MacArthur draft retained the emperor as a "symbol," but as the draft gave sovereignty to the people, it was unnecessary to follow the organization of the Meiji Constitution. The Belgian Constitution of 1838, for example, is known to be founded on "basic principles of democracy and liberalism, though formally a monarchy."[72] The position and powers of the monarch are defined in the second chapter of Section 3, "The King and the Ministers," which follows Section 1, "The Territory and Its Divisions," and Section 2, "The People and Their Rights."

The SCAP draft followed the organization of the Meiji Constitution because Government Section insisted that it was not framing a new constitution for Japan but merely amending the Meiji Constitution. But why was "amending," as opposed to "framing," important? Government Section offered its official explanation in *Political Reorientation of Japan*, noting that it concerned the Hague Convention on Land Warfare. Article 43 of the Convention says:

The authority of the legitimate power having in fact passed into the hands of the occupant, the latter shall take all measures in his power to restore and ensure, as far as possible, public order and safety, while respecting, unless absolutely prevented, the laws in force in the country.

Government Section made the judgment that "from a purely legalistic point of view, no machinery existed for complete revision within the framework of existing organic law and the establishment of such machinery *could well be considered* improper interference by the military occupant in violation of the Hague rules."[73] In other words, according to the Hague rules, the occupant had to "respect the laws [the Meiji Constitution] in force." And in the absence of a legal procedure for completely rewriting the Meiji Constitution, Government Section's revision took the form of an amendment to the Meiji Constitution in order to ensure legal continuity.

This thesis, however, contradicts rather sharply SCAP's own interpretation of international law and the occupation of Japan. The *Political Reorientation of Japan*, the official view of Government Section, elsewhere interprets the Japanese occupation in the following way:

The surrender of Japan and its occupation by the forces of the victorious Allied Powers presented a new problem in international law. . . . A familiar incident of military occupations of the past has been either the outright annexation of the country occupied or the establishment of a regime regarded as sympathetic toward the occupant. . . . In no case, however, did this involve major organic changes imposed by the occupant. . . . The basis for governmental reform—constitutional revision—in Japan by the Japanese people, was laid in the Potsdam Declaration.[74]

However, the Potsdam Declaration is then interpreted in this way:

It was clearly stated [by the Declaration] at the outset that the Allied Powers expected the Japanese people to undertake their own reforms. Pursuant to this clear declaration, the United States Government prepared an initial postsurrender policy directive for the guidance of General MacArthur in his occupation of Japan as Supreme Commander for the Allied Powers.[75]

In other words, the Japanese occupation was interpreted as different from "a familiar incident of military occupations of the past" and as "raising new problems of international law in which rules such as Article 43 of the Convention which stipulates respecting, unless absolutely prevented, the laws in force in the country, can to some extent be changed."[76] In the memorandum that Whitney sent to MacArthur on February 1, 1946, just before the drafting had begun, he advised:

You now have the unrestricted authority to take any action you deem proper in effecting changes in the Japanese constitutional structure.[77]

Given this interpretation, it would only have been necessary to follow the organization of the Meiji Constitution in framing the draft constitution if "customary international law, concerning the Hague treaty and occupation of enemy territory, is applied during a belligerent occupation,"[78] and if the basis for the framing procedure were the Hague Convention on Land Warfare. Why, then, was the revision procedure based on the Hague Convention? The answer seems to be that practical politics were considered to be more important than logic. An important phrase in the official Government Section view quoted earlier is worth repeating here: "[Complete revision of the constitution, that is, the framing or writing of one] *could well be considered* improper interference by the military occupant in violation of the Hague rules."[79]

Government Section's apparent desire to respect international legal procedure as much as possible, while quietly carrying out radical political reform, probably accounts for the organization of the SCAP draft being at once conservative and very similar to the Meiji Constitution.

Notes

1. "Kyokutō shimon iinkai futaku jōkō," in *Nihon senryō oyobi kanri jūyō bunshoshū*, ed. Gaimushō tokubetsu shiryōbu hen (Tokyo: Tōyō Keizai Shimpōsha, 1949), 1:24.

2. The Secretary of State to the Chairman of the Far Eastern Advisory Commission (McCoy), November 27, 1945, *Foreign Relations of the United States* (hereafter, *FRUS*) (1945), 6:870.

3. Gaimushō, *Nihon senryō*, 1:172–174.

4. Ibid.

5. Hussey Papers, reel no. 5.

6. The Acting Political Adviser in Japan (Atcheson) to the Secretary of State, November 25, 1945, *FRUS* (1945), 6:870.

7. Translation of a draft constitution prepared by a private study group known as the Constitution Investigation Association, December 28, 1945, Hussey Papers, reel no. 5.

8. Takayanagi Kenzō, Ōtomo Ichirō, and Tanaka Hideo, eds., *Nihonkoku kenpō seitei no katei*, vol. 1 (Tokyo: Yūhikaku, 1972), complete translation following p. 26.

9. Ibid., translation pp. 2 ff.

10. Ibid., translation pp. 412 ff.

11. Ibid., p. 131.

12. Ōmori Minoru, *Sengo hishi* (Tokyo: Kōdansha, 1975), 5:221.

13. See *FRUS* (1946), 6:882–884.

14. Robert E. Ward, "Presurrender Planning: Treatment of the Emperor and Constitutional Changes," in *Democratizing Japan*, ed. Robert E. Ward and Yoshikazu Sakamoto (Honolulu: University of Hawaii Press, 1987), p. 65.

15. General of the Army Douglas MacArthur to the Chief of Staff (Eisenhower), January 25, 1946, *FRUS* (1946), 8:396.

16. Planning Group, Public Administration Branch, memorandum by Courtney Whitney, January 28, 1946, GHQ/SCAP bunsho, Kokkai Toshokan shozō, microfiche GS (B)00567.

17. Gaimushō tokubetsu shiryō, 1:111 ff.

18. Frank E. Hays, Memorandum for the Chief, Government Section, GHQ/SCAP bunsho, Kokkai Toshokan shozō, microfiche GS (B)00567.

19. Hussey Papers, reel no. 5.

20. This translation can be found in Tanaka Hideo, *Kenpō seitei katei oboegaki* (Tokyo: Yūhikaku, 1979), p. 55.

21. Douglas MacArthur, *MacArthur kaisōki* (Tokyo: Asahi Shinbunsha, 1964), 1:346–351; Courtney Whitney, *MacArthur: His Rendezvous with History* (New York: Knopf, 1956), pp. 130, 136; Charles A. Willoughby and John Chamberlain, *MacArthur, 1941–1951* (New York: McGraw-Hill, 1954), p. 213.

22. The New Zealand Minister, Washington to the Minister of External Affairs, January 29, 1946, *Documents on New Zealand External Relations*, ed. R. Kay (Wellington, 1982), 2:324.

23. Memorandum by Secretary General of the Far Eastern Advisory Commission (Johnson), January 30, 1946, *FRUS* (1946), 8:124–125.

24. R. Kay, ed., *Documents on New Zealand*, 2:324–327.

25. Takayanagi, Ōtomo, and Tanaka, eds., *Nihonkoku kenpō*, 1:91.

26. Courtney Whitney, Memorandum for the Chief, Government Section.

27. Charles Kades, Memorandum for the Chief, Government Section, GHQ/SCAP bunsho, Kokkai Toshokan shozō, microfiche GS (B)00567.

28. Takayanagi, Ōtomo, and Tanaka, eds., *Nihonkoku kenpō*, 1:43.

29. Tanaka, *Kenpō seitei*, p. 46.

30. On this point Kojima Noboru, *Shiroku Nihonkoku kenpō* (Tokyo: Bungei Shunjū, 1972), p. 206, says that Whitney and Kades at "the meeting on December 31 made the decision to draft a revised Constitution." But Tanaka Hideo, who has criticized this, favors the thesis that the decision was made on February 3, 1946. See the discussion with Satō Tatsuo and others, "Problems on the Process by Which the Japanese Constitution Was Written," *Jurist*, no. 531 (May 1, 1973).

31. Takayanagi, Ōtomo, and Tanaka, eds., *Nihonkoku kenpō*, 1:99.

32. Ibid., p. 101.

33. Ibid., pp. 111–112.

34. Tanaka, *Kenpō seitei*, pp. 70–73.

35. Shūkan shinchō, ed., *MacArthur no Nihon* (Tokyo: Shinchōsha, 1970), p. 116.

36. Sodei Rinjirō and Fukushima Chūrō, eds., *MacArthur* (Tokyo: Nihon Hōsō Shuppan Kyōkai, 1982), p. 246.

37. MacArthur, *MacArthur kaisōki*, 2:164.

38. Inumaru Hideo, "Kenpō no sensō hōki jōkō no kisōsha ni tsuite," *Kokusai shōka daigaku ronsō*, no. 27 (January 1983).

39. Theodore McNelly, "General Douglas MacArthur and the Constitutional Disarmament of Japan," *The Transactions of the Asiatic Society of Japan*, 3d ser., 17 (October 1982).

40. Takemae Eiji, *Nihon senryō—GHQ no shōgen* (Tokyo: Chūō Kōronsha, 1988), p. 60.

41. Inumaru Hideo, "Hussey bunsho to kenpō seitei katei," *Hōgaku Seminar* (August 1981): 175 ff.

42. Takayanagi, Ōtomo, and Tanaka, eds., *Nihonkoku kenpō*, 1:393.

43. Takano Yūichi, "Kenpō dai kyūjō," in *Bunken senshū: Nihonkoku kenpō*, ed. Fukase Tadakazu (Tokyo: Sanseidō, 1977), 3:132.

44. United Nations Charter, Article 2.

45. Takayanagi, Ōtomo, and Tanaka, eds., *Nihonkoku kenpō*, 1:105.

46. Nakagawa Tsuyoshi, "Nichihi ryōkoku kenpō ni miru ruien," *Chūō kōron* (May 1987): 185.

47. Sodei and Fukushima, eds., *MacArthur*, p. 254.

48. Shindō Eiichi and Shimokabe Motoharu, eds., *Ashida Hitoshi nikki* (Tokyo: Iwanami Shoten, 1986), 1:79.

49. Sodei Rinjirō, *MacArthur no nisen nichi* (Tokyo: Chūō Kōronsha, 1964), p. 38.

50. Tanaka, *Kenpō seitei,* pp. 73, 132.

51. Takayanagi, Ōtomo, and Tanaka, eds., *Nihonkoku kenpō,* 1:219, 221.

52. Ibid., p. 223.

53. Susan J. Pharr, "The Politics of Women's Rights," in *Democratizing Japan,* ed. Ward and Sakamoto, p. 472.

54. Takagi Yasaka, Suenobu Mitsuji, and Miyazawa Toshiyoshi, eds., *Sekai jinken sengen shū,* p. 215.

55. Takayanagi, Ōtomo, and Tanaka, eds., *Nihonkoku kenpō,* 1:205.

56. Tanaka, *Kenpō seitei,* p. 134.

57. Takayanagi, Ōtomo, and Tanaka, eds., *Nihonkoku kenpō,* 1:207.

58. Tabata Shinobu, *Sasaki hakase no kenpōgaku* (Kyoto: Ichiryusha, 1964), pp. 146 ff.

59. Tanaka, *Kenpō seitei,* pp. 73–74.

60. Jichi daigakkō, *Sengo jichi shi* 2 (1961): 10.

61. Tanaka Jirō, "Rengōkoku sōshireibu to chihō seido no kaikaku no tsuite," *Sengo jichi shi,* 2:239.

62. Takayanagi, Ōtomo, and Tanaka, eds., *Nihonkoku kenpō,* 1:239.

63. Ibid., p. 237.

64. Tanaka, *Kenpō seitei,* p. 167.

65. Takayanagi, Ōtomo, and Tanaka, eds., *Nihonkoku kenpō,* 1:301.

66. Rengōkoku saikō shireibu minseikyoku, "Nihon no shinkenpō," in Kenpō chōsakai jimukyoku, *Kenshi sōdai ichigō,* p. 50.

67. Ibid., p. 120.

68. Takayanagi, Ōtomo, and Tanaka, eds., *Nihonkoku kenpō,* 1:121.

69. Ibid., p. 121.

70. Rengōkoku saikō shireibu, "Nihon no shinkenpō," p. 47.

71. Takayanagi, Ōtomo, and Tanaka, eds., *Nihonkoku kenpō,* 1:129.

72. Miyazawa Toshiyoshi, ed., *Sekai kenpō shū* (Tokyo: Iwanami Shoten, 1983), pp. 69 ff. See p. 66 for Kiyomiya Shirō's "interpretation" of the Belgian Constitution.

73. Miyazawa, *Sekai,* p. 29.

74. Ibid., p. 19.

75. Ibid., p. 20.

76. Furukawa Jun, "Kenpōshi no ronten: Nihonkoku kenpō seiritsushi o chūshin ni," *Jurist*, no. 731 (January 1981): 33.

77. Takayanagi, Ōtomo, and Tanaka, eds., *Nihonkoku kenpō*, 1:97.

78. Ashibe Nobuyoshi, *Kenpō kōgi nōto* (Tokyo: Yūhikaku, 1986), 1:91.

79. Rengōkoku saikō shireibu, "Nihon no shinkenpō," p. 29.

5

A Second Defeat
"Imposed" on Japan?

Appraisal of the Matsumoto Draft

While Government Section was working feverishly—and in complete secrecy—to complete a draft constitution for Japan, it was simultaneously demanding that the Japanese government submit its own draft. On February 8, 1946, the chairman of the Government's Committee to Study Constitutional Problems, Matsumoto Jōji, sent to SCAP a "Gist of the Revision of the Constitution" along with a general explanation of the revision. But SCAP apparently did not interpret this as a formal government action; it was described instead as "an informal submission by the Japanese side."[1] Furthermore, Government Section did not recognize this "Gist of the Revision of the Constitution" as a formal Japanese government draft. There is no reference in the U.S. documents to a "Government draft"; rather, the "draft revision" that Matsumoto submitted on February 8 was designated "Matsumoto Draft (A)."[2]

Be that as it may, the public administration branch of Government Section, which had received the Matsumoto draft, completed a memorandum criticizing it on February 12, precisely the day the SCAP draft was completed.[3] As might be expected, when the SCAP draft was finished, the U.S. criticisms of the Japanese draft became quite clear. The criticisms were arranged in ten points, with each point evaluating whether or not the draft "fulfill[ed] the objectives set forth in the Potsdam Declaration." The first point dealt with the position of the emperor.

> There should be . . . "established in accordance with the freely expressed will of the Japanese people a peacefully inclined and responsible government." (paragraph 12 of the Potsdam Declaration) This means that sovereignty is to rest in the people.
>
> Comment: a) Chapter I, Articles 1 to 6 are revised only to the extent that the word "sacred" in Article 3 is changed to "supreme." This makes no basic

change in the concept of sovereignty, leaving it wholly vested in the Emperor. b) No change has been proposed in Article 5 whereby the Emperor continues to exercise the legislative power. c) The Emperor can still dissolve the House under Article 7, as the Matsumoto Draft (Gist, Paragraph 2), makes no material change.

Comments that followed covered the people's sovereignty, limits of legislative power, human rights, local government, and so forth. By contrasting Matsumoto's draft with the Potsdam Declaration in this way, Government Section's memorandum made a thorough criticism of the Japanese document.

Presenting the MacArthur Draft

Having produced both a proposed draft constitution and a critique of the Matsumoto draft, SCAP was at last ready to meet the Japanese on February 13, 1946. The director of the first section of the legislative bureau, Satō Tatsuo, who was deeply involved in negotiations with SCAP, wrote in later years on the history of the framing of the constitution: "It was indeed on this historical day that, one might say, 'the Japanese Constitution was conceived.'"[4]

For the Japanese side, however, February 13, 1946, was nothing more than the day when they were to receive SCAP's response to the Matsumoto draft, which had been submitted five days earlier. They never imagined that a U.S. draft would be presented to them. In the sunroom of the foreign minister's official residence in Azabu, where the two sides met, Foreign Minister Yoshida, State Minister Matsumoto, adviser to the Central Liaison Office Shirasu Jirō, and a Foreign Ministry interpreter, Hasegawa Motokichi, awaited the Americans. Lying open on a table in front of them was the Matsumoto draft. At precisely 10:00 A.M. General Courtney Whitney, chief of Government Section, arrived with Kades, Rowell, and Hussey.[5]

A written record of this meeting was made both by the Japanese and American participants. The Japanese record totaled eight hundred words. The document was not signed, but it was probably written by the interpreter, Hasegawa.[6] On the other hand, the U.S. record of the meeting was approximately seven times as long. It was written and signed by Kades, Rowell, and Hussey.[7] Despite the difference in length, the contents of the two documents do not differ significantly.

Let us attempt to reconstruct what happened based on both records. The Japanese record noted that "Whitney spoke first; he said the Japanese draft was completely unacceptable, and presented a draft which they had prepared and brought along." It then continued: "After Minister

Matsumoto read it once . . ." But the SCAP account describes differently the appearance of the Japanese as they took the SCAP draft: "At this statement of General Whitney, the Japanese officials were obviously stunned—Mr. Yoshida's face particularly manifesting shock and concern. The whole atmosphere at this point was charged with dramatic tension."

Facing the four Japanese, Whitney began by saying, "As the draft of constitutional revision which you have submitted to us is wholly unacceptable, we have prepared a draft." The SCAP draft was then distributed by Kades and the others to the four shocked and surprised Japanese, who had only expected to hear the U.S. reaction to Matsumoto's draft. The SCAP draft had been typed on legal-sized paper and contained twenty-one bound pages. SCAP had made twenty copies and numbered them consecutively. The paper was of poor quality and quite thick. Copies one and two were given to MacArthur; copies three, four, and five were kept by Government Section; and copies six through twenty were brought to the meeting. Copy six was handed to Yoshida, copy seven to Matsumoto, and eight to Hasegawa. The number of each copy was written in small letters on the lower right side of the cover, but none of the Japanese had the time to notice.

After copies nine through twenty were given to Shirasu, Kades handed him a piece of paper on which was typed: "Fifteen copies, numbered six though twenty, of the document, Draft of the Japanese Constitution, received from Colonel Kades."[8] Shirasu signed it with a pencil and returned it to Kades.[9] Next Whitney announced that "in order that you gentlemen may freely examine and discuss the contents of the document, my officers and I will now withdraw." He then went out into the garden.[10] According to the SCAP record, the time was 10:10 A.M. After twenty or thirty minutes, Whitney and his officers returned to the sunroom and resumed the meeting. Whitney then explained the reason for presenting the SCAP draft. The Japanese record summarized this in the following way:

> Although we have no intention of forcing on you either the contents or the form of this draft, the Supreme Commander in order to defend the Emperor in the face of strong pressure in the United States, has with painstaking and deliberate consideration had a draft prepared which he thinks would protect the Emperor. And observing recent conditions in Japan, he believes that this document will also satisfy the wishes of the Japanese people.[11]

In short, Whitney said that although there was no thought of forcing the SCAP draft constitution on the Japanese government, it was being offered for the purpose of protecting the emperor. Furthermore, the essence of the SCAP draft agreed with the consciousness of the Japanese people. The SCAP account of Whitney's comments does not differ significantly from the Japanese. Still, the SCAP record recounts this scene in a very concrete and lively manner. In later years the SCAP account became the subject of much controversy. Although somewhat long, it is worth quoting in part.

> General Whitney spoke as follows: The Supreme Commander has observed various party platforms recently published having for their primary purpose constitutional reform, and he has observed a growing consciousness on the part of the people of the need for constitutional reform. It is his purpose to see that the people get constitutional reform. As you may or may not know, the Supreme Commander has been unyielding in his defence of your Emperor against increasing pressure from the outside to render him subject to war criminal investigation. He has thus defended the Emperor because he considered that that was the cause of right and justice, and will continue along that course to the extent of his ability. But, gentlemen, the Supreme Commander is not omnipotent. He feels, however, that the acceptance of the provisions of this new Constitution would render the Emperor practically unassailable. . . . The Supreme Commander has directed me to offer this Constitution to your government and party for your adoption and your presentation to the people with his full backing if you care to do so, yet he does not require this of you. He is determined, however, that the principles therein stated shall be laid before the people—rather by you—but, if not, by himself.[12]

Following Whitney's statement, Minister Matsumoto raised questions about the unicameral legislature provided for in the SCAP draft. At the end of the meeting both sides agreed to keep strictly secret the fact that this meeting had occurred and that the SCAP draft had been presented to the Japanese. According to the Japanese record, it was Whitney who requested this secrecy, while according to the SCAP record, it was Yoshida. This is the sole point of difference in the two records. The meeting concluded after eleven o'clock.

As already indicated, on February 13—at the moment when the "day of the conception was announced"—there was, according to the public record, almost complete agreement and very little about which the two sides quarreled. There is no evidence to conclude that SCAP "forced" the American draft on the Japanese. To the contrary, Whitney stressed that they were not "compelled" to accept the draft. The Japanese indicated in their own record that this was the case. It was somewhat later that this point became an issue. In fact, for several days after February 13 the Japanese side was optimistic and had little sense of "defeat." Matsumoto, especially, was in good spirits.

Yoshida, meanwhile, stayed in the background; his secretary, Shirasu, made all of the contacts with SCAP. Shirasu had gone to England at age eighteen and had graduated from Cambridge University. Afterward he enjoyed a warm friendship with Yoshida, then ambassador to England, and became "a person behind the scenes" who acted on Yoshida's behalf. He not only acquired an excellent command of English but "his smooth and frank manner of speaking completely captivated Yoshida."[13] Consequently, he was just the right person to negotiate with SCAP.

Kades relates an interesting episode that illustrates Shirasu's tendency to manipulate. "He came almost every day to our office. But instead of passing through the executive office he came in the back way, knocked at the door, and said as he came in: 'It's the milkman! Does anyone want milk?'"[14] In England the milkman would go around offices every day at three o'clock, ringing a bell and offering tea and cookies. This incident indicates the wit and nerve of Shirasu. But since the business of adopting a constitution was in effect a "dirty business," it is difficult to estimate the extent to which Yoshida saved his own political life by staying in the background and directing Shirasu to do that work for him. Had there been no Shirasu, perhaps Yoshida would not have become prime minister several months later.

The Japanese Government's Reaction

Shirasu spent much of the afternoon of February 13 and the next day talking to Whitney at SCAP headquarters. Though the subject of their conversation is not clear from the record, we can guess its content from a letter in English that Shirasu delivered to Whitney on February 15. This is usually referred to as the "Jeep way letter."[15] Surprisingly, Shirasu said in the letter that "Dr. Matsumoto was quite a socialist in his young days," thus indirectly trying to convince Whitney of Matsumoto's progressive views. He acknowledged that the SCAP draft came as "a great surprise" but asserted that it and Matsumoto's draft were "one and the same in spirit." Shirasu continued:

> He and his colleagues feel that yours and theirs aim at the same destination but there is this great difference in the routes chosen. Your way is so American in the way that it is straight and direct. Their way must be Japanese in the way that it is round about, twisted and narrow. Your way may be called an Air way and their way a Jeep way over bumpy roads.

Skillfully using simile, he emphasized that Matsumoto's draft was not really conservative and that there were no differences in the two drafts. The goals are the same; the differences lie only in the process. He attempted to confuse the other side, but this time he would not succeed. "This time," because—as their previous six months under military occupation showed—it was typical of Japanese conservative politicians, when pushed into a corner, to avoid intellectual confrontation and attempt to win over their opponent by assuming a polite air. When Japan accepted the Potsdam Declaration, for example, because the declaration did not mention Japan's imperial institution, the government interpreted this to mean that no change had taken place in the "Emperor's sovereign right to rule the country" and announced publicly that the "kokutai [national polity] had been preserved."[16]

On February 16 Whitney wrote Shirasu a letter repeating that unless the government accepted SCAP's draft, "it is quite possible that a constitution might be forced upon Japan from the outside." In that case it might be "a constitution which well might sweep away even those traditions and structures which the Supreme Commander by his instrument makes possible to preserve."[17] Whitney repeated his warning to the Japanese government and showed no interest in the "Jeep way letter." Meanwhile, the government could not understand that SCAP's draft was the final draft that would protect the imperial institution.

Matsumoto tried to approach SCAP in a different way than did Shirasu. To Matsumoto the SCAP draft was nothing more than a draft written by amateurs who were ignorant of the law. When he questioned the SCAP draft's unicameral legislature at the February 13 meeting, Matsumoto thought Whitney's reply was especially off the mark. Years later Matsumoto remembered the event as follows: "As far as I know I can't think of any major country which has a unicameral legislature. So when I asked for what reason they had included it [in their draft], he said that Japan was nothing like the American states. Therefore, they had not recognized the necessity of an upper chamber. A unicameral legislature was thus simpler. He used the word 'simpler' in responding to my question. This is the response of someone who knows nothing about the parliamentary system."[18]

Thereupon, Matsumoto Jōji, Doctor of Law, informed them that a bicameral system is necessary as a check and balance mechanism. When they heard this, "the faces of all four of the SCAP officials looked like they had understood it. I was very surprised that their faces seemed to indicate that for the first time they understood that the purpose of a bicameral system is to serve as a check and balance. And I was thoroughly alarmed about a constitution made by such people."[19]

His interpretation of their reaction was typical of "the self-confident" Matsumoto. However, as we have already said, the unicameral system of the SCAP draft was something that Kades had inserted very purposely in the last stage of drafting, knowing that it "might be useful in negotiating" with the Japanese government. But to Matsumoto "the self-confident one," what appeared to be looks of acknowledgment were probably looks that meant, "You've done just what we expected!" Nothing is more dangerous than over-confidence. This was Matsumoto's weakness. He thought that "since they seem to know little about constitutions, and apparently don't understand the bicameral legislative system, wouldn't it be better if I taught them a little something?"[20] On February 18 he thus prepared a second explanatory letter with the title "Supplementary Explanation of Proposed Constitution Revision" and had Shirasu deliver it to Whitney.

After saying that "the United States Constitution and the English Constitution are the best examples of democratic constitutions in the world," Matsumoto noted their differences in form. Those differences are due to differences "in customs and traditions, and historical backgrounds between the two countries. . . . The laws of a nation are largely the product of its own history." Although the Weimar Constitution has been called the most democratic constitution possible, "not only did it fail to achieve its objectives but on the contrary was abused in the most undemocratic manner possible." He continued:

> The constitution of a country can achieve the desired ends only when it is adapted to its national circumstances. . . . The new draft constitution submitted the other day may seem outwardly meagre in bulk and of a rather neutral character. That is because the proposed revision aims to leave the existing constitution untouched as far as possible to avoid arousing needless antagonism on the part of the great majority of our people, who are neither radicals nor communists. On the other hand, the revised constitution marks, in practice, a big step forward toward parliamentary democracy after the English pattern. . . . Metaphorically speaking, the new constitution is a tablet sugar-coated for the benefit of the masses.[21]

Matsumoto concluded that the mass media were critical of his draft because they were "largely and distinctly left," and warned that "it would be dangerous to overlook the silent majority of conservative thought" or to ignore "those without a voice." Finally, as Shirasu had earlier, Matsumoto said: "Having carefully studied your counter-proposal, I have arrived at the conclusion that although the formula appears to be diametrically opposed to our own, in their underlying principles the two do not stand so widely apart as seems at first sight."

Whitney replied that Matsumoto's draft did not merit examination and asked whether SCAP's draft had been presented to the cabinet. When Shirasu replied that it had (in fact, it had not), Whitney said that the Supreme Commander had no objections to minor changes being made in SCAP's draft according to the requirements of the people. However, he warned that the cabinet must decide within forty-eight hours that the principles of the SCAP draft were acceptable. Finally, he threatened that unless the decision was made, the Supreme Commander would "take the constitution [the SCAP draft] to the people directly and make it a major issue in the forthcoming [election] campaign."[22] The Japanese government was left with no further means of resisting.

Matsumoto's Report to the Cabinet

Five days had passed since the SCAP draft had been presented to the four Japanese, but the cabinet had not yet met. The only Japanese who knew about the SCAP demands were Prime Minister Shidehara and the four to whom the draft had been presented on February 13. Seeing no way out, Prime Minister Shidehara called a cabinet meeting on February 19. Now that events had come to such a pass, Matsumoto was in a state of dejection. Ashida Hitoshi, the minister of health and welfare, attended the cabinet meeting and described it in his diary in this way: "The regular Cabinet meeting began at 10:15 A.M. A pale Dr. Matsumoto Jōji asked to have the floor and said that an extremely serious incident had occurred."[23] Ashida wrote at length of Matsumoto's report concerning the February 13 meeting. In response to the report Home Minister Mizuchi, Justice Minister Iwata, and Prime Minister Shidehara all said, "We cannot accept the SCAP draft." But Ashida himself appears to have taken a somewhat different position.

> I said at this time that if the American draft were to be published, the Japanese newspapers would definitely pursue this and probably give their support to it. If at that point the present Cabinet were to refuse to accept responsibility and resign, it is certain that others who approve of the American draft would come forward. And the great influence this would have on the outcome of the coming general election is something about which we should be seriously concerned.[24]

Given these differences of opinion in the cabinet, it was decided that Prime Minister Shidehara should talk directly to MacArthur. Before discussing that meeting, however, we should first consider more carefully Matsumoto's report at the February 19 cabinet meeting, which later became a major issue. Ashida wrote that Matsumoto reported Whitney's statements of February 13 as follows:

> He related the following gist of what Whitney had said. "The Japanese draft is wholly unacceptable. Accordingly, a different draft has been prepared by SCAP. The United States and MacArthur have approved this document. Of course, we will not force this draft on you. We think this draft is truly one

which the Japanese people desire. MacArthur does support the Japanese Emperor, and this draft constitution is the only way of *protecting the person of the Emperor from those who are opposed to him.*"[25] (emphasis added)

However, when Matsumoto appeared before the Liberal Party's hearings on the constitution in July 1954, he testified that he was pressured to accept the SCAP draft because Whitney had said that "without the SCAP draft the person of the Emperor could not be guaranteed."[26] For more than forty years now the charge has been repeated that the constitution was "forced" on Japan and that the most extreme evidence of this originated with Matsumoto's 1954 testimony. Moreover, Matsumoto emphasized this charge time and again. Irie Toshio, director general of the cabinet's Legislation Bureau, also attended the February 19 cabinet meeting with Ashida and gave the following account of the event: "(According to Matsumoto's report, Whitney) said that if the Japanese rejected the SCAP draft, there would undoubtedly be a major change regarding the person of the Emperor. (Note: Whitney's words about the 'person of the Emperor' strongly struck Matsumoto, and he told Irie that it had made a powerful, unforgettable impression on him, a statement which he repeated elsewhere as well.)"[27]

In actual fact, then, what did Whitney say? To the extent that we can know from both the Japanese and SCAP public records, which have been cited at length, we see no evidence of the words used by Matsumoto. Those present at the February 13 meeting—Yoshida, Shirasu, Hasegawa, Rowell, and Hussey—have denied "hearing such words."[28] What remains is Matsumoto's report to the cabinet, which according to Ashida "[quoted Whitney as saying that] the SCAP draft is the only way of protecting the Emperor from those who are opposed to him." According to Irie, however, Whitney said, "If the Japanese side rejects this draft, there will be a major change regarding the person of the Emperor."

Both statements agree that Matsumoto used the English words "person of the Emperor," synonymous with the Japanese words "tennō no shintai." Yet the question is not whether Whitney used the words "person of the Emperor" but whether he used them in a threatening way, as Matsumoto testified. The *Ashida Hitoshi Diary*, on the contrary, viewed the words as a warning about protecting the emperor, and the records of the meeting agree with this. There is no evidence anywhere that supports Matsumoto's testimony.

If Matsumoto's testimony were accurate, however, he would have been inconsistent for not being gravely concerned from February 13 about the "threat" that Whitney supposedly uttered. But as we have seen, until at least February 18 Matsumoto was so full of confidence that he thought "it would be best to teach SCAP a thing or two." Thus even if he had reported the events of February 13 to the cabinet meeting on February 19, as he testified in 1954, that was after SCAP had completely rejected his "Supplementary Explanation" of February 18 and demanded a reply within forty-eight hours [to SCAP's draft]. In his distressed state of mind Matsumoto was convinced that Whitney had said on February 13, "Unless this (SCAP's draft) is accepted, the person of the Emperor cannot be guaranteed," rather than, "If the provisions of this new constitution are accepted . . . the Emperor will be secure." Perhaps it was indeed quite reasonable for Matsumoto to believe that the reason the Japanese were unable to refuse the SCAP draft was because of this threat.

The cabinet decided on February 19 that Shidehara should appeal directly to MacArthur. But since SCAP had ordered the Japanese on February 18 "to reply within forty-eight hours," Shirasu was again dispatched to SCAP headquarters, this time to implore Whitney to extend the deadline until February 22. The Japanese request was granted. In a memorandum to MacArthur Whitney explained the reason for the extension.

> I informed Mr. Shirasu that I considered the request for forty-eight hours extension to be quite reasonable as I felt sure that if the document was fully understood the members of the Cabinet would see in it a means of protecting the dignity and person of the Emperor and the Imperial institution in modified form; a means of assuming moral leadership among other nations of the world; a means of gaining great favor among the Allied nations; and a means of sharply reducing the period of Allied control over Japan.[29]

Here expressed very clearly is the political meaning of the SCAP draft. And in fact, Yoshida Shigeru, who had not at this point emerged as a central figure, said almost the same thing to the House of Peers when he became prime minister three months later.[30] In other words, the Japanese government only later came to understand the political significance of SCAP's draft.

Accepting the SCAP Draft Constitution

On February 21 Prime Minister Shidehara called on MacArthur at his SCAP headquarters, and following three hours of discussion, was persuaded by MacArthur's oratory. The next morning he reported on the meeting to the cabinet. According to Irie Toshio, Ashida Hitoshi recorded the proceedings of that meeting. And according to Ashida's account, MacArthur had spoken to Shidehara in the following manner:

> "We are working sincerely on behalf of Japan. Since meeting the Emperor, it has been my intention to do whatever I can to ensure his security. I also un-

derstand that you, Count Shidehara, are working with sincere good faith for your country. But I have heard reports that the recent discussions among the members of the Far Eastern Commission in Washington were most unpleasant. I have heard that they were worse for Japan than you could ever imagine. I myself do not know how long I can remain in the position as Supreme Commander, and when I think of what might happen after that, I am filled with apprehension. The Soviet Union and Australia fear a war of revenge from Japan and are doing their utmost to prevent this from ever happening. . . . What we mean by Basic Forms is in the first chapter of the draft which provides for the abolition of war. I think that by declaring that it will abandon war Japan will be able to grasp moral leadership."

Shidehara at this moment seized on the word "leadership" and said that probably nobody would become followers. MacArthur replied that "even without followers Japan has nothing to lose. Those who do not support this are bad." . . . [MacArthur said] chapter one (the Emperor as symbol and popular sovereignty) and abolishing war were the essential points; he gave the impression that there was room for negotiating the other matters of the draft. The Prime Minister expressed the opinion that MacArthur's attitude was one of understanding.[31]

According to Irie,[32] the cabinet expressed unanimous approval of the SCAP draft, but according to Ashida's account, Matsumoto in fact was opposed, while Shidehara, Home Minister Mizuchi, Agriculture Minister Fukushima, and Ashida himself favored accepting the draft. In any case, SCAP's draft was accepted at the cabinet meeting and the Japanese government proceeded to prepare its own draft based on it.

It is unclear, however, to what extent cabinet members understood the SCAP draft. Perhaps they understood no more than "the Emperor as symbol" and "renunciation of war," for it is highly probable that prior to the draft's acceptance at this cabinet meeting, no more than three ministers—Shidehara, Yoshida, and Matsumoto—had actually seen the document. As we have seen, Government Section gave fifteen copies of its draft to the Japanese government. Although not enough copies for all ministers, the only possible reason for SCAP's decision to provide fifteen copies—at a time when convenient copy machines did not exist—was to facilitate immediate debate by the cabinet.

However, there is no evidence that copies of the SCAP draft were ever distributed to the cabinet. A study of Foreign Ministry records[33] suggests that copy six, given to Yoshida on February 13, was passed on to Shidehara; copy seven was retained by Matsumoto; copy eight, given to the interpreter Hasegawa, ended up with Yoshida; copy nine was later (February 26) passed to Satō Tatsuo, the head of the first section of the cabinet's Legislation Bureau;[34] and copy ten was, according to the record, in Yoshida's possession but was probably kept by Shirasu. All of the remaining copies appear to have been left with the Foreign Ministry's chief of documents section. What happened to the original document, or at least to the translation of it? Amazingly, when the SCAP draft was accepted at the February 22 cabinet meeting, the Foreign Ministry's Japanese translation of Chapter 1 on the emperor and Chapter 2 on renouncing war were given to cabinet ministers. "The Japanese translation (by the Foreign Ministry) of the complete American draft was distributed in mimeograph form for the first time at a Cabinet meeting on February 26."[35]

At the February 19 cabinet meeting, despite the fact that six days had passed since the SCAP draft had been received, the draft was discussed without a Japanese translation, and at the meeting on February 22, when for all practical purposes the decision was made to accept the U.S. draft, only the first two chapters had been translated into Japanese.

It seems clear that the text was purposely not distributed in order to keep it secret. Perhaps secrecy was good policy. Beyond secrecy, however, there was another explanation for the draft's lack of circulation. Institutionally speaking, there was no tradition of carrying on debates in the cabinet. Throughout the process of adopting the present constitution, whether it was the Konoe draft or the Matsumoto draft, the whole matter was actually treated as a private affair. At this final critical hour, there was no precedent for conducting a calm, reasoned debate. Aside from their discussion about protecting the emperor and "preserving the national polity," the cabinet ministers accepted the SCAP draft without a meaningful constitutional debate pitting ideas one against another. At this juncture the wheel of Japanese history took a dramatic turn.

This was Japan's second surrender following the first on August 15, 1945. The "imposition" of this draft constitution meant the defeat of a political ideology and a historical consciousness and signified the decisive defeat of Japanese constitutional ideas.

Notes

1. Takayanagi Kenzō, Ōtomo Ichirō, and Tanaka Hideo, eds., *Nihonkoku kenpō seitei no katei* (Tokyo: Yūhikaku, 1972), 1:79.

2. According to a paper in the Kades personal file, C. L. Kades, "Japanese Constitution—Formation during Diet Debate and Preliminary Proposal," University of Maryland, McKeldin Library, *Gokuhi* (top secret) is stamped at the top of the "Kempō kaisei yōkō" (Matsumoto draft "A"), which is labeled "No. 28 of 30 Copies." The title of Matsumoto draft "A" was rendered in English as "Tentative Revision of the Meiji Constitution by Joji Matsumoto, 4 January, 1946." It is not clear when it was received from the Japanese government.

3. Takayanagi, Ōtomo, and Tanaka, eds., *Nihonkoku kenpō,* 1:81–89.

4. Satō Tatsuo, "Nihonkoku kenpō seiritsushi—'MacArthur sōan' kara 'Nihonkoku kenpō' made," part 2, *Jurist,* no. 82 (May 15, 1955): 13.

5. Hays was not actually present at this meeting. *Ed.*

6. Gaimushō gaikō bunsho microfilm, reel no. A'0092 (hereafter, Gaimushō microfilm).

7. Takayanagi, Ōtomo, and Tanaka, eds., *Nihonkoku kenpō*, 1:323–325.

8. Gaimushō microfilm.

9. Kades personal file.

10. Takayanagi, Ōtomo, and Tanaka, eds., *Nihonkoku kenpō*, 1:323.

11. Gaimushō microfilm.

12. Takayanagi, Ōtomo, and Tanaka, eds., *Nihonkoku kenpō*, 1:327–329.

13. Aragaki Hideo, *Gendai jinbutsuron* (Tokyo: Kawade Shobō, 1950), p. 278.

14. Takemae Eiji, *Nihon senryō—GHQ kōkan no shōgen* (Tokyo: Chūō Kōronsha, 1988), p. 93.

15. Takayanagi, Ōtomo, and Tanaka, eds., *Nihonkoku kenpō*, 1:337–341.

16. See the telegram the Japanese government sent to the Allied countries concerning acceptance of the Potsdam Declaration, August 10, 1945, Gaimushō tokubetsu shiryōbu hen, *Nihon senryō oyobi kanri jūyō bunshoshū* (Tokyo: Tōyō Keizai Shinpōsha, 1947), 1:14.

17. Takayanagi, Ōtomo, and Tanaka, eds., *Nihonkoku kenpō*, 1:347.

18. Matsumoto Jōji kōjutsu, "Nihonkoku kenpō ni tsuite," Kenpō chōsakai jimukyoku, *Kenshi, sō dai nijūhachi gō* (October 1958): 11–12.

19. Ibid., p. 12.

20. Ibid., pp. 12–13.

21. Gaimushō microfilm.

22. Takayanagi, Ōtomo, and Tanaka, eds., *Nihonkoku kenpō*, 1:369.

23. Shindō Eiichi and Shimokabe Motoharu, eds., *Ashida Hitoshi nikki* (Tokyo: Iwanami Shoten, 1986), 1:75.

24. Ibid., p. 77.

25. Ibid., pp. 75–76.

26. Matsumoto Jōji kōjutsu, "Nihonkoku kenpō ni tsuite," p. 10.

27. Irie Toshio, *Kenpō seiritsu no keii to kenpōjō no shomondai* (Tokyo: Daiichi Hōki Shuppan, 1976), p. 199.

28. Takayanagi, Ōtomo, and Tanaka, eds., *Nihonkoku kenpō*, 1:58.

29. Ibid., p. 373.

30. Yoshida's explanation of the reason he submitted the bill to revise the constitution to the House of Peers appears in Dai kyūjūkai teikoku gikai kizokuin giji sokkiroku daini gō (June 23, 1946), p. 17.

31. Shindō and Shimokabe, eds., *Ashida Hitoshi nikki*, 1:78–79.

32. Irie, *Kenpō seiritsu*, p. 203.

33. Gaimushō microfilm.

34. Satō Tatsuo, "Ma sōan no bangō," *Jurist*, no. 472 (February 1971): 10.

35. Irie, *Kenpō seiritsu*, p. 204.

6

The Struggle to Japanize
the American Draft

Preparing the Japanese Draft

After very reluctantly accepting the SCAP draft, the Japanese government finally set about making a "Japanese draft" modeled on SCAP's version. It is fitting to refer to this as a "Japanese draft." That is, it is usually said that the government draft was a "translation" of the SCAP draft. But the process of making a Japanese draft was not simply one of translating or adhering faithfully to the SCAP draft, for it took the considerable skill of the Legislation Bureau officials to "Japanize" the document.

The initial, partial Japanese translation of the American draft, produced by Matsumoto Jōji, was presented to the cabinet on February 22, 1946. This was not a complete translation, however, as it only included Articles 1 through 9. Chapter 1, "The Emperor," comprised eight articles, or one more than SCAP's draft; and Chapter 2, "Renunciation of War," became Article 9. The Foreign Ministry's translation, presented at the cabinet meeting of February 26, was complete, and unlike the Matsumoto translation, faithful to the original, almost a literal rendering.

Following the cabinet decision of February 26, Irie Toshio, deputy director general of the Legislation Bureau, assisted by Satō Tatsuo, chief of the first section of the bureau, began the next day the task of writing the provisions of a Japanese draft constitution. The goal was to complete the document by March 11.[1] They were assigned a radio broadcasting studio in the prime minister's official residence as a place where they could work in total secrecy. Aside from its use as a recording studio, this room was used mainly as a place where the elderly Prime Minister Shidehara took his afternoon naps. A sound-proof broadcasting room was certainly an appropriate place for naps as well as for highly secretive projects of this sort. Satō Tatsuo has written of the drafting process:

Because we were required to maintain the strictest secrecy, we could neither discuss the matter with our colleagues of the Bureau nor borrow the reference works we needed. . . . In any case, working under a strict deadline, we very anxiously scrutinized the MacArthur (SCAP) draft, pondering various points and did our level best to write out our own draft quickly.[2]

Adding Chapter 3 (people's rights and obligations), which Satō drafted, to Matsumoto's preliminary draft of Chapters 1 and 2, Irie and Satō produced their first draft. They then proceeded to write a second draft by adding Chapter 4, "The Diet," and Chapter 5, "The Cabinet," from the Matsumoto draft. Irie and Satō met with Matsumoto twice during this time. Along with Miyazawa Toshiyoshi, this was the same group that had written the Matsumoto draft for the Committee to Study Constitutional Problems. With his work for the government completed, Miyazawa had meanwhile ended his association with Matsumoto, Irie, and Satō.

Although from the outset the plan was to complete the draft by March 11, SCAP began almost immediately to press them to speed up their work. On March 2 Satō and the others hastily put their draft in order, and without translating it into English, made thirty mimeographed copies for submission to SCAP.[3] This preliminary draft is commonly referred to as the "Japanese draft" or the "March Second draft." Here in summary form is what we shall call for now the "Japanese draft."[4]

The Japanese draft differed from the American draft in several ways. For one thing, it had no preamble. The arrangement of its chapters was also somewhat different. For purposes of comparison, we will contrast several of the articles of each draft in the following section. As we have seen, the SCAP draft was translated by the Foreign Ministry. To better understand the SCAP draft, however, we will use here the translation by Tanaka Hideo.[5]

American Draft

Article 1. The Emperor shall be the symbol of the State and of the Unity of the People, deriving his position from the sovereign will of the People, and from no other source.

Article 2. Succession to the Imperial Throne shall be dynastic and in accordance with such Imperial House Law as the Diet may enact.

Japanese Draft

Article 1. The Emperor derives his position from the supreme will of the Japanese People, maintaining his position as a symbol of the State and as an emblem of the Unity of the People.

Article 2. The Imperial Throne shall be dynastic and succeeded to in accordance with the Imperial House Law.[6]

Article 1 of the American draft stated that the emperor's position was "derived from the sovereign will of the people." But Article 1 of the Japanese draft changed that to "derived from the supreme will of the Japanese people." In other words, in contrast to the SCAP draft's opening with a clear statement of the people's sovereignty, the Japanese draft used the word "supreme." This was, in fact, a very intentional avoidance of the word "sovereignty."

As we have seen, the SCAP draft was translated by the Foreign Ministry and in part by Matsumoto. The Foreign Ministry translation stated that "the Emperor's position is derived from the sovereign will of the People,"[7] while Matsumoto's said that "The Emperor is based on the People's will."[8] Both explained the position of the emperor as being determined by the will of the people. However, when Prime Minister Shidehara saw the two translations, he thought "sovereign will" should be changed to "supreme will," thus using the unfamiliar term *shikō* (supreme) instead of sovereign.[9] As we shall explain later, this one word became a serious problem during the Diet deliberations on revising the constitution, and subsequently the wording of the SCAP draft was restored.

It may appear that there is little difference between Article 2 of the SCAP draft and of the Japanese draft, but indeed there is a major difference. The SCAP draft provides for succession to the throne in accordance with such "Imperial House Law as the Diet may enact." The Imperial House Law is enacted by the people's representatives in the Diet; that is, it is a statute. In the Japanese draft the words "enacted by the Diet" are missing. In essence this is the same as Article 2 of the Meiji Constitution: "The Imperial Throne shall be succeeded to by Imperial male descendants according to the provisions of the Imperial House Law." Only the phrase "Imperial male descendants" was omitted from the Japanese draft. And it was omitted because it would contradict the provision for sexual equality in the draft constitution. For the same reason the thought was that the Imperial House Law should not be a law but an imperial rescript or a government ordinance. When writing the provisions concerning the emperor, the Japanese drafters took pains to use terminology as similar as possible to that of the Meiji Constitution. For example, Article 6 of the American draft said: "Acting only on the advice [*jogen*] and with the consent of the Cabinet, the Emperor, on behalf of the people, shall perform the following state functions." But the Japanese draft said: "On the advice [*hohitsu*] of the Cabinet, the Emperor shall . . . on behalf of the people." This must be considered a conscious effort by officials of the Legislation Bureau to preserve the phrase in Article 55 of the Meiji Constitution: "The respective Ministers of State shall give their advice [*hohitsu*] to the Emperor."

Next, let us consider the provisions on the renunciation of war.

SCAP Draft

Article 8. War as a sovereign right of the nation is abolished. The threat or use of force is forever renounced as a means for settling disputes with any other nation.

No army, navy, air force, or other war potential will ever be authorized and no rights of belligerency will ever be conferred upon the State.

Japanese Draft

Article 9. War, as a sovereign right of the nation, and the threat or use of force, is forever abolished as a means for settling disputes with other nations.

The maintenance of land, sea and air forces, as well as other war potential, and the right of belligerency of the state shall not be recognized.

Although there are differences in the wording of the two drafts, there are virtually no differences in meaning.

Modeling Human Rights on the Meiji Constitution

The next issue is human rights. We noted earlier that the SCAP draft's provision granting equal protection and guarantees of the rights of foreigners living in Japan was one of its special features. The Japanese draft changed that in the following way.

SCAP Draft

Article 13. All natural persons are equal before the law. No discrimination shall be authorized or tolerated in political, economic or social relations on account of race, creed, sex, social status, caste or national origin.

No patent of nobility shall from this time forth embody within itself any national or civic power of government.

No rights of peerage except those of the Imperial dynasty shall extend beyond the lives of those now in being. No special privilege shall accompany any award of honor, decoration or other distinction; nor shall any such award be valid beyond the lifetime of the individual who now holds or hereafter may receive it.

Article 14. Aliens shall be entitled to the equal protection of the law.

Japanese Draft

Article 13. All the people are equal under the law and there shall be no discrimination in political, economic, or social relations because of race, creed, sex, social status, or family origin. No special privilege shall accompany any title and court rank, award of honor or other distinction.

Article 14. Aliens shall have the right of equal protection of the law.

First of all, by changing "all natural persons" in Article 13 of the SCAP draft to "all the people" and by changing "caste or national origin" to "family lineage," the Japanese draft limited the object of equal protection in Article 13 to "all the people." But since the Japanese draft's guarantee of the rights of aliens in Article 14 was almost exactly the same as the SCAP draft's, one might think that, taken as a whole, the Japanese draft was in no way different from the SCAP draft. Yet at this stage the concept of "the people" (*kokumin*) was unclear and was later defined by statutory law. With the complete elimination of Article 14, however, the rights of foreigners were excluded from protection by the constitution. We shall return to this point again later.

The greatest difference in the human rights articles of the two drafts concerned the right of freedom. Take, for example, "freedom of expression."

SCAP Draft
Article 20. Freedom of assembly, speech and press and all other forms of expression are guaranteed. No censorship shall be maintained, nor shall the secrecy of any means of communication be violated.

Japanese Draft
Article 20. All the people shall, within limits not prejudicial to peace and order, have the freedom of speech, writing, publication, assembly and association.
No censorship shall be maintained except as specifically provided for by law.
Article 21. The secrecy of correspondence and other communications of all the people shall not be violated. Measures necessary to maintain public peace and order shall be provided for by law.

The SCAP draft recognizes very clearly freedom of expression as an unlimited constitutional right. By contrast, the Japanese draft goes no further than to recognize the freedom of expression "within limits not prejudicial to peace and order" or "within the limits of the law." It seems certain that when Irie and Satō drafted this provision they had in mind Article 29 of the Meiji Constitution, which concerned freedom of expression. Nothing in this portion of their draft is essentially different from the Meiji Constitution.

Moreover, some of the human rights articles in the SCAP draft were omitted entirely from the Japanese draft. One example is SCAP's Article 28, which provided for the state ownership of land. Another is the social rights provisions, including the rights of women, which Beate Sirota and others had so strongly advocated during the drafting in SCAP's subcommittee on civil rights. The provisions in SCAP's Article 24 on free and universal education and the prohibition of exploitation of children were incorporated into the Japanese draft, but the provisions requiring improvement of public health and providing a system of social security were omitted.

Also, the SCAP draft's provision for a unicameral legislature, to which Minister of State Matsumoto had objected from the moment the draft was handed to him, was changed to a bicameral system: "The Diet shall consist of two houses, namely the House of Representatives and the House of Councillors." And with regard to the method of electing the House of Councillors, Article 45 [of the Japanese draft] envisaged a dual system of members elected from "the various districts or professions" and members appointed by the cabinet. In view of the fact that the earlier Matsumoto drafts (the tentative draft and drafts "A" and "B") provided for a new institution, the House of Councillors, to replace the House of Peers, it seems reasonable to conclude that in the inclusion of an article providing for a bicameral system we see a revival of Matsumoto's idea.

Finally, let us consider the chapter on local government. We have already described SCAP's chapter on local government. The Japanese fundamentally revised this part of the SCAP document. First of all, the title of the chapter was changed from "Local Government" to "Local Self Government." Second, while the SCAP draft mentioned such concrete local government bodies as "prefectures" and "cities and towns" and defined their authority, the Japanese eliminated all of these and created a new concept of all-inclusive bodies called "local public entities." Matsumoto, Irie, and Satō drafted this chapter. Satō relates how, "from the notion that we would go beyond the restraints of such fixed constitutional ideas" as the "prefectures" and "cities and towns" contained in the SCAP draft, they came up with the term "local public entities."[10] However, the change did not stop with new wording; a completely new article was inserted at the beginning of the "Local Self Government" chapter, which read:

> Article 101. Regulations concerning organization and operations of local public entities shall be fixed by law in accordance with the principle of local autonomy.

In other words, nothing concerning local self-government was to be determined by the constitution. Rather, everything was to be left to statutory law (the Law on Local Self Government). Satō subsequently explained that, "When we wrote this chapter, we had the most difficulty finding a way of expressing the first article (101)."[11] But it is hard to overstate the significance of this article for the Japanization of local self-government.

Thirty Hours of Negotiations

On Saturday, March 2, 1946, Irie and Satō made thirty mimeographed copies of the Japanese draft in preparation for Minister Matsumoto's scheduled report to SCAP's Government Section at 10:00 A.M. on Monday, March 4. Early Monday morning Matsumoto suddenly asked Satō, who had just arrived at the office, to accompany him to SCAP headquarters. Taken aback, Satō "rather reluctantly went along with the Minister."[12] The conference took place in room 602 of the Daiichi Seimei Building, where the SCAP headquarters was located. The sixth floor was the top floor of the building and the heart of SCAP's operation; here MacArthur, his chief of staff, his adjutant, and Government Section all had offices.[13] Waiting for Matsumoto to arrive were Shirasu Jirō and two Foreign Ministry interpreters, Hasegawa Motokichi and Obata Kaoru.

Matsumoto met first with the head of Government Section, General Whitney, and handed over the Japanese draft with the comment: "This draft has not yet been discussed and approved by the Cabinet. It is nothing more than a preliminary draft which we are submitting to you."[14] Two American interpreters joined the Japanese interpreters and all set to work promptly to translate the draft into English. As the examination of the document began, Colonel Kades noticed that the preamble was missing. Turning to Satō, Kades said sharply: "You can't omit the preamble. Add a preamble that is precisely the same as the one in the MacArthur draft."[15] Thus from the outset the situation took a perilous turn. Satō had no choice but to attach the American preamble that had been translated by the Foreign Ministry. The situation became increasingly tense and threatening.

Before translation of the article on the emperor had been completed, Kades summoned Shirasu. He pointed out that Article 1 of the SCAP draft declares that the emperor derives his position from the sovereign will of the people, then adds further: "and from no other source." In a scathing manner, Kades told Shirasu that these words were missing from the Japanese draft. Furthermore, whereas Article 2 of the SCAP draft stated that succession to the throne shall be in accordance with "such Imperial House Law as the Diet may enact," Kades noted that the Japanese draft had omitted "as the Diet may enact."[16] But Kades [and his interpreters] finished reading the article on the emperor without noticing that the SCAP draft's "sovereign will of the People" had been written in the Japanese draft as "*supreme* will of the people" (*kokumin shikō*) before being translated back into English as "*sovereign* will of the people."

As the translating proceeded, Kades became increasingly angry. He pointed to the use of the word *hohitsu* (from the Meiji Constitution) in the words "on the advice and with the consent" of the cabinet (Article 6).[17] Meanwhile, Matsumoto did not remain silent, but countered with explanations for each of Kades's objections. But no matter what he said, nothing could convince the Americans. This must have been unprecedented for the self-assured Matsumoto, who had never met anyone who argued with him the way that Kades did. Moreover, from Matsumoto's perspective Kades was nothing more than a forty-year-old upstart. In Matsumoto's long experience no young scholar had ever really challenged him. Since discussions and debates had always progressed to his satisfaction, one can imagine how angry he became during this confrontation with Kades. On the other hand, Kades must have been surprised by Matsumoto's angry manner. Matsumoto later described this encounter:

> He [Kades] was extremely upset, his hands were shaking so hard that they shook the table. I was upset too. I couldn't wait for Shirasu to translate what Kades was saying. I finally began to respond directly in my broken English. I even asked him, "Have you come to Japan to correct our Japanese?" I was so mad that I even said something like that. He too was very angry at that point, and we couldn't get anything done. About that time somebody said "let's eat" and we took a break for lunch. We had some American army food, some beans or something in a can, with a little pork. It was really terrible! There is an expression in Japanese, "to chew wax," and that food tasted exactly like chewing wax. I did eat it, even though I didn't want it.[18]

It is difficult to believe that the Americans were eating food that was worse than anything the Japanese had, but for Matsumoto taking food from an impudent upstart whom he detested must have been extremely distasteful. When he had finished lunch, Matsumoto returned to the prime minister's office, informing Satō that he had to attend a meeting of cabinet members on some economic affairs.[19] However, this appears to have been merely an excuse. Matsumoto himself later explained his reason for leaving: "Since we were arguing about every article there was the danger that a fistfight might break out. That is one reason I thought it might be wise to leave at this juncture. So I said I had something to do and left."[20] Matsumoto subsequently sent back word to Satō at Government Section, saying only: "I can't go back because I'm not feeling well; you should use your own discretion."[21] Matsumoto never again went back to SCAP headquarters. Thus, except for interpreters, Satō literally was left alone in this forlorn battle against a besieging enemy. The work of translating the Japanese draft into English lasted until evening. Satō recalls:

> Shortly after six P.M. I was suddenly told by the Americans, "We have to make a final draft this evening. General Whitney says he will wait until

twelve o'clock. If it can't be done by then, he will wait until six o'clock tomorrow morning." I had gone to MacArthur's headquarters that day without any preparation just to help the Minister with the translation. The Japanese document itself was just a rough draft that we were still working on, something we had expected to go over again and again while negotiating with the Americans and making revisions. So I was greatly surprised to hear Whitney's statement.[22]

But Satō did not leave the meeting, nor could he. He continued his negotiations with Government Section officers, examining the draft article by article. It was about this time that the number of Americans present greatly increased. As negotiations began, Satō noted in pencil "a conference of about seventeen people" in the margin of his mimeographed copy of the Japanese draft.[23] This included Kades, Hussey, Rowell, and others of Government Section, who were all watching with a critical eye. The interpreter for Government Section was Beate Sirota, the woman who had worked for the inclusion of civil rights provisions in the subcommittee during the preparation of the SCAP draft. Satō was satisfied with Sirota's interpreting. He noted that "she understood Japanese well, was sharp, and conveyed to the other side exactly the meaning of what I said."[24]

Nevertheless, the image of Satō standing alone, surrounded by such a large number of Government Section personnel, certainly reinforces the idea that the Americans "imposed" their draft constitution on Japan. Robert Ward, a professor of political science at the University of Michigan, first advanced in his 1957 article the thesis that the constitution was imposed, describing this scene in some detail. He concluded that "forcing on the Japanese people a Constitution that is not in accord with the political ideas and political experience of the great majority of Japanese will not in the long run serve the cause of democracy."[25] We may not agree with that conclusion today. But the scene at Government Section was unusual, not merely because of the number of people present but because negotiations went on throughout the night and until the evening of the next day—an exceptionally long period of time.

To his credit Satō never wavered, persevering until the very end. Chapter 2, "Renunciation of War," did not produce much opposition, and was completed with a few minor revisions. Next came Chapter 3, "Human Rights." Recall that Article 13 of the Japanese draft had omitted SCAP's phrase "national origin" but had guaranteed the human rights of foreigners residing in Japan by incorporating Article 16 of the SCAP draft into Article 14. The Americans immediately questioned the removal of the words "national origin." To this, Satō in turn questioned the reason for including Article 16 in the SCAP draft and drew the response that the reason for guaranteeing the human rights of foreigners was because they were equal to Japanese. If that is so, Satō replied, there is no need to make a provision specifically designed to protect the rights of foreigners. He suggested the elimination of Article 14 of the Japanese draft and the inclusion of a clause on the human rights of foreigners in Article 13. Agreement was soon reached on the wording of the new Article 13: "All natural persons are equal under the law and there shall be no discrimination in political, economic, or social relations because of race, creed, sex, social status, or family origin."

In short, the phrase "all the people" in the Japanese draft was cut out and the wording in SCAP's draft, "all natural persons," was restored. In addition, the prohibition against discrimination because of "national origins" in the SCAP draft was restored as a prohibition against discrimination because of "nationality." Satō thus succeeded in weakening the general provision giving protection to foreigners in Article 14 of the Japanese draft. However, he realized that even though he had won a partial victory, he was still "in a bind."[26] For the moment, though, he was content with this. And the next day, after the Diet had begun its session, he renewed his effort to eliminate entirely from the constitution the provision for protection of foreigners.

When the examination came to the "rights and duties of the people," the Americans said that "chapter three of the Japanese draft is so completely different from the MacArthur (SCAP) draft it would be meaningless to examine it."[27] SCAP's view seems to have been quite reasonable, for as we saw when we discussed the "freedom of expression," the Japanese provisions were indeed very different from those in the American version, resembling more closely those of the Meiji Constitution. Understandably, then, the Americans doubted that the Japanese provisions would really guarantee the freedom of expression.

Satō explained that the Japanese draft included the clause, "to the extent that they do not conflict with the public order and peace," because "we think it is necessary to recognize an exception in law for obscene pictures and so forth."[28] But he could not convince the Americans, who argued, "There is a danger that it would be abused."[29] Subsequently, this and other civil rights provisions were written much as they had been in the SCAP draft. Nor would the Americans allow the elimination of articles on public health and social security from the social welfare provisions. In the end, they were restored in the newly drafted Article 23: "In all spheres of life, laws shall be designed for the promotion and extension of social welfare and security, and of public health, freedom, justice and democracy."

Thus the article-by-article deliberation proceeded in this fashion through Chapter 5, "The Cabinet," and Chapter 4, "The Diet." Satō made handwritten revisions on the Japanese draft, and after each section had been reviewed with SCAP, had a cabinet assistant secretary named Kiuchi take them one by one to the prime minister's office. As Chapter 4 ("The Diet") was finished, "the first light of dawn appeared in the sky through the window."[30] The all-night review of the Japanese draft had at last come to an end. But Chapter 6 ("The Judiciary") and other chapters still remained to be examined. After finishing breakfast at about seven o'clock, the Japanese and American teams resumed their deliberations.

None of Chapter 6 or the following chapters in the Japanese draft were acceptable to the Americans. Revisions were no longer entered on the mimeographed copies of the Japanese draft but instead were written double-spaced on new sheets of lined paper, with any revisions written in the margins.[31]

With work proceeding in this way, the rewriting of the Japanese draft finally reached an end at four o'clock in the afternoon of March 5. Satō left Government Section and returned to the prime minister's office, having worked some thirty hours without a wink of sleep. At the end of a memorandum he later wrote about this event, Satō expressed his feelings in this way:

> I deeply regret the fact that, being unprepared and with little talent and, moreover, under extreme time constraints, I had no opportunity to question their views in detail or to explore their arguments fully. While it was unavoidable under the circumstances, I felt deeply dejected on considering my failure to perform this important responsibility satisfactorily and returned to the Prime Minister's office with my head hanging.[32]

One might say in Satō's defense, however, that in his more than thirty hours of agony he performed an indispensable function as an official of the Legislation Bureau under a conservative government and succeeded in Japanizing the SCAP draft. Unlike Matsumoto, Satō fully understood the role that he could play in the circumstances. That is, with respect to SCAP's constitutional ideas—MacArthur's three constitutional principles (the emperor as head of the state, renouncing war forever, and abolishing the peerage system)—he avoided unnecessary verbal battles with the Americans, and in a technical, legal sense, attempted a last-ditch resistance by adjusting Japan's legal tradition in a way beneficial to Japan's conservative institutions.

The first instance of Satō's success in Japanizing the SCAP draft had to do with terminology. Two classic examples illustrate this: First, he avoided the phrase "sovereignty of the people" by using "supreme will of the people" in its place; and second, in all the places where the SCAP draft said "the Japanese people" and the Foreign Ministry's translation [of the SCAP draft] had used [the progressive] *Nihon jinmin* to translate this phrase, Satō used [the conservative] *Nippon kokumin*. This effort later opened the way (in the Citizenship Law) to a statutory definition of the term *kokumin*. T. A. Bisson, a member of Government Section who did not take part in writing the SCAP draft and who represented the leftist position within SCAP, offered this judgment:

> It is true that in the negotiations the bungotai [literary] translation of the English draft which Government Section had prepared was used. What was most essential for the Americans as they undertook the work of approving the Japanese text of the Constitution was to be proficient in Japanese. In this kind of give and take the highly trained Japanese bureaucrats, even though few in number, were probably justified in thinking that they could easily outdo the many Nisei [second generation Japanese-Americans] interpreters and translators.[33]

There is a second example of Satō's success in Japanizing the SCAP draft. On the pretext of making the constitution brief, Satō used the tactic of excluding any concrete definition of rights from articles of the constitution, leaving them to statutory laws rather than making them constitutional rights. An example of this is Article 101 of the Japanese draft, the provision on local government, which he drafted.

The Honorable Defeat of Matsumoto Jōji

March 5, 1946, the day that Satō returned to the prime minister's office with pangs of conscience and "head bowed," was doubtless the same day that Matsumoto, who had been captivated by the emperor system, was awakened to the reality of Japan's having lost the war.

After his departure from Government Section at noon on March 4, Matsumoto never again engaged in negotiations with SCAP. Not only that, but while he still held his position as minister of state during the remaining month of the Shidehara cabinet, he never again made a constructive utterance about the constitution. Even years later Matsumoto could say, "Actually I haven't even read what is in the Constitution. I came to hate it that much."[34] For Matsumoto, the confrontation with Kades on March 4 was perhaps the day of his defeat as a legal scholar, or one might say his *gyokusai* (honorable defeat or death). Matsumoto's son-in-law, Tanaka Kōtarō, who rose from the position of professor of commercial law at Tokyo University to serve as the minister of education in the Yoshida cabinet and later as chief justice of the Supreme Court, commented as follows on Matsumoto the person and his scholarship:

Professor Matsumoto, being an impatient person, could not acquire an interest in such a leisurely past-time as fishing. He also disliked such competitive games as shogi and go. That was because of his extreme aversion to losing. But, in the end, weren't the legal debates and litigation, which he enjoyed more than eating, a form of competition? I think they definitely were a kind of contest. But Professor Matsumoto was confident that in such contests he would lose to nobody, and since he was convinced that victory belonged to him, he enjoyed it as a unique sport. Even if he lost a case, of course that was naturally due to the stupidity of the judge. . . .

His view of the character of the Constitution collided head on with SCAP's policy and he suffered a bitter defeat. I wonder if it wasn't due to this aspect of his character that it ended tragically for him. His ideas about constitutions were from the nineteenth-century, purely legalistic and negative, whereas the constitution required by the times had to have substantial political principles and exhibit the most common ground of the political parties. But, even if he was not completely suitable [for the task of constitutional revision], who besides him could have been equal to the task? I have the feeling that the way he thought about things, the way his mind worked, was more like a natural scientist than a social scientist, a philosopher or an intellectual. That is probably a temperament that he inherited from his father, a preeminent technician, Doctor of Engineering Matsumoto Sōichirō.[35]

Matsumoto apparently thought that logic ("a good mind") and legal technique (legal interpretation) were all that was required of a lawyer. He regarded the concept of human rights, which marked the opening of a new era, as being of little concern to the legal scholar. To him everything began with the "legal text." Subsequently, he never questioned that text within the framework of the emperor system, nor did he appear to have entertained any doubts about living under the protection of that system. But his defeat in the "contest" with SCAP is not something that he could easily forgive, even late in his life. Miyazawa Toshiyoshi relates the following conversation he had with Matsumoto:

He said quite seriously that he did not actually understand the meaning of "the Japanese people." He said he did not know whether or not they understood events. In short, because he thought an angry populace would be dangerous, he had decided when drafting the constitution not to use such words as "sovereignty resides with the people," which deny Imperial sovereignty.[36]

It is extremely interesting that Matsumoto, who thought the judge was stupid if he himself lost a court case, seemed to be blaming the people when he lost to SCAP. Even though he had provided imperial sovereignty for the Japanese people, he was sure they would not understand. Perhaps his reaction was only natural. One wonders whether Matsumoto ever seriously considered the thoughts of the "stupid" people of Japan. A review of public opinion polls published by the newspapers at that time quickly reveals that the Japanese people did not desire imperial sovereignty. A mere 16 percent of the people supported a status for the emperor identical to that in the Meiji Constitution, as Matsumoto had proposed in his draft, whereas about half wanted the emperor's [constitutional] position to be no more than a "center of morality."[37] It is clear that the majority of authors of the various private draft constitutions also preferred popular sovereignty. Before and during the war, both Takano Iwasaburō and Suzuki Yasuzō had resisted government oppression and had developed the ideas that would protect the lives and human rights of those people who suffered under that oppression, thus inspiring them to include these ideas in their private drafts.

A modern constitution is, in truth, most concerned with guaranteeing the human rights of those people who are suffering under oppression.

Miyazawa Toshiyoshi's "Revolution"

What was happening in the meantime to another constitutional scholar, Miyazawa Toshiyoshi? From about the middle of February 1946, Miyazawa began to entertain ideas about constitutional reform that were completely different from those he had had earlier when working on Matsumoto draft "B" as a member of the Committee to Study Constitutional Problems. A fragment of his new thinking was published as an article, "On Constitutional Reform," in the March 1946 issue of the journal *Kaizō*. Miyazawa himself noted that "by the time this manuscript appears in print, the contents of the Government's draft for reform will have been made public,"[38] leading us to surmise that the article was written in February and appeared after March 6, the day the government's summary draft was published. Miyazawa advocated in this article ideas of constitutional reform that, to anyone who knew that he was the author of Matsumoto draft "B," can only be regarded as out of the blue.

> I think that the ideal of constitutional reform at the present time is, briefly put, the construction of a nation of peace. . . . If one seeks the real meaning of rebuilding Japan as a truly peaceful nation, I consider it essential that we have the determination to establish a great national policy of not just making the present dissolution of the military a temporary phenomenon but of moving forward to make Japan—and this alone will assure a truly peaceful country—a nation without arms forever.

The worst thing we can do is to think that we can carry out limited constitutional reform in order to meet our obligations under the Potsdam Declaration, and get through the current crisis, without possessing the high ideal of truly building a nation of peace. Such thinking is frequently described as "bureaucratic." In fact bureaucrats think in this way. But that won't do. Japan has been *stripped clean and is at the point where it must make a fresh start.*[39]

Is this not exactly the "renunciation of war" found in the SCAP draft? This and the fact that he claimed "some part is missing" from the draft[40] indicates without a doubt that he wrote this only after he learned of the SCAP draft. Etō Jun criticized Miyazawa's article, considering it to be Miyazawa's declaration of ideological conversion after stealing a peek at the SCAP draft.[41] Of course, it could also be that the real object of Etō's criticism was the "younger generation" of scholars who inherited Miyazawa's views on the constitution. However, we need to consider this issue with greater emotional detachment.

After all, it was not only Miyazawa who saw the SCAP draft—despite the strict secrecy—prior to the publication of the Japanese government's draft on March 6. According to Tanaka Jirō, Suehiro Kentarō—a Tokyo University professor who was a member of the Labor Legislative Investigation Committee studying the bills of three labor laws—had said at a meeting of the Committee on Constitutional Research of Tokyo Imperial University (established February 14, 1946, and chaired by Miyazawa Toshiyoshi) that "the MacArthur draft was presented [to the organizing committee of the Democratic People's Front]."[42] Hani Setsuko has written in detail about what happened at a meeting of the organizing committee:

The organizing committee, which began as a preparatory committee, just at the time that SCAP had given up on the draft which the Japanese Government had submitted and had prepared its own model constitution, and before that had been made public, Professor Suehiro Kentarō, one of our committee organizers, brought a copy of the draft with him, introduced it and began reading it article by article in front of everybody. The presiding chairman, Yamakawa Hitoshi, and Takano Iwasaburō, who had drafted a republican constitution, started asking questions and said to Professor Suehiro that they wanted SCAP to be cautious. Thus on this one rare occasion, while the Constitution was being written, I was allowed to study it fully.[43]

Given the fact that SCAP was trying so hard to keep the draft secret, it seems unlikely that only Miyazawa was quietly and deliberately given a look at it. Rather, one can easily imagine that, even though Suehiro's action was rather rash, SCAP boldly offered a preview of the draft in order to solicit the opinions of such scholars as Miyazawa, a leading intellectual, and Suehiro, who, as a member of the Committee to Investigate Labor Legislation, was concerned with drafting a bill on the labor standards law and was in a position directly concerned with the constitution.[44]

In any case, Miyazawa demonstrated in the *Kaizō* article a major change in his postwar ideas about the constitution from the Matsumoto draft "B" to the SCAP draft. He later spelled out the related legal principles in his article, "The Meaning of the August Revolution in Constitutional History," published in the May issue of *Sekai Bunka*.[45]

In this article he wrote, first of all, that "the most important point (in the Government's draft, which is based on the SCAP draft) is, needless to say, the theory of the people's [*kokumin*] sovereignty, or popular [*jimmin*] sovereignty." The government's draft offers a change "from the principle of theocratic rule to rule by the people." What is the basis of that innovation? Miyazawa finds it in Article 12 of the Potsdam Declaration: "The ultimate form of the Japanese government . . . shall be established by the freely expressed will of the Japanese people." Such a reform "was not something that the Japanese Government could logically bring about. Even if it were the will of the Emperor, it could not be done legally. Consequently, constitutionally speaking, this reform must be thought of as a *revolution*."[46] Miyazawa's thesis of the "August Revolution," which was later to become famous, is still debated today, having received renewed attention since the recent publication of Etō's article.

How, then, should we explain such a change in Miyazawa's postwar consciousness and his thoughts about the new constitution? One view is that "by examining Miyazawa's prewar constitutional theories, one can see the preliminary work for this thesis of the August Revolution was for the most part already present in his prewar writings."[47] But the more his consistency is emphasized, the more one must ask why he did not use that preliminary work earlier. Why did the August Revolution thesis not appear until eight months after the August Revolution? On this point, Ukai Nobushige, professor at Keijō Imperial University until the end of the war and immediately thereafter professor at the Social Science Institute of Tokyo University, offered the following background on how the thesis originated, although he cautioned that his explanation was based on hearsay:

In the Law Faculty of Tokyo University a Constitution Research Seminar (he probably means the Committee on Constitutional Research of Tokyo Imperial University) was organized, and study was begun on a new form of constitution. Senior professors and progressive scholars engaged in easy argument and debate in an atmosphere of freedom and emancipation. At a time when there was a strong feeling that the old Japan had passed away, Professor Maruyama Masao, a specialist in political and intellectual history, made the following remark. "Isn't it the case that the basic principles of the Japanese Constitution collapsed on August 14 [1945], and new basic principles were born? And wouldn't it be accurate, speaking historically, to call that an August revolution?" (Of course, because Ukai was not a member of the seminar, he refers to this as "hearsay.")[48]

But as Ukai pointed out in a different essay, "There is no room for the concept of revolution in a constitution, especially in the present Constitution; that is primarily a matter of concern to scholars."[49] His point is certainly well taken. No matter how good Maruyama's idea was, it was probably not his intention as a political scientist to announce publicly an "August Revolution thesis." That is because, like a weather forecaster explaining after a typhoon has passed that "that was definitely a typhoon," he could not make light of it. And then a legal scholar [Miyazawa], who wished to offer a theoretical interpretation ("From the standpoint of the Constitution it was a kind of revolution") to the academic community, published his argument as an issue of legal interpretation in a general journal that did not specialize in legal matters.

Miyazawa was stimulated by Maruyama's idea, the essential part of which did not exist in Miyazawa's own prewar notions of constitutionalism. It appears that Miyazawa's thesis also grew out of his experience with occupation policies on constitutional reform. As we have seen, there was the early period of "initial probing" when MacArthur suggested to Konoe that the constitution should be revised. At that point there was good reason for the existence of Miyazawa's interpretation of the Meiji Constitution. However, from the moment that the Far Eastern Commission became involved, SCAP's attitude toward constitutional reform changed dramatically.

At this stage of the military occupation, toward the end of 1945, indirect rule was the form of authority being exercised, as provided in the Instrument of Surrender, which stated: "The authority of the Emperor and the Japanese Government to rule the state shall be subject to the Supreme Commander of the Allied Powers." But this was by no means absolutely binding, for the United States Initial Post-Surrender Policy for Japan gave MacArthur the authority to "act directly if the Emperor or other Japanese authority does not satisfactorily meet the requirements of the Supreme Commander."[50] In other words, this policy essentially allowed for direct military occupation, provided that MacArthur deemed it necessary.

At this time it became clear that the Committee to Study Constitutional Problems (Matsumoto Committee), including Miyazawa, did not understand the Potsdam Declaration and occupation policy. It was clear, too, that "the Supreme Commander's requirements were not satisfactorily being met," and that, as can be seen after February 13, SCAP had begun to take "direct action." However, this does not mean that, from SCAP's perspective, "indirect rule" and "direct rule" existed in international law as clearly distinguishable concepts. Nor does it mean that in fact there were serious differences between these two forms of rule.

In its dealings with the FEC, SCAP was confused about the interpretation of Article 43 of the Hague Convention on War [which called for the observance of existing laws], and this seems to have dogged them to the end; moreover, there was discord within MacArthur's headquarters. And, after the decision of February 1, SCAP moved toward the drafting of the constitution that has already been described. In the midst of all of this, Miyazawa, having learned indirectly of the SCAP draft, again read the Potsdam Declaration. This is when he apparently noticed its "revolutionary character" and rushed to make that public in his article.

Nevertheless, one must say, as the constitutional scholar Higuchi Yōichi has pointed out, "that the very person who proclaimed the 'August Revolution thesis,' cannot evade responsibility because he could not point it out in August, 1945, or at least before February, 1946, when he was stimulated by the exhibit of the MacArthur draft, which was done because the Government's Matsumoto Committee draft was so very conservative."[51]

Miyazawa himself must be criticized not only because he failed to provide an intellectual accounting of his connection with the SCAP draft constitution, but because, with respect to his relationship with the Matsumoto Committee, he told younger constitutional scholars that "having lost my passion for attending meetings of the Matsumoto Committee, I was only a nominal member of that Committee."[52] In the postwar period most constitutional scholars have consistently acted from the posture of defenders of the constitution, but Miyazawa came to this position only much later. He once testified before the Liberal Party's Constitutional Investigation Committee that, "While I have given much thought to the problem of revising Article 9 of the Constitution, I do not have the confidence to tell you with conviction that this should be done, or that if we do it Japan's future will be secure . . . or that this is the road with the least danger for the country."[53]

Miyazawa seems to have escaped by a side road. In any case, unlike Matsumoto, he did not fight to the end, but came to understand the fact of Japan's defeat somewhat earlier than did Matsumoto and prepared himself to deal with the postwar reality.

The Japanese government emerged from a "long tunnel" some twenty days after February 13 and somehow struggled along toward the publication of a draft constitution. However, following the all-night negotiations of March 4–5, the government again attempted to rework the SCAP draft more to its liking. The specific issue at this point was the provision guaranteeing the rights of foreigners.

At midnight on March 4, a day before the draft was published, Satō Tatsuo had reached agreement with SCAP concerning the provision for foreigners' rights in Article 13:

> All natural persons, whether Japanese citizens or not, are equal before the law. No discrimination shall be authorized or tolerated in political, economic or social relations on account of race, creed, sex, social status, caste or national origin.

But Satō was dissatisfied with this. He wished to eliminate from this article two phrases: "whether Japanese or not" and "national origin." [The word "caste" had been dropped when the SCAP draft was translated into Japanese.] Shortly after returning to the prime minister's office, where he was busily finalizing the draft for publication the following day and preparing for the start of a cabinet meeting, Satō placed a telephone call to Government Section.

The direct negotiation was handled by Shirasu, who spoke English fluently. Satō's proposal was quickly accepted and agreement was reached on the following wording: "All of the people are equal under the law . . . [and there shall be no discrimination] because of . . . social status or family origin."[54] With this change, the provision that specifically guaranteed the rights of foreigners disappeared from the draft constitution. And the "Japanization" of the SCAP draft was more or less complete, at least with respect to this article. There are no reliable documents that explain how the Japanese presented the proposal to eliminate the reference to foreigners' rights, nor why the Americans agreed to accept it. But in light of the fact that on May 2, 1947, the day before the constitution took effect, an Ordinance on Alien Registration (the last imperial ordinance) was issued for the purpose of controlling Koreans residing in Japan, we have to wonder whether it was not intended to replace the provision in the SCAP draft that guaranteed the rights of foreigners.[55]

Publication of the Summary Draft Constitution

The effort at "Japanization" continued until just prior to the publication of an "outline," or summary, of the draft constitution on March 6. The document appeared in the press the following day.

As the Japanese people had heard nothing about the government's draft constitution since the Mainichi "scoop" of February 1, they were quite surprised that, in only one month, such a different draft had been produced by the same Shidehara cabinet. Yokoto Kisaburō, a professor of international law at Tokyo University, expressed the prevailing sentiment in a newspaper article: "Probably everybody is surprised at the very radical revised draft."[56]

In a statement accompanying the draft, the government did not explicitly deny the SCAP connection. Prime Minister Shidehara first issued some "respectful remarks" following the emperor's rescript about the publication of the new draft. After reporting that the emperor approved the revised draft "with extremely firm resolve," Shidehara then ended with the following sentence: "The Government has decided to publish this outline of a revised draft Constitution in close consultation with the Supreme Commander for the Allied Powers."[57]

MacArthur issued a statement at the same time, which opened as follows:

> It is with a sense of deep satisfaction that I am today able to announce a decision of the Emperor and Government of Japan to submit to the Japanese people a new and enlightened constitution which has my full approval. This instrument has been drafted after painstaking investigation and frequent conference between members of the Japanese Government and this headquarters following my initial direction to the cabinet five months ago.[58]

Neither of the statements denies collaboration with SCAP. About the only difference is that Shidehara issued his statement in the presence of the emperor and inserted the phrase "close consultation" at the end, while MacArthur triumphantly announced the SCAP connection at the outset and "expressed satisfaction."

Immediately following the publication of the March 6 draft, the general affairs bureau of the Foreign Ministry produced a document with the title, "The Domestic and Foreign Reaction to the Draft Constitution Summary (One)."[59] It gives a general sense of the Japanese reaction: "We have a strange feeling about the summary because of the enormous gap between it and the Government's earlier draft which was until now widely talked about"; "It gives the impression of being a translation"; "It attempts to strike a balance between retaining the Emperor system and the concept of popular sovereignty"; and "It gives one a sense of relief." Although these are extremely general views, they seem to be fairly accurate representations of Japanese reactions at the time.

Perhaps the most common reaction to the March 6 draft was one of bewilderment. But if we analyze individual and party views, a clear pattern emerges. First of all, reaction from the political parties: the two major parties, the Liberal Party and the Progressive Party, expressed their "approval in principle." They could agree because the two were very similar parties. The view of the Liberal Party was that the major points of the draft—preservation of the emperor system, respect for basic human rights, and renunciation of war—"coincide precisely with the principles of the draft of a revised constitution which our party published."[60] If we recall the two drafts that the Liberal and Progressive parties published a mere two months earlier and how much they resembled the Meiji Constitution, we must question the notion that their major points "coincide precisely" with those of the March 6 draft. At the same time, we are reminded of Shirasu's "Jeep way letter," sent on behalf of Yoshida to Whitney immediately after the SCAP draft was shown to the government, which said that the objectives of the SCAP and Matsumoto drafts were the same.

On the other hand, the Socialist Party, although expressing approval of the "demonstration of the faithful fulfillment of the Potsdam Declaration and zeal for democratic government," was "greatly disappointed with the provisions on the authority of the emperor," and requested changes in four points concerning the emperor and the Diet.[61]

The Communist Party displayed an attitude of substantial opposition and identified five items which it opposed, including the emperor system. The party offered a statement on the rights of working people,[62] which appeared in June in a concrete proposal titled "New Draft Constitution" (usually called "Constitution of the People's Republic of Japan").

And then there was Suzuki Yasuzō of the Constitutional Research Association, who was strongly critical of the March 6 draft. The association's own draft constitution had influenced the SCAP draft somewhat, and of the many drafts published by private organizations, it was the most like the government's March 6 summary and perhaps most like the SCAP draft as well. Yet Suzuki took issue with a number of provisions in the March 6 draft. His main objections appeared in three articles published in *Yomiuri Hōchi Shinbun* in early March 1946.[63] Considered to be the most comprehensive statement of his views, the articles can be summarized as follows.

First of all, concerning the emperor's accession to the throne, the March 6 draft constitution "does not provide that the Diet and the people should approve and authorize it each time." Second, regarding human rights, Suzuki noted several weaknesses: The draft contains no article prohibiting "racial discrimination," no provision on correcting economic inequality, and the provision on workers' right of existence is not concrete. In addition, he said, "It is desirable . . . to have in the Constitution very specific provisions to liberate women and raise their status."

It is astonishing indeed that the day after the publication of the March 6 draft he presented in a coherent fashion these and other issues that were to become the focus of important constitutional debate for the next forty years. He pointed out precisely those human rights that were excised in the process of "Japanizing" the draft, that is, the "human rights of foreigners" and the "human rights of women" (although at the time, the words "female [*fujin*] liberation" were used, as the expression "women's [*josei no*] liberation" was not common). Shortly afterward, Suzuki put together the opinions of the Constitutional Research Association regarding the March 6 draft and presented them to Professor Kenneth Colegrove when he arrived in Japan as a special political adviser to SCAP on constitutional matters.[64]

Miyazawa Toshiyoshi's views of the new draft are also of interest. Miyazawa, after pointing out that the preamble of the draft resembled that of the U.S. Constitution, praised its three distinctive features: "the doctrine of democracy," renunciation of war, and respect for human rights, including social rights. He expressed broad approval in these words: "From all angles, it is the expression of the intention to try to construct something new which simply did not exist in Japan before August 15 [1945], and it is a draft Constitution which has as its purpose to become the Magna Carta of the New Japan."[65]

What pattern emerges from a review of reactions to the March 6 draft? The groups and individuals who were concerned with constitutional revision in the earliest stages and who were thinking in terms of broad or thorough revision of the Meiji Constitution were critical of the government's draft outline. On the other hand, those groups and individuals who advocated only the most minor revisions of the Meiji Constitution supported the draft.

On April 10, 1946, only a month after the March 6 draft was published but before the complete text of the draft constitution had been published, the first general election of the postwar period was held. The election was also the first to be held following revision of the electoral law of the House of Representatives, the first in which women exercised their right to vote and to stand for election, and the election that chose the members of the Diet who would take part in the deliberations on the bill to revise the constitution. In short, it was through this election that the Japanese Constitution was created, based on the Potsdam Declaration's "freely expressed will of the Japanese people."

Why was such an important election held even before the complete text of the new draft constitution had been published? We will discuss this soon, but for the moment let us examine to what extent the people expressed their views on the draft constitution through their selection of representatives and political parties. A review of a poll conducted by the Commission on the Constitution reveals that the draft constitution was hardly an issue at all.[66] Using a standard sample survey, the poll investigated the political opinions carried in official bulletins of the 535 official candidates in eight electoral districts who were still living: Hokkaido's first district,

Fukushima prefecture, Ibaragi prefecture, Shizuoka prefecture, Osaka's first district, Hiroshima prefecture, Ehime prefecture, and Fukuoka's first district. The survey found that only 17.4 percent of the candidates even mentioned the draft constitution. Of these, 12.3 percent supported it, 1.0 percent opposed it, and 4.1 percent did not make their opinions clear. Of the 82.6 percent who never mentioned the outline draft, 16.1 percent did say they supported constitutional reform, while 66.5 percent never mentioned the draft constitution or raised the issue of constitutional reform.

It was under such conditions that the members of the House of Representatives of the Diet (the Ninetieth Imperial Diet) who would adopt the new constitution were elected. The Liberal Party won 139 seats; the Progressive Party, 93; the Socialist Party, 92; the People's Cooperative Party, 14; and the Communist Party, 5—an overwhelming conservative victory. The Yoshida Shigeru cabinet was formed in the following month.

The Draft Constitution in the Vernacular

The complete text of the government's March 6 draft was published on April 17, a week after the general election. The Japanese people got a strong sense of the new era as they opened their newspapers on April 18. The government draft constitution that appeared before them, unlike the earlier draft—indeed, unlike all the laws published since the Meiji period—was written in colloquial Japanese. Today we can hardly appreciate the novelty of such a change, but at the time it was a revolution in legal texts. Its influence in popularizing Japan's present constitution was incalculable.

In early 1980 a publisher in Tokyo assembled the entire text of the Japanese Constitution in very large letters, with the Japanese interpretation of the wording in footnotes, and sold it under the simple title, "The Japanese Constitution." It became a best-seller.[67] Skeptics claimed it caught the public's fancy because of the scenic photographs displayed on every other page. But one could also say that it became popular because many Japanese found the constitution quite appropriate to read aloud.

It is often said that the constitution reads like a translation. And the charge cannot be denied. One must say, however, that it still does not have the vagueness of the text of the Meiji Constitution. As the writer Marutani Saiichi said: "The present constitution is not outstanding prose, but even so the writing is far superior to that of the Meiji Constitution. It expresses very clearly what the writer wanted to say, and is relatively free of ambiguity. There is little room for misunderstanding it."[68]

How and by whom was this "legal textual revolution," from literary to colloquial Japanese, carried out? Several people who participated in the revolution have written personal accounts of how it happened. As in any "successful revolution," however, it is difficult to determine who was the driving force behind it.

First, in late March 1946 there was the following proposal from the People's National Language Movement:

> His Excellency, the Prime Minister of Japan, Count Shidehara Kijūrō
> Subject: A Proposal Concerning the Writing of Laws
> Generally speaking, any written material that is important to the people must be written in a manner that is easily understood by them. In spite of this, everybody admits that on this score the laws and other public documents have until now been remiss. We think that there is little chance for success in trying to mobilize the strength of all the people to build a new Japan if we leave this absurd situation as it is.
>
> We believe that now, at this new starting point of our history, it is obvious that the Government expects much of the people. In order to arouse their consciousness and courage, reforming the way the laws and public documents are written at this time would be a very desirable step. With the above concern in mind, we would like to request that the writing of all laws and public documents be changed in the following ways: that they be written in colloquial Japanese; that if at all possible they not use difficult kanji [Chinese characters]; that they avoid obscure and difficult words and expressions; that the number of kanji used be reduced; and that standard marks be used to indicate sound changes in the phonetic script, such as voiced consonants.
>
> We propose that the laws and public documents now in force quickly be rewritten according to the above principles and that hereafter new laws and public documents be written in this way.
>
> [Signed] Andō Masaji, Representative of the People's National Language Movement. March 26, 1946.[69]

Andō, Yamamoto Yūzō (a writer), Yokota Kisaburō (a professor of international law), and Miyake Shōtarō (a judge) presented this petition to the prime minister's office in the afternoon of March 26.[70]

They met with Minister of State Matsumoto Jōji and Director General Irie Toshio of the Legislation Bureau. Matsumoto's reaction appears to have been rather cool. Miyake recalls: "The Minister's response was very polite, but Yamamoto and I felt somewhat disappointed as we left the meeting."[71] This was not the end of the matter, however. Irie picks up the story:

> Since becoming a councillor in the Cabinet's Legislation Bureau in the late 1920s, I had been interested in simplifying the terminology of laws and government regulations. So the proposal of the Citizens' Language Movement appealed strongly to me. When I discussed the matter with Watanabe Yoshihide, a young councillor of the Legislation Bureau who was helping me write the draft constitution and who had an excellent understanding of this problem, he agreed wholeheartedly and said that unless we seized this op-

portunity it would be extremely difficult to achieve the goal of writing laws and government regulations in the spoken language. And I had exactly the same feeling.[72]

With the support of members of his department, Irie strongly recommended to Minister Matsumoto that the draft constitution be written in the spoken language. Matsumoto reacted differently to Irie, commenting that "since the Constitution sounds so much like a translation, it might at least seem a little more Japanese if we were to write it in the spoken language."[73]

It is interesting to note that although Matsumoto still did not agree with the use of the spoken language for the purpose of "making it easier for the people to read," as the petition had urged, he thought that the use of colloquial Japanese would get rid of the "translation odor" of the document. To Matsumoto, a constitution should be a thing of dignity, like the Meiji Constitution. But the draft constitution, even when rewritten and Japanized, could not be made to sound dignified. Matsumoto blamed this on the fact that it was a translation, but the real problem lay in its contents. Whatever the form of the draft constitution, it was in essence a declaration of human rights. For Matsumoto, it was impossible from the outset to bring the solemnity of the existing Meiji Constitution into a declaration of human rights.

Miyake Shōtarō, who had written legal opinions in the colloquial language as early as 1929, criticized the use of the literary language in this way:

It's fine to protect the dignity of the law by using the literary language. However, can we be sure that in protecting this dignity we are not enhancing unreasonable authority or glossing over defects of logic? What I have noticed is that among those who have opposed judicial decisions written in the spoken language are many who are tinged with militarism. I have the feeling that it is no accident that their cries of opposition were the loudest when the tide of militarism was the highest.[74]

In any case, Irie succeeded in obtaining the approval of Minister Matsumoto and ordered Watanabe Yoshihide to begin rewriting the draft in colloquial Japanese. Watanabe happened to live in Mitaka, a suburb in the western part of Tokyo. As luck would have it, Yamamoto Yūzō, one of the men who had taken the petition to the prime minister's office, lived nearby. Watanabe sought his assistance for the project. Yamamoto discussed the matter with a scholar of international law, Yokota Kisaburō, who lived in nearby Kichijōji. According to Yokota's memoirs, when Yamamoto consulted him about what form of the spoken language should be used, he urged adopting the form used by newspapers and journals. "Yamamoto said, 'That would probably be fine. No, that would certainly be fine. We definitely should use that form.'"[75] But Yokota also remembers that "a councillor of the Legislation Bureau sitting beside him, apparently very surprised, said 'No, that won't do!'"[76] The reference is clearly to Watanabe, but his and Irie's memories of this event are quite different. Yokota says that he himself was more positive about the project than was the Legislation Bureau.

In any case, Yamamoto and Yokota proceeded to write a draft in colloquial Japanese. Yamamoto wrote the preamble and Yokota wrote Chapters 1 ("The Emperor") and 2 ("Renunciation of War"); they finished the draft in one evening. The next day, Yokota recalls, the two of them spent seven hours scrutinizing their work and preparing a "sample copy in the colloquial language."[77] Let us look at a part of the preamble and Article 1 of the draft that they produced in this way.

> Preamble. We, the Japanese people, love truth, freedom and peace. We will exert all of our strength for the search and realization of these for the benefit not only of ourselves and our descendants but for the people of the whole world, and do not wish ever again to be drawn into war by a few leaders. We hereby proclaim through our duly elected representatives in the National Diet that sovereignty resides in the wishes of the people and do establish this Constitution.
>
> Article 1. The Emperor is the symbol of the state and of the unity of the people, and his position is derived from the will of the people who possess sovereignty.[78]

On April 3, despite the fact that it was a holiday, Irie, Satō, and Watanabe spent the whole day putting the draft constitution into colloquial language based on the preliminary work done by Yamamoto and Yokota.[79] On April 5 the rewritten draft won approval of the cabinet.

Comparing this "Revised Draft of the Japanese Constitution" with the preliminary Yamamoto-Yokota version, we note the following changes. Note, however, that the English translation cannot capture the many stylistic differences between literary and spoken Japanese:

> Preamble. We, the Japanese people, acting through our duly elected representatives in the National Diet, determined to establish peaceful cooperation with all peoples and to assure the benefits of liberty throughout the land of Japan, and resolved that never again shall the horrors of war arise through the action of government, do proclaim the supremacy of the people's will and establish this Constitution.
>
> Article 1. The Emperor is the symbol of the Japanese nation and the symbol of the unity of the Japanese people. His position is based on the supreme will of the Japanese people.

Although the Yamamoto-Yokoto preliminary draft did manage to preserve an underlying tone of the colloquial style, the style was not always preserved in the substantive points of the revised draft. The old form of *kana* (phonetic script) was used, but that was because the Japanese Language Commission did not issue its report on "Modern Kana Usage" until September 21, 1946. The government's "notification" on adopting the new kana usage was not issued until November 16, immediately after the promulgation of the constitution.

On April 17, 1946, the "Draft of the Revised Japanese Constitution," printed in *hiragana* (cursive phonetic script) and colloquial Japanese, was published. Yokoto recalled this experience as "truly an unexpected and delightful surprise."[80] And Miyake, who for many years had continually advocated the use of colloquial language in laws, court decisions, and other public documents, wrote afterward: "That year [1946] is a year that should be remembered forever for this event alone, even if nothing else had happened."[81]

The accomplishment of a month and a half—which began with the first Japanese draft, progressed to a summary draft, and ended with the draft of the revised constitution—was nothing less than the "Japanization" of the SCAP draft. If the Japanization of the text of the constitution, which was mainly advocated by officials of the Legislation Bureau, can be called "bureaucratization," then one can perhaps refer to the use of the colloquial language in the draft as the "popularization" of the constitution.

Notes

1. Irie Toshio, *Kenpō seiritsu no keii to kenpōjō no shomondai* (Tokyo: Daiichi Hōki Shuppan, 1976), p. 204.

2. Satō Tatsuo, "Nihonkoku kenpō seiritsushi—'MacArthur sōan' kara 'Nihonkoku kenpō' made," *Jurist* 3, no. 83 (June 1955): 8. (Hereafter cited as *Jurist* issue number and date.)

3. Ibid., p. 8.

4. Gamushō gaikō bunsho, microfilm reel no. A'0092. (Hereafter, Gaimushō microfilm.)

5. Takayanagi Kenzō and others, *Nihonkoku kenpō seitei no katei* (Tokyo: Yūhikaku, 1972), 1:267–303.

6. The "Japanese drafts" all appear in the Gaimushō microfilm already cited.

7. Satō Tatsuo, *Jurist*, no. 82 (May 15, 1955): 14.

8. Satō Tatsuo, *Jurist*, no. 83 (June 1, 1955): 8.

9. Ibid., p. 9

10. Ibid., no. 84 (June 15, 1955): 12.

11. Satō Tatsuo, "Kenpō dai hasshō oboegaki—sono seiritsu keika o chūshin shite," in *Chihō jichi ronbunshū*, ed. Jichichō hen (1954), p. 40. This is examined in detail by Amakawa Akira, "Chihō jichihō no kōzō," in *Senryōki Nihon no keizai to*

seiji, ed. Nakamura Takahide (Tokyo: Tokyo Daigaku Shuppankai, 1979), pp. 124 ff.

12. Satō Tatsuo, *Jurist,* no. 85 (July 1, 1955): 8.

13. See GHQ telephone directory in Fukushima Yasurō, ed., *GHQ no soshiki to jinji, September 1946* (Tokyo: Gannandō, 1984).

14. Matsumoto Jōji kōjutsu, "Nihonkoku kenpō no sōan ni tsuite," Kenpō chōsakai jimukyoku, *Kenshi, sō dai nijūhachi gō* (October 1958): 21.

15. Kenpō chōsakai, *Kenpō seitei no keika ni kansuru shōiinkai dai nijūgo kai gijiroku,* p. 2. Satō Tatsuo testifying.

16. Satō Tatsuo, *Jurist,* no. 85 (July 1, 1955): 10.

17. The full text reads: "Acting only on the advice and with the consent of the Cabinet, the Emperor, on behalf of the people, shall perform the following state functions."

18. Matsumoto, "Nihonkoku kenpō no sōan ni tsuite," pp. 22–23.

19. Satō Tatsuo, *Jurist,* no. 85 (July 1, 1955): 8.

20. Matsumoto, "Nihonkoku kenpō no sōan ni tsuite," p. 23.

21. Satō Tatsuo, *Jurist,* no. 85 (July 1, 1955): 9.

22. Ibid., p. 8.

23. Satō Tatsuo kankei bunsho, National Diet Library.

24. Satō Tatsuo, *Jurist,* no. 85 (July 1, 1955): 10.

25. Robert E. Ward, "The Origins of the Present Japanese Constitution," *American Political Science Review* (January 1957): 1001–1002 and 1010.

26. Satō Tatsuo, *Jurist,* no. 85 (July 1, 1955): 13.

27. Satō Tatsuo, *Jurist,* no. 86 (July 15, 1955): 46.

28. Ibid., p. 47.

29. Ibid., p. 46.

30. Satō Tatsuo, *Jurist,* no. 87 (August 1, 1955): 24.

31. Satō Tatsuo kankei bunsho.

32. Satō Tatsuo, *Jurist,* no. 88 (August 15, 1955): 33.

33. Thomas A. Bisson, *Nihon senryō kaisōki,* trans. Nakamura Masanori and Miura Yōichi (Tokyo: Sanseidō, 1983), pp. 244–245.

34. Matsumoto, "Nihonkoku kenpō no sōan ni tsuite," p. 29.

35. Tanaka Kōtarō, *Watakushi no rirekisho* (Tokyo: Shunjūsha, 1961), pp. 259, 263.

36. Miyazawa Toshiyoshi, "Shinsei Nihon no dōhyō," in *Shōwashi tanpō,* ed. Mikuni Ichirō (Tokyo: Banchō Shobō, 1975), p. 161.

37. See, for example, the Public Opinion Research Center's poll published by *Mainichi Shinbun,* February 4, 1946. Of the 5,000 people polled, 2,400 responded. Sixteen percent supported continuing the emperor system unchanged, twenty-eight percent favored the sharing of political power by the emperor and the Diet, and forty-five percent wanted the emperor to be outside the realm of politics and to be a patriarch and moral center for the Japanese. Kenpō chōsakai, *Kenpō seitei no keika ni kansuru shōiinkai dai yonjūnana kaigiroku,* p. 189.

38. Miyazawa Toshiyoshi, "Kenpō kaisei ni tsuite," *Kaizō* 27, no. 3 (March 1946): 23.

39. Ibid., pp. 25–26.

40. Dialogue between Miyazawa Toshiyoshi and Kobayashi Naoki, "Meiji kenpō kara shin kenpō e," *Shōwa shisōshi no shōgen* (Tokyo: Mainichi Shinbunsha, 1968), p. 169.

41. Etō Jun, ed., *Senryō shiroku,* vol. 3 (kaisetsu) (Tokyo: Kōdansha, 1982); and "'Hachi ten ichigō kakumei setsu' seiritsu no jijō: Miyazawa Toshiyoshi kyōju no tenkō," *Shokun* 14, no. 5 (May 1982).

42. See Tanaka Jirō's comments in "Zadankai: kenpō sanjū nen o kaiko shite," *Jurist,* no. 638 (May 1977): 9.

43. Hani Setsuko, *Tsuma no kokoro* (Tokyo: Iwanami Shoten, 1979), p. 176.

44. Takemae Eiji, *Sengo rōdō kaikaku* (Tokyo: Daigaku Shuppan, 1982), pp. 81–82.

45. Miyazawa Toshiyoshi, *Konmentaaru Nihonkoku kenpō, bessatsu furoku* (Tokyo: Nihon Hyōronsha, 1955), pp. 380 ff.

46. Ibid., p. 315.

47. Takami Katsutoshi, "Furui kawabukuro to furui sake—hachigatsu kakumei setsu e no isshikaku," *Jurist,* no. 796 (August 1, 1983): 73.

48. Ukai Nobunari, "Miyazawa Toshiyoshi hōgaku kanken," *Jurist,* no. 807 (February 15, 1984): 28.

49. Ukai Nobunari, *Shihō shinsa to jinken no hōri* (Tokyo: Yūhikaku, 1984), p. 404.

50. Gaimushō tokubetsu shiryōbu hen, *Nihon senryō oyobi kanri jūyō bunshoshū* (Tokyo: Tōyō Keizai Shinpōsha, 1947), 1:96.

51. Higuchi Yōichi, "Tabū to kihan," *Sekai* (June 1983): 42.

52. Comment by Kubota Kinuko in "Zadankai: Miyazawa Toshiyoshi sensei no hito to gakumon," *Jurist,* no. 634 (March 26, 1977): 141.

53. Miyazawa Toshiyoshi, "Kenpō kaisei no zehi," *Saiken* 8, no. 7 (September 1954): 48.

54. Satō Tatsuo, *Jurist,* no. 88 (August 15, 1955): 35.

55. Ōnuma Tomoaki, *Tan'itsu minzoku shakai no shinwa o koete—zainichi kankoku chōsenjin to shutsunyū kanri taisei* (Tokyo: Tōshindō, 1986), pp. 259 ff.

56. *Tokyo Shinbun,* March 12, 1946.

57. Satō Isao, *Kenpō kaisei no keika* (Tokyo: Nihon Hyōronsha, 1947), p. 105.

58. Ibid., p. 273.

59. Gaimushō microfilm.

60. *Mainichi Shinbun,* March 8, 1946.

61. Ibid.

62. Ibid.

63. This newspaper series has been included under the title "Kenpō kaisei sei-fuan ni taisuru iken," in Suzuki Yasuzō, *Minshu kenpō no kōsō* (Tokyo: Kōbunsha, 1946), pp. 157–176.

64. Suzuki Yasuzō, *Kenpō seitei zengo* (Tokyo: Aoki Shoten, 1977), p. 230.

65. *Mainichi Shinbun,* August 3, 1946.

66. Kenpō chōsakai, *Kenpō seitei no keika ni kansuru shōiinkai dai yonjūnana kai gijiroku,* pp. 449–450.

67. Yoraku henshūbu, *Nihonkoku kenpō* (Tokyo: Shōgakkan, 1982).

68. Marutani Saiichi, *Bunshō dokuhon* (Tokyo: Chūō Kōronsha, 1977), p. 59.

69. Irie Toshio bunsho, National Diet Library.

70. Satō Tatsuo, *Jurist*, no. 96 (December 15, 1955): 33.

71. *Miyake Shōtarō zenshū* (Tokyo: Kōgakusha, 1950), 3:231.

72. Irie Toshio, "Kenpō sōan yoroku," *Hōsō*, no. 56. (1955): 8.

73. Ibid.

74. *Miyake Shōtarō zenshū*, 3:248.

75. Yokota Kisaburō, "Kenpō no hiragana kōgo," in *Hō to Nihongo*, ed. Midori-umi Jun'ichi (Tokyo: Yūhikaku, 1981), p. 267.

76. Ibid.

77. Ibid., pp. 268–269.

78. Satō Tatsuo kankei bunsho.

79. Watanabe Yoshihide, "Hōseikyoku kaisō," in *Shōgen, kindai hōsei no kiseki*, comp. Naikaku hōseikyoku hyakunenshi henshū iinkai (Tokyo: Gyōsei, 1985), p. 102.

80. Yokota, "Kenpō no hiragana kōgo," p. 272.

81. *Miyake Shōtarō zenshū*, 3:231.

7

Macarthur Against the Storm

Colegrove Visits Japan

General MacArthur reigned over the Japanese government as a transcendental "giver of the law," and his headquarters staff, with unwavering confidence, strictly followed the orders that the Supreme Commander gave. But such political methods could not help but create conflict within the framework of the postwar international society. On March 6, 1946, the draft of a revised constitution was suddenly published by the Japanese government. MacArthur's immediate public announcement approving the document greatly irritated the eleven member nations of the newly established Far Eastern Commission, as well as the U.S. government, especially the State Department. The atmosphere of tension and distrust, along with MacArthur's uncompromising counterattack, created a far more serious matter than one might expect.

At the end of February, as this crisis was about to erupt, Kenneth Wallace Colegrove, a political scientist at Northwestern University, departed from his home in Evanston, Illinois, for Washington, D.C. Colegrove was born in Iowa in 1886, and after graduating from Iowa State Teacher's College, earned his Ph.D. in political science at Harvard. In 1926 he became a professor of political science at Northwestern University.[1] Before World War II Colegrove had shown interest in Japanese politics, writing books and articles on Japanese militarism and the Meiji Constitution.[2] Intellectually conservative, he bluntly stated his anticommunist arguments, especially during the early days of the Cold War in the 1950s.[3] During the war, however, he had published much factual research in the left-wing journal *Amerasia* and elsewhere.

Colegrove is known in Japan as the scholar who watched over Ōyama Iwao during his period of exile in the United States. In 1926 Ōyama, a professor of political science at Waseda University, organized the *Rōnōtō* (Workers and Farmers Party) and served as its chairman. But faced with continuing government repression, he sought refuge in the United States in 1932. From 1933 until 1947 Ōyama worked as research assistant to

Colegrove at Northwestern University.[4] That Ōyama became Colegrove's assistant appears to have been entirely fortuitous.[5] But fortune has a way of influencing people's lives.

Shortly after Ōyama arrived at Northwestern University in 1933, Charles Burton Fahs left Northwestern for Japan. From 1934 to 1936 Fahs studied constitutional law and politics in the faculty of law at Tokyo Imperial University with Professor Minobe Tatsukichi. Among the foreign students there at the time were Hugh Borton and Edwin O. Reischauer, members of the first generation of Japan specialists in the United States.[6] Fahs later served as a Japan specialist and chief of the Far Eastern Division in the wartime Office of Strategic Services (OSS) and later as chief of the Far Eastern Intelligence Section of the State Department. In the early 1960s he served as minister in the American embassy when Reischauer was ambassador to Japan.[7] Fahs was a close friend of Colegrove. When he arrived in Japan, Fahs received from Colegrove a copy of Minobe's *Annotated Commentary on the Constitution of Japan*. This was indeed a stroke of luck because shortly afterward, in May 1935, as the criticism of Minobe's book on the "Emperor as Organ Theory" mounted, the sale of the *Commentary* was prohibited.

Translations were especially important at a time when the study of Japan in the United States was just beginning. Colegrove was aware of this. At the end of 1938, just back from a trip to China, he wrote a letter to T. A. Bisson of the Foreign Policy Association requesting help in finding a translator for Minobe's *Commentary* and for Hozumi Yatsuka's *Principles of the Constitution*. Colegrove ended his letter to Bisson with the following words:

> For many years American scholars in the field of comparative law, who do not read Oriental languages, have been handicapped by the lack of translations of Japanese treatises on constitutional law and government. It is believed that the translation of the two leading treatises on Japanese constitutional law will greatly repair this deficiency.[8]

Who Bisson recommended as a translator is not known. But it is clear that Colegrove did not ask Ōyama, at least at this point, despite the fact that he was near at hand. Ōyama did not undertake the translation of the *Commentary on the Constitution* until early 1941.

Ōyama's work on the translation, despite substantial progress, was never completed.[9] Yet there is no doubt that through the partial translation of this book Colegrove absorbed Minobe's ideas and interpretation about the Meiji Constitution. It served him well as he prepared his lectures for Northwestern's Civil Affairs Training School, established during the war to train civil affairs personnel for the occupation of Japan. In

1944–1945 Colegrove taught courses on Japanese political organization. His lecture outlines, which have survived, provide details about the special features of Japan's emperor system, the development of political institutions, and bureaucratic organization.[10]

As one of the few prewar U.S. scholars of Japanese politics and the Meiji Constitution, Colegrove continued his study during the 1941–1945 interruption in U.S.-Japanese relations and developed many personal contacts. Now the time had come to put his knowledge to practical use. Colegrove was already sixty years old, but of the diplomats in Washington and the leaders of MacArthur's Government Section, only Colegrove had the detailed knowledge of Japanese politics and personal connections to help him in his new role.

On February 24, 1946, Colegrove left behind a snow-covered Chicago and headed for Washington, D.C. He had been appointed political consultant on Japanese constitutional matters to MacArthur's headquarters in Tokyo.[11] He was to attend the Far Eastern Commission's first general meeting, scheduled to take place in the former American embassy on February 26.

On February 25 the Japanese government announced that elections for the House of Representatives would be held on April 10. Because it was fully expected that the National Diet members chosen at this election would be those who would enact the constitution, the U.S. State Department, and of course the Far Eastern Commission, were on edge about MacArthur's actions. In Washington Colegrove met with General Frank R. McCoy, the U.S. member of the Far Eastern Commission, and was briefed on conditions in the commission. He also heard the thinking of the U.S. government, especially of the State Department, from his old friend Charles Fahs, now head of the Far Eastern Information (Intelligence) Office of the State Department. Moreover, General McCoy gave Colegrove a letter of introduction to MacArthur and other high-ranking U.S. military officials in Tokyo. Fahs provided a letter introducing him to civil officials in MacArthur's headquarters. Colegrove arrived in Tokyo, via San Francisco, at the beginning of March (unfortunately, the date cannot be confirmed), immediately before the publication of the Japanese government's March 6 draft.

Though Colegrove had many old friends among the Japanese, having a letter of introduction from Ōyama gave him a feeling of reassurance. Ōyama introduced him to many well-known Japanese politicians, scholars, and critics. The politicians included such Socialist Party leaders as Katō Kanjū, Katō Shizue, and Suzuki Mosaburō. Among the scholars were such constitutional law specialists as Sasaki Sōichi (Kyoto University), Minobe Tatsukichi (emeritus professor at Tokyo University), former Keijō (Seoul) University professor Ukai Nobushige, and Takano

Iwasaburō and Suzuki Yasuzō of the Constitutional Research Association. Others included the political scientist Yabe Teiji (Tokyo University) and economist Arisawa Hiromi (Tokyo University), and many other intellectuals.[12] Ukai and Yabe were friends who had visited Ōyama in Evanston in 1940 and 1935, respectively. As a constitutional law scholar fluent in English, Ukai had served as an interpreter for Colegrove, contributing greatly to his research.

A Shock to the State Department

The publication of the Japanese government's draft summary on March 6, 1946, was a complete surprise to the State Department. The then acting director of the Japan Office of the department, Hugh Borton (later professor of Columbia University), described conditions in Washington at the time:

> [When the Far Eastern Advisory Committee visited Japan in January 1946,] they had been told by General Whitney that the problem of constitutional reform was a matter for the Japanese to consider and that no work had been undertaken by SCAP. Their charge that they had purposely been kept ignorant of what was transpiring was made all the more difficult to refute in view of the fact that the United States government had not been kept informed of the activities of [MacArthur's] Government Section in February and March, 1946. There were no copies of the new draft Constitution available in Washington when it was published in Tokyo.[13]

It was not only Washington that was surprised. Even the office of the political adviser, which represented the Department of State in Tokyo, had not been informed before the fact. Max Bishop of that office wrote to the secretary of state on March 8, the day after the draft had been published in the newspapers, but instead of sending a telegram he sent a letter and a copy of the draft by post so that SCAP would not see it.

> There has not been time to prepare a careful analysis of the new draft, the sudden announcement of which came as a surprise. It is apparent from General MacArthur's press release and from the Imperial rescript that the Government's draft was carefully considered by Headquarters and was approved by the Supreme Commander and by the Emperor before its issuance.[14]

Bishop's report reached the State Department on March 16, but Secretary Byrnes was questioned about the issue by reporters at a news conference on March 12, before the report had arrived.

> Question: Was the proposed Japanese Constitution submitted for approval to the other major Allied powers before publication?

Answer: My information is that it was not. The Japanese Constitution was drawn up by the Japanese Government under its right to do so.

Question: Will the Constitution be submitted to the Allied Council for Japan under the terms of Paragraph 6, Section B, of the Moscow Conference decision on a Far Eastern Commission and Allied Council for Japan which gives a Council member the right to disagree on "fundamental changes in the Japanese constitutional structure" and the right of appeal to the Far Eastern Commission?

Answer: One would have to look at the exact language of the Agreement to determine what section would apply to it, but before the Constitution becomes effective, it will in some way or other come before the Far Eastern Commission.[15]

While the secretary of state was responding to these painful questions, inquiries were coming to the department from the Far Eastern Commission. But the inquiries could not be sent directly from the State Department to MacArthur in Tokyo; they had to go through the Joint Chiefs of Staff and the army chief of staff. On March 10 the army chief of staff sent the following inquiry by telegram to MacArthur:

It is understood that in view of Moscow Communique certain members of the Far Eastern Commission may question your right to approve new Japanese Constitution with[out] directives from the Commission. Accordingly, State Department is informally asking the War Department to ascertain basis of your approval.

View of War Department has been that if Japanese Government were to proceed with constitutional reforms prior to action in December [the signing of the Moscow Agreement, which established the Far Eastern Commission], you would intervene only if such reforms were inconsistent with directives already issued by you. It appears therefore that your action in personally approving this new Constitution is consistent with War Department view since (a) the Constitution was issued not by your Headquarters but by Japanese Emperor and Government in compliance with directives issued by you prior to Moscow Conference, and (b) constitutional reforms appear to be consistent with directives received by you.

Request your early confirmation of views expressed in para[graph] 2 above or comments thereon.[16]

The question is such that it already contains half the answer. Furthermore, its underlying assumption—that if one considered the process of constitutional revision to have begun before the signing of the Moscow Agreement, then according to the principle of non-retroactivity it was not restricted by the accord—is precisely the reason that Whitney recommended to MacArthur that the drafting should be undertaken within SCAP. MacArthur quickly responded to the War Department in a telegram on March 12: "The reasoning advanced by you is correct." But he did not forget to add:

> On the recent visit to Tokyo of the Far Eastern Advisory Commission . . . , I explained that for several months the revision of the constitution had been in progress in accordance with the directives covering this matter which I had already received and that I expected an acceptable draft revision shortly. No expression of dissent was offered. The proposed new constitution is still subject to acceptance or rejection by the Japanese people in the coming election.[17]

It is unclear whether the State Department circulated MacArthur's telegram to the U.S. representative on the Far Eastern Commission. But whatever the case, by this time the legitimacy of MacArthur's draft constitution and the scheduling of the general election had become a major issue within the Far Eastern Commission.

The Far Eastern Commission Requests an Election Delay

On March 20 the FEC decided by unanimous vote to dispatch the following inquiry to MacArthur.[18] First, concerning holding the general election as early as April 10:

> The members of the Commission are not without the apprehension that the holding of the election at such an early date may well give a decisive advantage to the reactionary parties and thus create the embarrassment of a Japanese Government . . . which might not, in fact, truly represent [the people's] wishes, and with which it might prove impossible for the Supreme Commander to cooperate.

Moreover, at a time when Japan's economy was still in doubt and the number of the electorate was uncertain: "The Commission does not think the Japanese people will express their fully instructed, intelligent and authoritative views on their political future." Concerning the constitution, "the Japanese people have little time to consider it." The commission, having expressed these opinions, in the end solicited MacArthur's views:

> The Far Eastern Commission would be most grateful if the Supreme Commander could let them have a very early expression of his views generally, and in particular on the following questions: Does the Supreme Comman-

der share the apprehensions expressed above? If so, would he consider it possible and desirable to require a further postponement of the Japanese elections, and in that case, for what period? If the Supreme Commander should not consider a further postponement desirable at this late date, would he express his views on the desirability, as an alternative, of publicly prescribing that the forthcoming election will be regarded as a test of the ability of Japan to produce a responsible and democratic government in full accordance with the wishes of the people and that further elections will be held at a later date?

MacArthur offered a total refutation on March 29 in reply, sending a return telegram four times as long as the commission's letter of inquiry.[19] After pointing out that the election law had been reformed; that voting age had been lowered; that women had been given the right to vote; that reactionary elements had been purged by the directive removing undesirable personnel from office; that since Japan's was not a parliamentary-cabinet system, a government bill would provide no advantage to any specific political party; and that the election battle was currently being fought, his answer to the FEC's three questions was completely negative: 1. No. 2. No. 3. Absolutely no need for a declaration [prescribing the election as a test case].

As relations between MacArthur and the FEC began to take a perilous turn, the U.S. representative, General McCoy, apparently began to suffer from spells of dizziness.

Born in Pennsylvania in 1874, McCoy graduated from West Point and entered the Department of the Army, where he served for forty-five years until his retirement in 1938. During that time he had many contacts with Japan, serving as head of the commission to aid Japan after the Kantō earthquake in 1923 and as a member of the League of Nations Commission on Manchuria (Litton Commission) in 1932, among others.[20] Although six years older than MacArthur, he never rose higher in military rank than major general. Consequently, he seems to have shown a deference to MacArthur, who in 1930 at the age of fifty was promoted to general and army chief of staff. When he was appointed FEC chairman, McCoy wired a personal message to MacArthur, saying: "You may rest assured of my determination to safeguard your interests at all times."[21]

But even McCoy felt he had to criticize MacArthur for rushing through the process from the general election to enactment of the constitution. Immediately after the FEC's initial decision of March 20 to obtain information from MacArthur, McCoy sent MacArthur an urgent message explaining why he had not exercised his veto to block the FEC's decision. The content of his message was almost the same as the FEC's inquiry of March 20, with the addition of one sentence at the end: "The fact that the draft Constitution is now an election issue has been unduly influenced in favor of the party in power by your recent expression of approval thereof in the press."[22]

MacArthur's immediate response was almost the same as the reply he had sent to the FEC. He held staunchly to his position that the April 10 election would elect the National Diet that would enact the Constitution. He did add that "postponement of the election has been supported by practically only the Communist element."[23]

The Question of a Constituent Assembly

Needless to say, MacArthur insisted on forcing the adoption of the constitution in this way in order to prevent the FEC from interfering. But there was another consideration. It appears that there was growing apprehension about certain political developments in Japan. The Japanese people had become more vocal about constitutional revision, expressing quite strongly their views that a special National Assembly should be created solely for the purpose of enacting a new constitution and that this should be done only after electing representatives for that purpose.

As the so-called Food May Day, the "people's conference to obtain food," indicates, for most people the food shortage was the problem that required an urgent solution. The priority of the Japanese people was finding food to eat, not enacting a constitution. In that sense, the slogan "food rather than a Constitution" had its foundation in the hearts of the masses—indeed, in the pits of their stomachs. It is understandable, then, that they did not perceive, as MacArthur did, the need to rush toward the adoption of the constitution.

The leading members of the Constitutional Research Association, Takano Iwasaburō and Suzuki Yasuzō, called for the creation of a Diet to adopt a constitution, as they were opposed to the united front organization that was making preparations with the Socialist Party and the Communist Party. On March 14 the sponsors of the Democratic People's Front, which had been formed on March 10, adopted a resolution that said, "The new Constitution should be enacted by the people themselves." The resolution was confirmed at the preparatory meeting of the Front's parent federation on April 3. Participating in this event were Ishibashi Tanzan, Ōuchi Hyōe, Nosaka Sanzō, Morito Tatsuo, Yamakawa Hitoshi, and Yokota Kisaburō.[24]

That such thinking was quite widespread can be discerned from public opinion polls of the time. The results of a survey by the Public Opinion Institute published on February 3 were as follows: 20 percent favored the emperor submitting a revision bill according to Article 73 of the constitution; 24 percent favored having the Diet Committee on Revising the Con-

stitution present a revision bill; and 53 percent supported the public election of a special committee to revise the constitution, with the direct representatives of the people publicly debating a revision bill.[25]

Such expressions of public opinion influenced the Japanese government as well. Irie Toshio, who was then deputy director general of the
Cabinet Legislation Bureau, remembers:

> There was the view among the citizenry that the Government ought to cre-
> ate a constitutional investigation committee and listen to the wishes of the
> people. And many thought that even if the matter were presented to the Im-
> perial Diet, deliberations in the Privy Council and House of Peers, with their
> conservative attitudes, would not be in keeping with the fundamental posi-
> tion of constitutional revision. . . . Narahashi (Chief Cabinet Secretary) and
> Ishiguro (director general of the Legislation Bureau), and I all agreed that
> given such a radical reform of the Constitution, it would be only natural to
> radically reform the deliberative procedure and move forward under a new
> procedure.[26]

Thus Irie and the others came up with two plans for revising the constitution and presented them to the cabinet. Plan "A" provided for a special session of the Imperial Diet to deliberate on a constitutional revision
bill from May 10 to July 10 and then to promulgate it. Plan "B" provided
for a special session of the Imperial Diet to meet in May and June to revise Article 73, which provided for constitutional amendments. It would
then revise the laws of both houses of the Diet with a view to abolishing
the House of Peers and establishing a House of Councillors. After that,
the Diet would elect the members of a Constitution Diet, allow two
months (from September 10 to November 10) for that body to complete
its work on a draft constitution, and then hold a national referendum on
the draft in the middle of November.[27]

Both plans were submitted to the cabinet on March 12. At the cabinet
meeting, however, both Minister of Justice Iwata and State Minister Matsumoto strongly opposed plan "B," and so plan "A" was adopted. Their
reasoning was that plan "B" was

> too idealistic, no more than a theoretical plan, and could not possibly be
> done in the time we have in the present circumstances. Also, there is no
> telling what might happen in such a leisurely scenario. Since this Cabinet
> has brought the issue of constitutional revision this far, it is certainly desir-
> able that we complete it quickly.[28]

Furthermore, on April 24, while deliberations were under way in the
Privy Council, Matsumoto spoke of shortening the schedule of delibera-

tions: "I expect the Diet to convene in mid-May, finish deliberations by mid-June, and promulgate the Constitution by the end of that month, convene the Diet in July for the purpose of revising supplemental laws and regulations, and have the Constitution take effect about the time the Diet closes at the end of this year."[29]

In short, only MacArthur and the conservative cabinet members of the Japanese government agreed that the Imperial Diet should establish the constitution as quickly as possible. It is possible that MacArthur refused to listen to the proposals of his own government and the FEC because he had such support from the Japanese government.

MacArthur Refuses to Listen

The day of the general election drew ever closer. As the U.S. position in the FEC grew increasingly difficult, McCoy, realizing that it was impossible to convince MacArthur to postpone the general election, retreated one step and decided to request an enactment procedure that could reflect the will of the Japanese people. He sent the following cable to MacArthur on April 9, 1946:

> [The] Constitution . . . should receive due consideration of [the] Japanese Diet and people, possibly over considerable time. Unless this is done, and unless [the] Commission has full opportunity to express itself before final adoption of document, there is grave danger that it will not be approved by the Commission. I should, therefore, appreciate being informed as to successive steps which will be taken by Japanese government and people in processing constitution and the time that you consider that Allied Powers should pass on it.[30]

On April 10, the day after McCoy's letter was sent and on the day of the general election, the FEC—unable to tolerate MacArthur's repeated faits accomplis—had already decided to ask MacArthur to send a representative to Washington to report on events and conditions.

> The Far Eastern Commission has unanimously requested its Chairman to consult with the Supreme Commander of the Allied Powers with a view to having him send a member of his staff to Washington to confer with the Commission in connection with the Commission's current study of the Japanese constitutional reform and of the basic principles which should determine its approval of any specific constitutional draft.
>
> Any officer selected by the Supreme Commander for this purpose should not only be familiar with the subject of Japanese constitutional reform in general, but should also be prepared to discuss with the Commission the

views and plans of the Supreme Commander's Headquarters in these matters and should be informed about the current developments within the Japanese Government and among the Japanese people on the subject of a new constitution.

The Commission, in its concern that any constitution adopted by the Japanese should embody the "freely expressed will of the Japanese people," is particularly interested in the procedures by which it is contemplated a new constitution will be adopted—whether, for example, by the Diet, by a constitutional convention, or by a plebiscite.[31]

MacArthur did not send a reply until May 4, almost a month later. However, his response to the FEC this time was more a thesis than a letter. In order to prove the correctness of his policy, he provided long quotes from SWNCC 228 ("Reform of the Japanese Governmental System") and other documents. It may have taken a month to prepare such a long argument, but the part that responded directly to the FEC's letter consisted of no more than the first few lines.

I am in full agreement with the need for a closer working arrangement and understanding between the Supreme Commander for the Allied Powers and the Commission and stand ready to do everything in my power to such end. I do not believe, however, that the dispatch of an officer from my staff to confer with the Commission would provide a solution to the problem. In the first place, as Supreme Commander I have given my personal attention to the matter of constitutional reform, and there is no other officer in position to express in detail my views on that subject.[32]

The State Department judged that it was not appropriate to send MacArthur's unresponsive letter to the commission. J. H. Hilldring, the State Department member of the State, War, Navy Coordinating Committee (SWNCC), proceeded to send another directive to MacArthur. He wrote: "This government believes that such personal contacts between GHQ and the Far Eastern Commission will be of great assistance to all concerned and are of special importance at the present time."[33] MacArthur's attitude did not change. Finally realizing that MacArthur would not modify his stance, the State Department sent his long letter to the Far Eastern Commission on May 29.[34] More than a month and a half had passed since MacArthur had received the commission's letter. McCoy attempted to justify the long delay to the FEC members as not deliberate but rather as the result of a misunderstanding.[35]

The Department of the Army could no longer remain silent. Assistant Secretary of the Army Howard Petersen sent a telegram to MacArthur, stating that it was essential that "the Far Eastern Commission be afforded an opportunity to examine the new Constitution before it takes effect."[36] But Petersen's telegram had absolutely no effect on MacArthur. In his reply MacArthur merely praised the contents of the draft constitution: "This draft provides one of the most liberal constitutions in the world— far more liberal than is that of Russia or China, and certainly no less liberal than that of the United States or of England."[37]

Nothing more need be said about MacArthur's relations with the FEC or with the State Department. Even his relations with the Department of the Army were hopeless. The Office of Far Eastern Affairs of the State Department had already concluded that it was impossible to persuade MacArthur to change his course on constitutional revision. Consequently, on April 19 the director of that office, John Carter Vincent, sent the following recommendation to Secretary of State Byrnes:

> There is general agreement among concerned American officials (a) that General MacArthur should not have approved the draft constitution; (b) that his defense is not to the point; (c) that in his address to the Allied Council in Tokyo on April 5, however, he carried out in a limited but sufficient measure the policy decision of the Far Eastern Commission of March 20 by indicating that changes in form and detail might result from examination of the draft constitution; and (d) that, therefore, no useful purpose would be served by any further discussion of this matter.[38]

The State Department had already given up in despair. Nor could the FEC continue to oppose indefinitely the April 10 general election, which by this time was a fait accompli. On May 13 the FEC reached a policy decision calling for a full consideration of the constitution by the elected representatives, informing MacArthur of the decision through the U.S. government.

> The criteria for the adoption of a new Constitution should be such as to ensure that the Constitution, when finally adopted, is, in fact, a free expression of the will of the Japanese people. To this end, the following principles should be observed:
>
> A. Adequate time and opportunity should be allowed for the full discussion and consideration of the terms of the new Constitution.
> B. Complete legal continuity from the Constitution of 1889 to the new Constitution should be assured.
> C. The new Constitution should be adopted in such a manner as to demonstrate that it affirmatively expresses the free will of the Japanese people.[39]

Colegrove's Role

It was in such circumstances that Colegrove, who had arrived in Japan in early March, began to carry out his responsibilities as political consultant to MacArthur's headquarters. He was given an office in the Government Section, in room 611 on the sixth floor of the Daiichi Insurance Building, where a few days earlier Satō Tatsuo and others had negotiated all night with Government Section officials about the draft constitution. In the next room was Kades. Sharing the office with Colegrove were T. A. Bisson and Cyrus Peake.[40] Bisson had come to Japan once in the fall of 1945 as a member of the Strategic Bombing Survey Team, but had returned briefly to the United States. He had been assigned to Japan—at about the same time as Colegrove—as a special assistant in Government Section.[41] Bisson was not involved in any way in preparing the SCAP draft, but he had previously known Colegrove. Cyrus Peake had participated in writing the SCAP draft as chairman of the subcommittee that prepared the chapter on the executive branch. He was a graduate of Northwestern University (1922), spoke both Chinese and Japanese, and had been an assistant professor at Columbia University since 1937.[42] Colegrove, Bisson, and Peake probably shared the same office, as their assignment was to assist Kades as Far Eastern specialists. Kades offered the following comments on their role:

> All of them were Japan specialists. I accepted their advice only in those cases when they agreed, and reported to General Whitney. The reason was that Colegrove was very conservative, Bisson was a member of the IPR (Institute of Pacific Relations), that is, left wing, and Peake was in the middle, and so their views tended to be at odds with each other. Their views did carry some weight, but as group, not as individual opinions.[43]

Before Colegrove left for Japan, Ōyama had given him letters to deliver to his Japanese friends. Colegrove personally handed letters to Katō Kanjū and his wife Shizue,[44] and asked Matsukata Yoshisaburō, chief editor of *Kyōdō Tsūshin*, to send Ōyama's letter to Kyoto University professor Sasaki Sōichi.[45] Since communications between Japan and the United States had been prohibited for so long, letters from Ōyama were without doubt an unexpected gift. By sending Ōyama's letters to numerous people, it appears that Colegrove had the opportunity to meet them and thus to increase his exposure to current Japanese views. Of course there were others, such as Suzuki Yasuzō, who met Colegrove when submitting comments on the draft outline. And there were people such as the then NHK director, Takano Iwasaburō, Tokuda Kyūichi, and Shiga Yoshio of the Japan Communist Party, who corresponded with Colegrove but did not meet him.[46] Of the intellectuals whom Colegrove met and whose views on the draft constitution he heard, many were affiliated with the League of Men of Culture, of which Sugimori Kōjirō was the chairman. Unfortunately, no individual records of conversations with the Japanese, except comments by Suzuki and Sasaki, exist. On the other hand, Colegrove in his meetings with them did not mention his reason for being in Japan. For example, even Irie Toshio could recall that "I don't know why he came to Japan. Didn't he often come?"[47]

Colegrove conveyed information to SCAP about the State Department and the Far Eastern Commission and offered advice to MacArthur and Whitney. He also wrote numerous letters about the conditions in Japan to U.S. representatives on the FEC, such as Chairman McCoy, Chief of the Secretariat Nelson Johnson, and Political Adviser George Blakeslee. With SCAP becoming increasingly isolated, Colegrove's activities provided an understanding of SCAP's position at a time of friction between the State Department and SCAP and helped gradually to nudge SCAP in a more positive direction in the process of enacting the constitution. When he conferred with the chief of Government Section, General Whitney, on April 22, Colegrove informed him frankly of the activities of each FEC member country and assured him that McCoy did not support MacArthur's position. He told Whitney:

> General McCoy and the State Department (i.e., John Carter Vincent and Dean Acheson) felt that you should not have approved the Constitution without first consulting the Far Eastern Commission. General McCoy believes that your approval has seriously embarrassed him in his relationship with the representatives of other nations.[48]

Since arriving in Japan, Colegrove had solicited Japanese views of the occupation in his meetings with Japanese intellectuals and had learned that the Japanese had a very good impression of the draft constitution. Colegrove met with MacArthur immediately after conferring with Whitney and then wrote a long letter to General McCoy, giving his first impressions of Japan and criticizing the attitude of the FEC toward the constitutional issue.

> The time has been short, but already I have had opportunity to renew my acquaintance with a number of Japanese scholars and publicists and to meet a few new Japanese. My conversations with them have given me a vivid impression that the success of the military occupation is largely due to the phenomenal esteem and confidence entertained by the Japanese people for the Supreme Commander. . . . They are particularly unanimous in saying that

the personality of the Supreme Commander is the foremost reason for the American success in Japan. . . . I realize that you are in a very delicate position as head of the American delegation and as Chairman of the FEC, and I do not like to add to your anxieties. But I must say that, as an American citizen, deeply interested in the achievements of this dangerous experiment in democracy in the Far East, I am worried over the ambiguous policy of the FEC toward the new constitution of Japan. The Shidehara draft of the new constitution has the approval of most of the well-informed Japanese people to whom I have talked. They seem to think that the sooner the constitution of 1889 is terminated and the sooner the new constitution is adopted, the better it will be for Japan. Furthermore, there is abundant evidence of the fact that the Japanese voters in the election of April 10 expected the new Diet not only to legislate for Japan but also to adopt a constitution as proposed by the Shidehara Government, with or without amendments. . . .

It is obvious that the political situation cannot be stabilized in Japan until the new constitution is adopted. At the same time it is intolerable to hold up for a considerable length of time the decision of a large nation until a commission in a distant capital gives its approval to every item in that document. There is no doubt but that such a delay will weaken the prestige of the Supreme Commander and jeopardize the success of the American experiment in democracy in the Far East.[49]

Thus Colegrove emphasized that, for political stability in Japan, putting the U.S. political position first and protecting SCAP were more immediately important than fulfilling an international political agreement. Colegrove's argument for protecting SCAP was that it had the support of the many Japanese intellectuals to whom he had spoken. The FEC had expressed dissatisfaction with MacArthur for having arbitrarily approved the draft constitution. But in a letter to Blakeslee, Colegrove stood this argument on its head: "Several Japanese scholars have asked me whether it can be said that the Constitution would be the 'will of the Japanese people freely expressed' in case their Constitution was at the mercy of a commission of foreign representatives sitting in a distant city."[50]

Receiving this letter in the "distant city" of Washington, Blakeslee immediately showed it to Johnson. Not to be outdone, Johnson quickly wrote to Colegrove defending the position taken by the FEC.

I think that someone there at SCAP must help SCAP to understand that the Far Eastern Commission has a very definite feeling of responsibility. This feeling of responsibility begins with the fact that the Secretary of State of the United States definitely said at the time when the draft constitution was published in Japan that this draft, or any other draft, must in some way come before the Far Eastern Commission.

Criticizing Colegrove for not understanding MacArthur's position despite the fact that he was "near the Supreme Commander," Johnson expressed a new fear that was already being whispered at the State Department and at the Far Eastern Commission: "An impression has been created here that General MacArthur intends to jam this particular draft constitution through this present Diet without debate."[51]

Johnson made the point in his letter in a rather diffident manner. The fact is, however, that within the State Department efforts were being made to avoid further conflict with MacArthur.

MacArthur's Compromise

The Far Eastern Commission's requests for careful deliberations, for a postponement of the election, and for a representative to come to Washington to explain the situation of the draft constitution had all been rejected by MacArthur. The State Department had heard, meanwhile, that MacArthur intended to have the government's draft—that is, "a particular draft Constitution"—passed by the Diet in two or three weeks. If he were to reject the FEC's "Criteria for the Adoption of a New Constitution" mentioned earlier and if the Shidehara government's draft were to be "rammed through the Diet without debate" in two or three weeks, the U.S. government's ability to conduct foreign policy could be questioned by the FEC nations. Faced with this serious impasse, the State, War, Navy Coordinating Committee had already concluded that the only way to persuade MacArthur to submit to the FEC was to have President Truman send him a letter. The committee had prepared a first draft of the letter for the president and had decided to send it to MacArthur as "information and guidance" on June 11, 1946.[52]

> It was recently reported that the Japanese Government expected the Diet to adopt a new Constitution by the end of June at the latest. It is difficult, as you have stated, to determine in advance the length of time necessary for the consideration of the Constitution. This Government, however, believes that a period of three or four weeks from the time of the introduction into the Diet of the Constitution is much too short. It is contrary to precedent in the United States where State Constitutions have required on the average nearly three and one-half months' consideration in the respective Constitutional Conventions. It is also contrary to precedents in Europe where the Constituent Assemblies after the first World War took on the average sixteen months each to complete their work. . . .
>
> Further, this Government believes that it would be advisable, provided it should be acceptable to the Japanese, to have the new Constitution receive final ratification by some media other than the present Diet: that is, by a specially elected Constituent Assembly or another Diet elected with the Consti-

tution as a campaign issue, or a popular referendum. In spite of pressure for the adoption of such a procedure from practically all other members of the Far Eastern Commission, General McCoy had made it clear in the Commission that the United States will not permit you to be embarrassed by a policy decision which would require a Constituent Assembly, a second Diet or a referendum. However, a final approval of the Constitution by either a Constituent Assembly or referendum or both would be in line with American precedents. . . .

This Government believes therefore that it would be advisable for you to discuss this matter with suitable Japanese leaders and make clear to them that there is no objection to final ratification of the Constitution by a Constituent Assembly or second Diet elected expressly for the purpose, or a referendum.[53]

The letter was never sent to the president or to MacArthur. The director of the State Department's Office of Far Eastern Affairs, John Carter Vincent, considered "the complexities of this problem" and apparently chose to leave the letter in draft form.[54] But did MacArthur surmise what was going on in Washington? On June 22, the day after the opening ceremony of the Ninetieth Imperial Diet, which was to debate the constitution, MacArthur issued the following statement to the Japanese people in which he accepted most of the FEC's May 13 policy decision. The statement is rather tedious, but if read against the background of the FEC-MacArthur dispute, it is obvious that it was not directed to the Japanese people; though nominally a statement to them, it was in fact MacArthur's response to his own government and to members of the FEC.

With the submission to the Diet of a proposed revision of the constitution, the Japanese people face one of the vital moments in the life of Japan. The fundamental charter of their existence will be determined by the action taken on this monumental question. In its solution, it has been and continues to be imperative (a) that adequate time and opportunity be allowed for the full discussion and consideration of the terms of such a charter; (b) that the procedure followed assures complete legal continuity with the constitution of 1889 now existing; and (c) that the manner of adoption of such a charter demonstrates that it affirmatively expresses the free will of the Japanese people. These criteria governing the mechanics involved in constitutional revision thus far have been scrupulously followed, and they must continue to guide now that the issue is before the National Diet. For over eight months the revision of the constitution has been the paramount political consideration under discussion by all parties and all classes of the Japanese people. Numerous drafts have been prepared by the various political parties, educational groups, publicists, and individuals of all shades of thought and opinion. The press and radio and every other medium of information have been employed to an extent seldom witnessed in any national forum. Rarely has a fundamental charter, regulative of national life, been more thoroughly discussed and analyzed. The Government Draft now before the Diet is a Japanese document and it is for the people of Japan, acting through their duly elected representatives, to determine its form and content—whether it be adopted, modified, or rejected.[55]

In the three months since the publication of the government's March 6 draft, which was based on the SCAP draft, MacArthur had continually rejected various requests from the FEC and the State Department. For the first time, however, he accepted several of those requests in his statement.

Minister of State Matsumoto had said at the April meeting of the Privy Council that the draft constitution would be promulgated at the end of June and take effect at the end of the year. The timetable had since been greatly revised. The new schedule called for the draft constitution to be debated in the Imperial Diet for roughly four months. As we shall see later, it was now possible for the draft to be amended in the Diet. The Japanese government was informed of this SCAP policy before the MacArthur statement, apparently just after the FEC's policy decision. On May 13, 1946, Matsumoto had told the Privy Council that "the Government cannot amend the draft."[56] But Prime Minister Yoshida, responding to a question in the Privy Council on May 29, changed this to: "It will be possible for amendments to be offered by the Imperial Diet."[57]

This was a significant change. The State Department's fear that the draft would be "rammed through the Diet without discussion" was now allayed. At the time the Japanese people were not informed that this change had taken place. We now know that behind MacArthur's acceptance of this change were the continued demands from the Far Eastern Commission and the State Department.

A Democratic Constitution Without Bayonets?

MacArthur not only ensured that the Ninetieth Imperial Diet would be the body that enacted the constitution, but he also made sure that only the government draft was placed before the Diet. Since arriving in Japan, Colegrove had considered MacArthur's plan for constitutional revision the correct one and had been trying to convince the FEC of that. On June 15, shortly before the convening of the Imperial Diet, Colegrove sent a long, well-argued letter to FEC Secretary General Johnson. One might call the letter a general report, the product of his grappling with the constitutional issue for some three months. Colegrove explained to Johnson how right, in the context of political conditions in Japan, MacArthur's course of action on constitutional reform had been.

The member states of the Far Eastern Commission who have tried to delay the reform of the political system in Japan are in effect serving the interests of Japan's reactionary elements, not the cause of democratization. Unless a liberal Constitution is adopted in the present democratic process, no matter how democratic it is, it would probably not be adopted without the coercion of the Allied bayonets. It is clear that such a Constitution would be worse than useless in the circumstances. The principal reason that the liberal reform of the political system in occupied Japan has made such conspicuous progress is because of MacArthur's unrivaled authority and incomparable reputation. The Japanese people's trust in his leadership today is creating the major element of the democratic Constitution. . . . Any delay in the adoption of the constitution will provide a favorable opportunity to the preliminary plans of the reactionary political leaders to ensure their conservative gains.[58]

The "Japanese people's trust" in MacArthur was certainly strong.[59] And yet that trust was not just the result of "a policy of democratization." The fact that MacArthur would import food from "rich America" to feed "starving Japanese" and would bring stability to their lives by rescuing them from starvation made that trust much greater. The Ninetieth Imperial Diet even passed a unanimous resolution expressing "gratitude to the Supreme Commander for the Allied Powers."[60] Nevertheless, the strength of his reputation should not by itself justify the means by which MacArthur enacted the constitution. On the other hand, Colegrove's political judgment that "no matter how democratic the Constitution, it would probably not be adopted without the coercion of the Allied bayonets" cannot be ignored, especially in view of the overwhelming majority of seats that the conservative forces controlled in the Diet.

The procedure for enacting the draft constitution had largely been established. There was no need for "coercion by bayonets" and there was no fear that the government's draft would "be rammed through without debate." Enough time had been allowed for the debate.

When the draft constitution was brought before the Diet for debate on July 16, Colegrove attended a meeting of the Committee to Revise the Constitution in the House of Representatives. This was the same day that the Plenary Session of the House adopted the resolution of thanks to MacArthur. The committee chairman, Ashida Hitoshi, interrupted the proceedings, invited Colegrove to the chairman's dais, and offered the following words of greeting in English:

> Professor Colegrove, on behalf of the members of this Committee, I want to express our greetings and sincere appreciation for the interest which you have taken in our business. I understand that you are going home soon. When you arrive in your homeland, please tell your countrymen that the Japanese people are doing their best to rebuild a new and democratic coun-

try and are looking forward to collaborating as soon as possible with the peace-loving peoples of the world.[61]

It was a memorable moment for them both. Ashida recorded the entire greeting in English in his diary, noting that "Colegrove responded to this with a short greeting of his own and was welcomed by a full round of applause."[62] And Colegrove preserved *Asahi Shinbun*'s July 17, 1946, report of this incident.[63] But what in fact did Ashida's greeting mean? Recall that Colegrove's objective in coming to Japan was, at this point, completely unknown to the Japanese. But was it known to Ashida? The expression he used—"for the interest you have taken in our business"—was exceedingly vague, all the more because it appeared that Ashida used the expression in order to hide Colegrove's mission.

Why, then, did Colegrove attend a meeting of the Committee to Revise the Constitution? SCAP's role in writing the draft constitution was the most secret of secrets, and of course neither Whitney nor Kades was present at the Diet. Colegrove was the only American there. And yet *Asahi Shinbun* identified him as "a political adviser to the Supreme Commander, and professor of Northwestern University." Still, as is evident in MacArthur's June 22 statement, SCAP continued throughout to say that the draft constitution was "a Japanese document." Only later was it revealed that it had been written with "SCAP's assistance." Was the purpose of this *Asahi Shinbun* report, which was published under strict SCAP censorship, to make the public aware that the draft had been written with "SCAP's assistance"? On the other hand, Colegrove made certain that the procedure for revising the constitution, which he had recommended, was welcomed by representatives of the Japanese people, and he felt the need to report this to the U.S. government.

The true story of how the constitution was imposed on Japan was first reported in Japan just before the end of the occupation in 1951, as described in the introduction to this book. But it was reported in the United States by a newspaper as early as June 1946. The *Christian Science Monitor* of June 25, 1946, carried a rather shocking article by its correspondent, Robert Peel, who was returning home from special assignment in Japan. The title was especially eye-catching:

> Reluctant Japanese Accept Constitution Dictated by MacArthur. First Sprouts of Democracy Withered by Sudden Action. The most important step in General Douglas MacArthur's "paper revolution" is the draft constitution for Japan written according to the Supreme Command's specifications. There is little question that it will receive a rubber-stamp approval by the Japanese Diet, since it is what General MacArthur wants—and those close to him have stated that it is his pet project.[64]

The article is rather short on specifics, but its publication, especially by such a reliable newspaper, was clearly not in SCAP's interest. Colegrove might have preferred that the article strike a different tone. Had he not been able to determine with his own eyes during his visit to the Diet that there were no "reluctant Japanese" present?

Colegrove departed from Japan on July 22. On July 29 he wrote a letter from Northwestern University to President Truman at the White House.

My observations on the spot lead me to believe that General MacArthur's policy toward the drafting of the new Japanese Constitution has been both timely and wise. Any change in this policy by a contrary directive from the Far Eastern Commission, sitting ten thousand miles from Japan, would confuse and bewilder the Japanese people and might lead to disaster. The Supreme Commander is eminently correct in his program of promoting the abandonment of the old autocratic Constitution and the adoption of a democratic Constitution in the shortest possible time.[65]

The Supreme Commander did manage somehow to get his way. Events developed more or less as MacArthur had planned. The fact that he treated the FEC's and the State Department's recommendations with contempt could not fail to produce its victims. In early July McCoy fell ill and remained in a New York hospital until late August. It was said that his fear that he had lost MacArthur's confidence was a serious psychological cause of his illness,[66] although it appears that the main cause was exhaustion from his work as the U.S. representative and chairman of the FEC, which put him in the thick of the fight with MacArthur. Colegrove informed Whitney of McCoy's illness at the end of July, but apparently MacArthur never even sent his old friend a card to wish him well. On August 10 Colegrove again sent a letter to Whitney, in which he wrote:

It is quite likely that General MacArthur has already sent a personal letter or radio to General McCoy, expressing his concern over the hospitalization and his delight at learning that his health was improving. If not, it might be well to send such a letter.[67]

Colegrove played the role of a mediator between the two generals until the very end.

Notes

1. Katherine H. Giese, "Kenneth Wallace Colegrove Papers" (hereafter, Giese, "Colegrove Papers"), 1977, Northwestern University Library Archives.

2. For example, his *Militarism in Japan* (World Peace Foundation, 1936); "The Japanese Emperor," *The American Political Science Review* 26, no. 4 (August 1932) and no. 5 (October 1932); and "The Japanese Constitution," *The American Political Science Review,* 31, no. 6 (December 1937).

3. Kenneth W. Colegrove, *Democracy Versus Communism* (Institute of Fiscal and Political Education, 1957).

4. Giese, "Colegrove Papers." Ninagawa Jō, "Ōyama Iwao nenpu," in *Ōyama Iwao,* ed. Maruyama Masao and others (Tokyo: Shin Hyōron, 1980), pp. 28, 257, gives his title as research associate. I follow Giese's interpretation of Colegrove's papers on this point.

5. According to his wife, Colegrove had written to Ōyama requesting materials on the Workers and Farmers Party, enclosing one dollar to pay for them. Ōyama had not sent the materials, and his reason for writing from Chicago was to return the money. "Memories of Ōyama Iwao," *Ōyama kai kaihō* 3 (August 1966).

6. Iokibe Makoto, *Beikoku no Nihon senryō seisaku* (Tokyo: Chūō Kōronsha, 1985), 2:196.

7. *Who Was Who in America with World Notables, 1977–1981*, vol. 7.

8. Colegrove to T. A. Bisson, November 22, 1938, Colegrove Papers, Northwestern University Library Archives.

9. In a 1946 letter to Colegrove, Ōyama wrote, "At the present time the translation is close to completion." See "The Life of Professor Ōyama Iwao in the United States," in *Ōyama Iwao zenshū,* vol. 5 (Tokyo: Chūō Kōronsha, 1949).

10. Colegrove Papers.

11. Giese, "Colegrove Papers."

12. Colegrove Papers.

13. Hugh Borton, *Japan's Modern Century* (New York: The Ronald Press Co., 1955), p. 424.

14. Max W. Bishop, of the Office of the Political Adviser in Japan, to the Secretary of State, *Foreign Relations of the United States* (hereafter, *FRUS*) (1946), 8:173.

15. FEC bunsho, kokkai toshokan shozō, microfiche bangō FEC(A)1245.

16. Colegrove Papers.

17. Ibid.

18. U.S. Department of State, *Activities of the Far Eastern Commission, Reported by the Secretary General* (Washington, D.C., 1947), pp. 58–59.

19. Ibid., pp. 59–63.

20. *Current Biography*, 1954, p. 428.

21. Personal Message to MacArthur from McCoy, W 99134, March 3, 1946, Colegrove Papers.

22. Ibid.

23. Personal Cable to MacArthur from McCoy, W 81600, March 22, 1946, Colegrove Papers.

24. Suzuki Yasuzō, *Kenpō seitei zengo* (Tokyo: Aoki Shoten, 1977), p. 138.

25. Of the five thousand people in the sample, twenty-four hundred responded. Kenpō chōsakai, "Kenpō seitei no keika ni kansuru shōiinkai dai yonjūnana kai gijiroku," pp. 188–189.

26. Irie Toshio, *Kenpō seiritsu no keii to kenpō no shomondai* (Tokyo: Daiichi Hōki Shuppan, 1976), p. 258.

27. Ibid., pp. 302–304.

28. Ibid., pp. 259–260.

29. Murakami Ichirō, ed., *Teikoku kenpō kaiseian gijiroku* (Tokyo: Kokusho Kankōkai, 1986), pp. 49–50.

30. Washington (McCoy) to CINCAFPAC (MacArthur), W 83719, April 9, 1946, Colegrove Papers.

31. Memorandum for the State Department Members of the State-War-Navy Coordinating Committee (Hilldring) to the Committee, April 12, 1946, *FRUS* (1946), 8:195–196.

32. General of the Army Douglas MacArthur to the Joint Chiefs of Staff, May 4, 1946, *FRUS* (1946), 8:220.

33. Memorandum from the State Department Member of SWNCC (J. H. Hilldring), proposed telegram to General MacArthur, May 8, 1946. National Archives 894.011/5–946.

34. U.S. Department of State, *Far Eastern Commission*, 1953, no hōyaku "Nihon shin kenpō to kyokutō iinkai" (Kenpō chōsakai jimukyoku, 1956), p. 13.

35. Ibid.

36. Assistant Secretary Petersen to General MacArthur, W 87958, May 15, 1946, Colegrove Papers.

37. From CINCAFPAC (MacArthur) to WARCOS (Petersen), C 61134, May 18, 1946, Colegrove Papers.

38. Memorandum by the Director of the Office of Far Eastern Affairs (Vincent) to Secretary of State, April 19, 1946, *FRUS* (1946), 8:211.

39. Gaimushō tokubetsu shiryōbu hen, "Criteria for the Adoption of a New Constitution," in *Nihon senryō oyobi kanri jūyō bunshoshū* (Tokyo: Tōyō Keizai Shinpōsha, 1949), 1:89–90.

40. "GHQ Tokyo Telephone Directory," in *GHQ no soshiki to jinji, September 1946*, ed. Fukushima Yasurō (Tokyo: Gannandō, 1984).

41. Thomas A. Bisson, *Nihon senryō kaisōki*, trans. Nakamura Masanori and Miura Yōichi (Tokyo: Sanseidō, 1983), p. 330.

42. Peake's curriculum vitae in Colegrove Papers.

43. Takemae Eiji, "Bei senryō seisaku no ito," *Chūō kōron* (May 1987): 201.

44. Colegrove sent Katō Kanjū a note of congratulations, dated March 18, 1948, when Katō was appointed labor minister in the Ashida Cabinet. Colegrove Papers.

45. Letter from Sasaki to Ōyama, in Sasaki Sōichi, *Sorin* (Tokyo: Kōbunsha, 1947), p. 183.

46. Takano sent a letter to Colegrove in Tokyo, dated July 2, 1946. Colegrove Papers. Since Colegrove sent letters of thanks for letters addressed to him, it would appear that he did not wish to meet Takano, Tokuda, or Shiga.

47. Irie, *Kenpō seiritsu*, p. 403.

48. Check Sheet from General Whitney to Commander in Chief, April 24, 1946, MacArthur Memorial Archives, Norfolk, Virginia.

49. Letter from Colegrove to General Frank R. McCoy, April 26, 1946, MacArthur Memorial Archives.

50. Colegrove to Professor George H. Blakeslee, May 17, 1946, Colegrove Papers.

51. Nelson T. Johnson to Colegrove, May 27, 1946, Colegrove Papers.

52. "United States Policy in Regard to the Adoption of a New Japanese Constitution," SWNCC 228/3, June 11, 1946, National Archives, Microfilm T 1205, Roll 8.

53. Ibid., Appendix "D."

54. *FRUS* (1946), 8:247, footnote 14.

55. *Asahi Shinbun*, July 17, 1946.

56. Murakawa Ichirō, ed., *Teikoku kenpō* (Tokyo: Kokusho Kankōkai, 1986), p. 62.

57. Ibid., p. 126.

58. Colegrove to Nelson, June 15, 1946, FEC bunsho, kokkai toshokan shozō, microfiche bangō FEC(A)1075.

59. For example, the collection of letters written by Japanese to MacArthur, Sodei Rinjirō, ed., *Dear General MacArthur* (Tokyo: Ōtsuki Shoten, 1985).

60. *Asahi Shinbun*, July 17, 1946.

61. Shindō Eiichi, ed., *Ashida Hitoshi nikki* (Tokyo: Iwanami Shoten, 1986), 1:119. It is written entirely in English.

62. Ibid.

63. Colegrove Papers. The section about Colegrove has been underlined.

64. *Christian Science Monitor*, July 25, 1946.

65. Colegrove to President Truman, June 25, 1946, Truman Presidential Library. Based on a copy of the letter in the possession of Professor Yamagiwa Akira, Yokohama City University.

66. Colegrove to General Courtney Whitney, August 10, 1946, Colegrove Papers.

67. Ibid.

8

The Draft Constitution in the Last Imperial Diet

For the Security of the Imperial Household

Even as MacArthur's relations with his government and the FEC began to improve, he faced a crisis of a completely different kind in the conservative political system of Japan. In the April 10, 1946, general election, held under the revised election law of the House of Representatives that took effect at the end of December 1945, Prime Minister Shidehara's Progressive Party won 94 seats and came in second to the Liberal Party's 141 seats. The Socialist Party, with 93 seats, followed the Progressives; the Communist Party won 5 seats in its first election since becoming a legal party; the People's Cooperative Party took 14; and various small factions and independents won 119 seats. Given the less than complete mandate for the Progressive Party, it was very difficult for Shidehara to maintain his cabinet.

He therefore concocted plans to form a coalition with the Liberal Party. But the Liberal Party, under Hatoyama Ichirō's leadership, declined to participate. The Liberals instead joined the four-party committee of Socialists, People's Cooperatives, and Communists to overthrow the Shidehara cabinet, which submitted its resignation on April 22. The Liberal Party then proposed an alliance with the Socialists, but the latter rejected the offer. Hatoyama at that point determined to form a Liberal Party government. But on May 3, as he was in the process of forming a cabinet, SCAP suddenly ordered that he be barred from holding public office. In place of Hatoyama, Yoshida Shigeru assumed the presidency of the party.

The food shortage by this time had become acute, and 250,000 people gathered in front of the Imperial Palace in a "Food May Day" rally. The shouts of the demonstrators reached into the grounds of the palace itself, and the prime minister's official residence was surrounded. To cope with the people's anger and to alleviate the shortages, Yoshida spent much time maneuvering to find a progressive scholar to serve as minister of agriculture. But the effort, which failed in the end, succeeded only in slowing the formation of a cabinet.

The first Yoshida cabinet was officially formed on May 22, 1946, precisely a month to the day after the Shidehara cabinet's resignation. This month has been called a period of a "political vacuum" by historians,[1] but it might more aptly be called a time of a "power vacuum" or perhaps a time of dynamic political developments. Indeed, it was nothing less than a crisis in Japan's conservative political system. Behind the crisis was the government's recent acceptance of the American draft constitution. Why did Shidehara and Yoshida give their support to a constitution that produced such a severe political crisis? As we have said, MacArthur had imposed the constitution upon both Shidehara and Yoshida. Yet by this time they had begun to accept the draft constitution's basic principles. What was their reasoning? On March 20, 1946, Prime Minister Shidehara offered the following explanation when he submitted the government's draft bill for revision of the constitution to the Privy Council:

> The Far Eastern Commission is a kind of legislative body which makes basic policy decisions with respect to the Far Eastern problem. At its first meeting in Washington on February 26 of this year the issue of revising the Japanese Constitution was debated. It was expected that there would be interference by the Commission in Supreme Commander MacArthur's policy of attempting to protect the Japanese Imperial Household. General MacArthur, in order to create a fait accompli before hand, rushed the announcement of the draft Constitution. I have heard that he was absolutely delighted to be able to announce this draft, which was put together in complete secrecy without a word leaking out. Considering these circumstances, I believe the completion of this draft before us today is something for which, for Japan's sake, we should be pleased. If this opportunity had been lost, I believe the Imperial Household would have been in grave danger and that we were within a hairsbreadth of a serious crisis.[2]

Yoshida also stated the matter bluntly. In reply to a question put to him in the House of Peers during his policy address on June 23, he said:

> The reason I would like to offer a word of caution here is that we have not presented this bill for the revision of the Constitution merely from the perspective of the Constitution as the nation's supreme law. At this moment of defeat in war, we have presented the bill having fully in mind the questions of how the nation can be saved and how the safety of the Imperial House can be assured.[3]

It seems that both Shidehara and Yoshida had finally realized that, in view of international circumstances, this constitution was the most appropriate way of formally protecting the emperor system. They asserted themselves in a way that was politically acceptable to SCAP. This defining characteristic of the first Yoshida cabinet first appeared during the Diet debates on the Constitution.

Profile of Kanamori Tokujirō

The Ninetieth Imperial Diet convened in June 1946 for the last time. (Strictly speaking, it convened twice again very briefly, but essentially this was the last Imperial Diet.) On the day before the Diet's opening ceremony, the Yoshida cabinet decided to appoint one additional minister. The cabinet had no initial plans to assign a minister to guide the draft constitution revision bill through the Diet, but then decided to modify a section of the imperial rescript, which provided for "Advice on Revision of the Constitution and the Legal Codes." This revision increased the number of cabinet posts by one, allowing for the appointment of a minister of state to take charge of the constitution.[4] Kanamori Tokujirō made his appearance at this point. Why Yoshida selected Kanamori for the post is not altogether clear. But, as we shall see, it appears Yoshida's principal concern was that Kanamori had been a "victim" of prewar militarism.

In 1934 Kanamori was appointed director general of the Legislation Bureau in the Okada cabinet, but soon drew criticism for his book, *Outline of the Imperial Constitution*. Written while he was a councillor of the Bureau, the book endorsed the "emperor as organ" thesis. His book, like that of Minobe's, did little more than state what was generally accepted at the time. That is, in the section that drew the critics' ire, Kanamori had written: "The Emperor is the natural person who ultimately and at the highest level determines ideas of State and unites in himself the State organs mentioned above."[5] Nothing more than this. In the 343 pages of the book, moreover, he touched on the "rights of subjects" on only forty-seven of those pages; the remaining pages deal primarily with his interpretation of the emperor and organs of government.

Kanamori was forced to resign in 1936 and remained outside government service until after the war. But the fact that Kanamori had resigned over the organ-theory controversy appealed to Yoshida, as he compared it to his own arrest by the secret police shortly before Japan's surrender (because of his involvement with Konoe's memorial to the throne about ending the war), which became a badge of honor after the war.

Furthermore, Kanamori did not have the appearance of a high-ranking bureaucrat. His house had been burned down in a bombing raid in 1945.

Ten members of his family lived in one room of a small house, and even after he was appointed to the cabinet, he obtained food for his family by cultivating a nearby field on Sundays.[6] During the Diet debates Kanamori dressed in a winter morning coat that had survived the fire-bomb raids, thus earning the nickname the "bombed-out minister."

Kanamori was quite a literary person with a talent for painting and writing essays. He was also highly articulate. His comments and responses to questions in the Diet debates did not sound like those of a bureaucrat. He spoke more than anyone else during the debates on the constitution, responding to questions and comments 1,365 times.[7] His longest response lasted for an hour and a half.[8] Despite all this, he never once conveyed an impression of being unwilling to respond to his interlocutors. Even his replies to questions by opposition party members seem unusually eloquent. Satō Isao, an official in the Legislation Bureau who observed the debates, recalled that "Kanamori's defense in the Diet was not in the least sullen. He responded very effectively, using skillful expressions and appropriate, familiar adages."[9]

At the same time, there is no denying that his "skillful expressions" often obscured the point at hand and tended to produce something of a smoke screen. The issue of greatest concern to all the political parties was whether the *kokutai* (national polity) would be changed by the new constitution. If Kanamori were to confirm its change, the government party would oppose, and if he were to deny any change, the opposition would object. Thus his answer was: "Even if the water flows, the river does not." When asked whether renouncing armaments under Article 9 would not endanger Japan's security, he replied: "A hard tooth breaks, but the soft tongue does not." Displaying the artistry of a master performer—unthinkable for a bureaucrat—Kanamori was able to escape from difficult positions through his clever responses. Furthermore, when the situation demanded, Kanamori could make good use of his knowledge of law and administrative rules. Kanamori's appointment brought incalculable benefit to the Yoshida cabinet.

Having secured the services of Kanamori, the Yoshida government faced the opening of debate in the Diet, one that would extend over a period of four months. What were the main points of contention in this debate? To make the complicated process somewhat easier to understand, it is necessary first to provide a general outline of the legislative proceedings.

After publishing the draft constitution, on April 17, 1946, the government referred the document to the Privy Council. Beginning on April 22, the draft was examined in eleven sessions of the Privy Council's investigation committee, chaired by Ushio Shigenosuke, and was approved on June 3 in a plenary session of the council, with only Minobe Tatsukichi opposing it. On June 25 the draft was then submitted to the Diet's House of Representatives. After three days in plenary session, it was sent on June 28 to the Special Committee on Revision of the Imperial Constitution, which was composed of seventy-two representatives appointed by the speaker. The Liberal Party's Ashida Hitoshi was elected from among the members as chairman. Following deliberations in the special committee, a subcommittee was established—also chaired by Ashida—and charged with producing an amended draft incorporating all changes agreed on by the members.

The subcommittee met for [secret] informal discussions from July 25 to August 20. The minutes of the subcommittee meetings were not even opened to the public until 1995. Chairman Ashida served as moderator, but no government officials were present. Although the special committee included members of all political parties, the subcommittee included no Communist Party or other minor party members. The subcommittee's common amended bill was accepted by the special committee on August 21, reported by Chairman Ashida to the plenary session of the House of Representatives on August 24, and approved on the same day. Members of the Communist Party and two independent members, eight all together, voted against the bill. Thereafter, the government's amended bill on revising the constitution was sent to the House of Peers for debate and returned on October 8 to the House for its consideration of amendments by the Peers and for final approval and adoption. Following another pro forma review by the Privy Council in October, the constitution was promulgated on November 3, 1946.

It will be apparent to the reader that during this period Ashida Hitoshi occupied an extremely important position. Ashida entered politics in 1945 after a diplomatic career, assisted Hatoyama Ichirō in organizing the Liberal Party,[10] and as we have seen, served as minister of welfare in the Shidehara cabinet. It is apparent that he felt greater pride in his work as chairman of the special committee and the subcommittee than he felt in his work as a minister. On the day that he became chairman of the special committee, he recorded in his diary: "I have been appointed Chairman of the Special Committee on Revision of the Constitution. Because of the epochal nature of this work, I think it is more prestigious than that of Welfare Minister or Minister of State."[11]

Satō Isao, a Legislation Bureau official who observed Ashida's performance in the Diet, recalled that "as chairman, Ashida was stately; he skillfully presided over the meeting. I would say that he certainly was a fine chairman. He himself was pleased with the position and seems to have taken pride in it."[12]

On June 29, immediately after becoming chairman of the special committee, Ashida ordered a new briefcase to be made with the words

"Commemorating Revision of the Constitution" written on the inside of the flap.[13] He was definitely well suited for the role of chairman, but this was not the only reason for his appointment. MacArthur's Government Section, aware of the fact that Ashida had frequently met with two Socialist Party members at his home in Kamakura during the war, "had a positive opinion of Ashida," believing that he possessed liberal tendencies.[14] SCAP's high opinion of Ashida was also behind his appointment to this important position.

The *Kokutai* Debate

At the plenary session of the House of Representatives on June 20, the question that attracted the most attention was *kokutai*, that is, whether the new constitution altered Japan's national polity. At the beginning of the session Kita Reikichi of the Liberal Party said:

> There are some people who say that the present Constitution invests sovereignty in the Emperor, and makes imperial sovereignty its basic premise. Others are amazed and angry because, they say, the bill on revision of the Constitution contradicts that, assigning sovereignty to the people, and makes a kind of change in the *kokutai*. But I think that in general the basic belief that the sovereign and the people have been reconciled has not changed. Therefore, is it all right to interpret the words "The Japanese people" that appear in the preamble of this bill of revision as including the Emperor? I am of the opinion that the Government has the responsibility and must drive home the point politely and fully that the draft Constitution does not change the *kokutai*.[15]

This comment was entirely in character for the younger brother of Kita Ikki, who had admired fascist government before and during the war.

In answer to Kita's interpellation, Prime Minister Yoshida rose and responded as though his view had been sought.

> I think the Japanese national polity itself has arisen naturally from the people because of the existence of the Imperial House. There is no difference between the Imperial House and the people. This is called the "oneness of ruler and subject," the ruler and subject are one family. . . . The *kokutai* is not changed one whit by the new Constitution.[16]

No matter how closely one reads the draft constitution, however, the words, "the ruler and subject are one family," cannot be found there. On the contrary, a careful reading of the articles about the emperor leads to the opposite conclusion.

Next, Kitaura Keitarō of the Liberal Party rose to his feet and offered this lament:

There is no doubt that this bill protects the Emperor System in a formal sense. In reality the beautiful Emperor System is protected in the provisions of Article 8. Through various provisions a flower is preserved. Although a flower is a flower, and there are seven or eight bunches of this flower blooming, this would indeed be a sad Constitution without even one mountain rose.[17]

Kitaura's "mountain rose Constitution" became quite a famous nickname for the draft constitution at the time. The conservative representatives pressed the government to state clearly that the *kokutai* had not been changed, and the government responded positively to their demand. Yet this was not the compliant Diet [*yokusan gikai*] that had existed during the war.

Shiga Yoshio of the Communist Party rose at the plenary session of the Diet and introduced a motion to suspend the session, arguing that no debate of the constitution by the Diet had meaning unless the people had already been given the opportunity to discuss it fully. When Shiga's motion was defeated, the Communist Party published its own "new draft Constitution." Nosaka Sanzō continued the sharp criticism of the government's replies to questions about the national polity at the plenary session, demanding that, "The Government must say clearly, without playing the sycophant, whether the people possess sovereignty, or whether the Emperor does."[18]

When the special committee reconvened, members of the Socialist Party also criticized the government's statement about *kokutai*. Mori Mikiji denounced the reply as sophistry. Oikawa Minoru asked, "Whose will is the 'will of natural persons' who constitute the supreme will of the nation? Is it the will of all the people, or the will of one ruler?" In short, he demanded to know whether the question was not the "location of sovereignty."[19] Kanamori responded:

That exists as the basis of our ties to the Emperor who is planted deep in our hearts. That is the *kokutai* that we believe in. . . . I acknowledge that the idea of the kind of *kokutai* that you have mentioned is one that at least a large proportion of scholars of law would share. However, not all of the Japanese people are familiar with the law, nor would they be sympathetic with the words of legal scholars, and it is extremely unlikely that they understand *kokutai* in such a sense. . . . Accordingly, is it not with our hearts that we best understand the essence of things?[20]

Kanamori's reply was certainly not the answer of a legal scholar. He later called the legal scholar's interpretation of *kokutai* "a form of government" (*seitai*), and maintained that *kokutai* was entirely a matter of the people's hearts. And, he continued, that had not changed.

In the House of Peers as well, Miyazawa Toshiyoshi and Nanbara Shigeru (who was both a political scientist and president of Tokyo University) argued that the government ought to acknowledge that the *kokutai* had changed.[21] The government still refused to do this. Kanamori even used the Copernican theory to illustrate his argument that the *kokutai* had not changed. "Whether the argument has been that the sun rotates around the earth, or that the earth rotates around the sun, the movement itself has not changed from ancient times to today."[22] This, like his proverb "Even though the water flows, the river does not," appears to have obscured the issue in the Diet and among the public, but perhaps his assertion that there was no "Copernican revolution in the Constitution with regard to the *kokutai*" was a superior metaphor. The Diet members, however, seemed in their own way to have recognized the fact that there had indeed been a change. It was about this time, according to Kanamori, that two poems were being circulated in the House of Peers. One asked the question: "Considering everything . . . Kanamori who fought so well . . . to what school of swordsmanship [*kenpō*, phonetically the same as the word for constitution] does he belong?" This second poem had this reply: "Kanamori belongs to the school of two swords, for he says the *kokutai* has not changed, even though he has changed it." Appreciating this play on words, Kanamori wrote in reply: "One sword of a master swordsman may look like two."[23]

The *kokutai* debate ended in a roll-call vote in the Diet. In a sense this was Kanamori's achievement. At the end of the debate, Chairman Ashida submitted to the full House his report about the special committee:

> When all is said and done, chapter one of the draft Constitution makes it clear that, based on the supreme will of the people, the Emperor's position as hereditary ruler who, coeval with Heaven and Earth, unites the people, has been assured. (applause) Thus while the Emperor is one of the people, he himself stands outside practical politics. Moreover, the confirmation of the certain fact that he possesses authority as the center of the people's lives and as their spiritual leader has been welcomed with the greatest of joy by an absolute majority of the Committee members.[24]

The major difference between the Meiji Constitution and the new constitution, as well as between prewar and postwar Japan, is this change in the emperor's position. Judging solely by constitutional provisions, there is no doubt that the change was substantial. But upon reading Ashida's report one would think that very little had changed in the ideology of the emperor system between prewar and postwar Japan. This is the clear limitation of "constitutional revision" when it is unaccompanied by social reform and a social movement.

Popular Sovereignty

Although the deliberations on Chapter 1 ("The Emperor") ended with a roll-call vote in the House, the debate had not necessarily proceeded at the pace that Yoshida and Kanamori had wished. This was a time when most Japanese, although calling for "food rather than a Constitution," were instead confronted by politics. Even though their stomachs were empty, or perhaps precisely because they were empty, politics was the priority of the time. It is different today when people feel no shame in saying "making money is [more important] than the Constitution."

The debate on *kokutai* ended with a vote in the Diet, but concern about the very crucial provision on the people's sovereignty continued. The rendering of "sovereignty of the people's will" in the SCAP draft as "supremacy of the people's will," as Shidehara had proposed, did not get very far in that form.

A council of two thousand "democratic scientists," founded in January 1946 to undertake research "to contribute to the welfare of the Japanese people and for world peace," made the people's sovereignty an issue at its second general meeting, held on June 1–2, 1946. The scientists passed a resolution calling for debate on the draft constitution to be conducted, not in the Imperial Diet, but "in a Diet especially elected to amend the Constitution, or by a special mechanism which can fully reflect the opinions of the people on the Constitution."[25] One reason for their concern was "the several important differences between the Japanese and English texts, creating a situation in which even the location of sovereignty is lacking in clarity."[26] Among the framers of the resolution was Nakamura Akira, former Taihoku University professor of government and constitutional law and later president of Hōsei University. Nakamura prepared the same announcement in English "to stimulate public opinion abroad."[27]

At the June 28 plenary session of the House Nosaka Sanzō was the first to raise questions about the "location of sovereignty" issue. The House was promptly thrown into disorder and heckling interrupted the proceedings. According to the minutes of the proceedings:

In the preamble of the draft Constitution are the words "kokumin no sōi ga shikōna mono de aru." In the English text this reads, "the sovereignty of the people's will." [interruptions] . . . Judging by the English version only, the new Constitution is very democratic [shouts of "retract that!" and many other interruptions].

President: Silence, please! Mr. Nosaka, I wish you would be more careful when you speak about the English version.
Nosaka: . . . But the Japanese original does not say this. It has many points that are extremely dubious and hard to understand. What is the opinion

of the Prime Minister with respect to this? (Many voices, "It's unnecessary to answer!" etc., etc.)[28]

Prime Minister Yoshida did not respond directly, and Kanamori said only that "the Constitution of Japan which was written in the Japanese language" is the official text. Another member of the committee on constitutional revision, Kuroda Hisao of the Socialist Party, also complained that the locus of sovereignty was not clear.[29] Still, the government's answer remained unchanged. This suggests, of course, that the government had assumed before the Diet convened that such questions would arise and had already developed its firm response.

In fact it was neither Nakamura nor Nosaka who initially made "supremacy" an issue. At the Privy Council hearings on May 3, Councillor Nomura Kichisaburō, a former admiral, ambassador to the United States in 1941, and an outspoken advocate of rearming Japan, had already done so.

Councillor Nomura: The phrase in the preamble, "The will of the people is supreme . . . ," is expressed in the bill as "sovereignty of the people's will." This can clearly be construed to have declared the sovereign power of the people. What is your opinion?

Director of Legislation Bureau Irie: "Sovereign power" in the terminology of constitutional law means anything that has a strong power, but so far as this bill is concerned, we understand that taken in its substantial sense, it means the will of the people has the highest nature.[30]

With Irie's answer as its guide, the Legislation Bureau immediately prepared a "Supplement to Likely Questions and Answers" before the opening of the Diet deliberations.[31]

The issue was not resolved in the Diet, however, and took an unexpected turn after Matsumoto Shigeharu's comment in a *Minpō* first-page article on July 7, 1946. After presenting both the Japanese and English texts, Matsumoto wrote:

"Sovereignty resides in the people's will . . ." is perfectly clear in the English translation, but the Japanese original lacks clarity in no small way and for some reason conveys the feeling that it has no direct relation to the problem of the location of sovereignty.[32]

The newspaper *Minpō*, a small daily published by Minpōsha, was founded by several former employees of Dōmei Tsūshin news service when the service was split after the war into *Kyōdō* and *Jiji*. Matsumoto was the president of the paper, first published in December 1945. It offered no home delivery and was sold only at railway stations in Tokyo. And it never printed more than twenty-five thousand to thirty thousand copies.[33]

Nevertheless, SCAP paid close attention to this small newspaper. The entire text of Matsumoto's commentary was translated into English by the Americans[34] and was widely read in Government Section. Bisson, Peake and Colegrove, advisers to Kades, prepared a joint memorandum on July 11 for the chief of Government Section, General Whitney, titled "Differences between Japanese and English Versions of the Draft Constitution."[35] According to Bisson's letter to his wife on July 19, this memorandum appears to have been sent immediately to Kades, Whitney, and MacArthur.[36]

There was an important reason that SCAP took such quick action. On July 2 the FEC in Washington had adopted a statement of policy titled "Basic Principles for Japan's New Constitution," and the Joint Chiefs of Staff had transmitted this document to MacArthur on July 6.[37] The statement began with the following sentence: "The Japanese Constitution should recognize that sovereign power resides in the people." Furthermore, it set forth detailed provisions on legislative, administrative, and judicial power to provide for "the people's sovereignty."[38] MacArthur understood that the FEC statement, if made public, would humiliate the Japanese government, and hurriedly replied to the Joint Chiefs:

> The Government's Bill on Revision of the Constitution is currently being debated in the Diet. It is in agreement in every respect with the fundamental principles set forth in the FEC statement.[39]

Once again MacArthur extended a helping hand to the Japanese government. The opposition parties were deprived of an issue, publication of the FEC statement was suppressed, and Kades was dispatched to the prime minister's office to convey SCAP's views. In a meeting with Kanamori, Irie, and Satō, Kades asked for an explanation of Kanamori's replies in the Diet regarding the *kokutai* and the position of the emperor. Kanamori wrote out his personal views one by one on a piece of paper and gave it to Kades. He also made the following general remark:

> Under the new constitution Japan's basic government structure with the Emperor as the center is radically modified. There are those who think that the basic government with the Emperor as the center constitutes Japan's national character. But that, I believe, is the form of government, and not the character of nationhood.[40]

This was essentially what he had often said in the Diet. But Kades was not satisfied and on July 23 called another meeting with Kanamori, Irie, and Satō. Irie gave the following account of this meeting:

> Kades spoke as follows. "Concerning the location of sovereignty, the words in the Japanese text are extremely vague. We want it stated clearly somewhere in the preamble or in the articles that sovereignty resides in the people. The preamble states that, 'We proclaim that the people's will is supreme.' It seems to me that this deliberately distorts the English words. It appears that sovereignty might reside in the state, or that sovereignty is divided among the Emperor, the cabinet, the Diet and the courts, or even that it is held jointly by those state institutions. An expression that can be understood in such a double meaning is a kind of deception. I want it stated clearly that 'sovereignty resides in the people.'" Kanamori responded to Kades's unusually impassioned speech in the following way. "I have often explained in the Diet that [the phrase in the preamble] is fine. And I believe it is fine. Therefore, if a change is being required, then I will have no choice but to resign my position. And I have no doubt that my successor would handle the matter appropriately."
>
> At this point Kades had a very perplexed look on his face, but repeated what he had said before, imploring Kanamori to give careful thought to this issue. . . . At the end of this very tense exchange, Kanamori finally said he would consider revising the phrase in the preamble that said "We do proclaim that the people's will is supreme," and the conversation ended.[41]

Satō Tatsuo also left an account of this event. While it differs in detail, the general sense is the same.[42] Satō explained the use of the word *shikō* (supreme) in this way: "Sovereign will literally translated is 'shuken ishi' but at the time it was considered 'undesirable from the standpoint of protecting the *kokutai* to speak openly of the people's sovereignty.'"[43]

We have seen that Shidehara had suggested the controversial word *shikō*. But where did he find it? A bit of research reveals that it came from Article 8 of the Privy Council Law, which stated: "Although the Privy Council shall serve as the Emperor's supreme [*shikō*] councillor in administrative and legislative matters, it shall not interfere in matters of government policy." In this context the word merely means the "highest" and has no conceptual relation to authority. Using *shikō* in this sense to replace *shuken* (sovereign) provided a significantly different interpretation of the entire constitution.

Once the government had agreed to adopt the word *shuken*, how was this presented to the Diet? In fact, instead of the government itself making a motion to this effect, the Liberal Party offered the motion to amend the draft. A proposal to amend was offered in the form of a joint motion by Kita Reikichi and the Progressive Party on July 25, the day after the bill moved from the special committee to the secretive subcommittee—that is, two days after the second meeting with Kades.[44] Given the fact that Inukai Takeru had read aloud Matsumoto Shigeharu's *Minpō* commentary at a Progressive Party meeting,[45] it would appear that the party acted because of Matsumoto's influence. In any case, the upshot was that the conservative parties, forever prisoners of the emperor system, forestalled both the Socialist Party and the Communist Party by proposing the amendment.

Kades, who learned of the amendment from the press, is said to have telephoned the government to say, "I am tickled to death."[46] MacArthur, who had proceeded along his own course of constitutional reform and had stood firm in the face of the FEC and Japanese government maneuverings to influence him, must have realized that this defiance by the Japanese government might pose a threat to his position. And the great significance of this amendment for Kades, who supported MacArthur, comes through clearly in his joyful telephone call.

Although temporarily defeated, Kanamori did not change his wily ways. He explained in the House of Peers that "the meaning of *shuken*, which the House of Representatives had adopted, was probably the same as *shikō*; only the characters had changed."[47] On the other hand, he could not hide his chagrin at losing. "I resisted," he said, "for a long time, but in the end adopted the plain expression out of respect for world opinion,"[48] as though the common word "sovereign" had taken on a negative connotation. Yet he did not fail to compose a suitable poem, scorning himself for not resigning, as he walked to his vegetable garden on a Sunday morning: "A poor wretched pumpkin—today still clinging to the vine."[49]

While the important concept "sovereignty" was being inserted into the Diet bill, what were the reactions of the scholars of constitutional law? Miyazawa Toshiyoshi, the first scholar to propound the "August Revolution thesis," commented as follows on the problem of the word "sovereignty" in a discussion carried in *Tokyo Shinbun*:

I think it is very clear that, if we ask how the problem of sovereignty in the draft constitution is to be determined, the doctrine that sovereignty resides in the people is to be the principle. But the word sovereignty is not used in the preamble or in any of the articles. I think the drafters deliberately avoided using the word. On that point, there is the influential view that one should not avoid using such words and that one should say in clear, common language that sovereignty resides in the people. I myself think that is a problem of semantics. Such slightly ambiguous expressions as this "people's will is supreme" is . . . well, I think that's fine.[50]

Looking back on this period years later, Miyazawa commented:

I had the feeling at that time that it was probably better not to make it too clear that popular sovereignty was the great rule of constitutional reform. My view was exactly the same as the one that Kanamori expressed.[51]

Consequently, it seems reasonable to conclude that at the time Miyazawa was not overly concerned with the notion of popular sovereignty. According to press accounts, Miyazawa, Sasaki Sōichi, Nanbara Shigeru, and some thirty members of the House of Peers, all of whom were well informed about the constitution, organized a committee to study the draft. They put together an amendment of as many as ten items, among which was the following: "In Article 1 replace 'symbol' with 'head of state' and after 'this position' insert 'Emperor as the head.'"[52] According to their plan, Article 1 of the Constitution would become:

The Emperor is the *genshu* [head or chief] of the Japanese state and the leader of the unity of the Japanese people, his position as the head is based on the supreme will of the Japanese people.

This amendment was not adopted, of course. Had the Diet adopted it, MacArthur certainly would have ceased such halfhearted measures as quietly sending Kades to the prime minister's office to remonstrate and would have moved the entire House of Peers to Ichigaya [the site of the war crimes trials].

To be sure, this does not mean that all scholars of constitutional law were unconcerned with issues of popular sovereignty and *kokutai*. It is well known that Sasaki Sōichi and Watsuji Tetsurō engaged in a public exchange about *kokutai* and that Miyazawa Toshiyoshi and Odaka Asao, a legal philosopher, carried on a debate about sovereignty. But to what extent did these debates contribute to the actual reform? The truth is that they were of no help at all in giving birth to the new constitution, which ultimately defined the principle of popular sovereignty. As for Miyazawa, he was touting his "August Revolution thesis" just a few months earlier, claiming that the government's draft meant a change from "theocratic rule" to "the principle of popular sovereignty." But in terms of concrete civil rights provisions, this meant choosing "supreme" rather than "sovereign" and "head" rather than "symbol." Thus the superficiality of Miyazawa's ideas, which did not fit the facts of his "August Revolution thesis," could not avoid being cast in bold relief.

Through this long journey it had become clear that sovereignty resides in the people. Such changes as substituting "supreme" for "sovereign" may seem small indeed, but the magnitude of their meaning was incalculable. Perhaps because the debate on Article 1 concentrated so much on the location of sovereignty, there was virtually no discussion of imperial succession and the emperor's accession to the throne. The Socialist Party, quite conservative when the draft constitution was written but suddenly progressive during the debate over the government's draft, did offer an amendment to require Diet approval "at the time of an Emperor's accession to the throne." But the proposal, which even today might be worth consideration, died with very little debate.

"Japanese People" and "Foreigners"

What do the words "the people" and "the people's sovereignty" as used in the constitution really mean? Article 10 of the constitution says: "The conditions necessary for being a Japanese national shall be determined by law." But neither the American draft nor the government draft originally contained this provision, although the Meiji Constitution did. Article 18 read: "The conditions necessary for being a Japanese subject shall be determined by law." The only difference is that "Japanese subject" in the Meiji Constitution became "Japanese national" in the new constitution.

How and why did Article 10 get inserted into the constitution? The government was negative about it even in the "Collection of Expected Questions and Answers," which was prepared before the draft was submitted to the House of Representatives.

> The category "the people" [*kokumin* or Japanese nationals] is something that is determined by custom and logic, and was not originally dealt with as a provision of law. Even under the present (Meiji) Constitution, not all cases are covered by the Nationality Law; some are determined by treaties. In sum, for the law to define "the people" as something existing in reality is impossible and inappropriate.[53]

The proposal to insert Article 10 was made simultaneously by the three conservative parties—the Liberal, Progressive, and People's Cooperative Parties—when the subcommittee was organized and each of the parties presented amendments to the government draft. The Socialist Party and several other parties also offered amendments, but Article 10 was not among them. At the subcommittee's fourth session on July 29, however, when the three conservative parties presented the amendment that became Article 10, Suzuki Yoshio of the Socialist Party said, "That is similar to a proposal we wish to make, and is something that most of the parties support." With broad support, the provision was adopted by the subcommittee without debate.[54] It is clear that as the representatives viewed it, this was not an important provision.

Hidden in it, however, was a very important legal technicality. Recall that the article stated, "The conditions necessary for being a Japanese national shall be determined by law." What exactly did "law" mean in this context? Some years later it came to mean the Law of Nationality, passed in 1950. By the provisions of this law "Japanese nationals" came to mean "holders of Japanese citizenship," and the words "the people" (*kokumin*) and "Japanese people" (*Nihon kokumin*) that appear numerous times in the Japanese Constitution came to be understood in that same sense. For example, the provision in Article 11, "The people shall not be prevented from enjoying any of the fundamental human rights," can be read to mean that foreigners shall be prevented from enjoying fundamental human rights. It is difficult to believe that such a strange thing could possibly be so. Another example: Because the National Pension Law defined the qualifications for an insured person as "a Japanese national between the age of 20 and 60 years who has a residence in Japan," a certain Korean resident in Japan was ineligible for a pension despite the fact that he had lived in Japan since 1910 and had made insurance payments for eleven years. In short, he was ineligible because he was not a "Japanese national."[55] Thus this provision regarding a "national" or "Japanese national" had very significant implications.

SCAP did not, of course, recognize such an anti-human rights provision. But as we have just indicated, when the Japanese draft was prepared, the government had insisted that *Nihon kokumin* was exactly the same as the English phrase "the Japanese people." Despite their doubts, the Americans grudgingly accepted it. But SCAP readily accepted the insertion of Article 10 in the draft, for the government appended an English translation when submitting it: "The conditions necessary for being a Japanese national shall be determined by law." In this case *Nihon kokumin* was translated into English as "Japanese national," or holder of Japanese citizenship, not as "Japanese people." There was absolutely no reason why the Americans would know that "Japanese people" and "Japanese national" were represented by the exact same words in Japanese.[56]

Did the three political parties propose this amendment after thinking through its implications? It seems highly unlikely that this was the calculation of Diet members. Although no documentary evidence exists that explains the origins of the amendment, it seems very likely that it was conceived by officials in the Legislation Bureau. It would appear that the bureau skillfully eliminated the human rights of foreigners in Japan in one fell swoop. But since it was not likely—given the government's negative reaction to the amendment in the "Collection of Likely Questions and Answers"—that the representatives themselves would propose this amendment, it is doubtful that the three conservative parties were its real authors. Certainly today, according to academic interpretations:

It appears natural from the perspective of constitutional principles of respect for human rights that to the extent possible foreigners also can enjoy equality under the law (Article 14) and social rights (Article 25). Reaching a firm conclusion from only the wording of provisions [of the constitution] is too formalistic and is contrary to reason.[57]

But it cannot be denied that in the process of framing the constitution some legislators intended to exclude the human rights guarantee for foreigners, especially as Koreans residing in Japan accounted for close to 90 percent of all foreigners.

Debate on the Rights of Women

The human rights provisions of the MacArthur draft drew on the traditions of the U.S. Constitution, and because the government's draft also used it as a model, guarantees providing for human rights were far stronger than those in the Meiji Constitution. But compared to the post-World War I Weimar Constitution (1919) and the Soviet Union's constitution (1936), the social rights provisions were considerably weaker.

In the Diet it was the Socialist Party that strongly championed the expansion of social rights, including the right of existence, labor, and women's rights. At the center of this effort was Representative Katō Shizue. Before the war Katō had promoted the birth control movement. Later she married Katō Kanjū, a member of the proletarian movement, became concerned for working women, and joined the proletarian movement with her husband. She was elected to the House of Representatives in the first postwar general election.

Given her own background, Katō believed the social rights provisions of the government's draft constitution to be extremely abstract and general. When the House committee on revision of the constitution began its hearings, Katō raised the following points about the protection of mothers and the rights of working women:

I think that the idea that must be clearly recognized in this article is the protection of motherhood in addition to legal equality for women. To put the matter very concretely, in the provisions on the rights of labor in Article 25 women's uniqueness must be recognized and provisions for the special protection of pregnancy, birth and care for children must be stated clearly.[58]

She advocated very concrete rights indeed. Would the male representatives have been able to address such issues? Women's suffrage in Japan was given new life by Katō. She later raised questions about the "right of livelihood for widows." At the time "widows" usually implied women widowed by the war. But Katō wanted to address the rights of all widows as well as the rights of divorced women, especially after the abolition of the legal family [i.e.] system. In the end she argued that the provisions on equality of men and women in the government's draft was no more than form, "and since it merely says mechanically in a provision of this Constitution that men and women are equal, in a real sense there will be no equality in real life."[59] When the subcommittee convened later on July 23, the Socialist Party proposed several broad amendments on the issues of the right of livelihood and worker's rights.

> Government Bill Article 23. In all spheres of life, laws shall be designed for the promotion and extension of social welfare and security, and of public health.
> Proposed Amendment to Article 23. Insert "All people shall have the right to maintain the minimum standards of wholesome and cultured living."
> Government Bill Article 25. All people have the right to work. Standards for working conditions, wages and hours shall be fixed by law. The exploitation of children shall be prohibited.
> Proposed Amendment to Article 25. All healthy people shall have the right and obligation to work. They shall have the right to receive fair compensation for fair labor. The State shall strive especially to ensure equal opportunity in employment and to prevent unemployment.
> Standards for working conditions, wages and hours shall be fixed by law. The exploitation of children shall be prohibited.
> Government Bill Article 26. The right of workers to organize and to bargain and act collectively is guaranteed.
> Proposed Amendment to Article 26. Add an article after Article 26 of the Government's Bill that provides: "People shall have the right of rest and relaxation. The State shall strive to enact a maximum eight-hour working day, a system of paid vacations, sanatoriums and nursing homes, and hours of social education."
> And, further, add the following to the Article. "The people shall have the right to be guaranteed security in their lives when they are elderly, ill, or unable to work. These rights shall be guaranteed by the broad development of social insurance, providing free facilities and furnishing of sanatoriums and so forth.
> The livelihood of women widowed by war damage and other causes shall especially be protected."[60]

Although Katō's provisions protecting working mothers were not included here, the right of livelihood for widows has been included. In addition, guarantees of the rights of livelihood, rest and relaxation, the eight-hour working day, and other concrete social rights were provided. One can see in the Socialist Party's amendments similarities to drafts of the Constitutional Research Association, Takano Iwasaburō, and the Socialist Party, influenced as they were by the constitutions of the Weimar Republic and the Soviet Union.

Let us consider now how these amendments were treated in the seventh meeting of the subcommittee. The Socialist Party was represented by Suzuki Yoshio, a former professor of administrative law at Tōhoku University, and Morito Tatsuo. Katō was not a member of the subcommittee. First to be debated was a proposal to insert a paragraph at the beginning of Article 23 of the government's bill. Just as the amendment was about to be adopted with the agreement of most of the members, Suzuki, either overconfident or having agreed in advance to this scenario, entered into a very important compromise: "If Article 23 is amended as proposed, we can eliminate the right of rest and relaxation, and provisions on assistance for the elderly and the ill which comes later."[61] A semantic debate ensued about "life of minimum cultural standards," actually settling on "life of lowest cultural standards." The other amendments were all disregarded.

Recall that the very same thing happened when the SCAP draft was written. Thanks in part to Beatte Sirota, the subcommittee draft concerning civil rights had included the humans rights articles of the American draft providing for "protection of motherhood" and other social rights. But in the final drafting stage they were eliminated because "they are not matters that should be included in the Constitution." At the time, to men in their prime years such things as the rights of motherhood and childhood, of the elderly, and of rest and relaxation for workers seemed distant ideals.

The amendment to Article 23 was inserted at the article's very end, but the first paragraph of that article in the government's bill later became the first paragraph of Article 25. Be that as it may, as is obvious from recent law suits regarding protection of livelihood, this provision was to become very important for people's lives.[62] If the right of rest and relaxation and the rights of working women, widows, and labor had been enacted as proposed in the amendment, perhaps such ideas as "quit work if you marry" would not have become quite as widespread and perhaps the comment that "welfare kills people" would not be heard quite as often as it is today.[63] Nor is it likely that, with these rights in place, Japan would have become the "economic superpower" that it is now.

The Extension of Compulsory Education

Another important social right, free elementary education (Article 26 of the constitution), was made much stronger through the Diet debates than it had been in either the American or the Japanese government drafts.

Moreover, although most of the amendments and supplements to the bill came from a few Diet members and bureaucrats, the provision concerning the right of education is the sole example of an amendment to the government's bill in which the voices of the people were directly reflected. In the government draft that was submitted to the Diet the provisions on the people's right of education were written as follows (Article 24):

> All people shall have the right to receive an equal education correspondent to their ability, as provided by law.
> All people shall be obligated to insure that all of the *children under their protection receive elementary education. This education* shall be free. (emphasis added)

This article remained substantially unchanged from the time the government's summary draft was published on March 6. The italicized portion in the second paragraph appeared as follows in the summary draft [in literary Japanese]: "All the people shall assume the obligation to have the children under their protection receive *elementary education. This education* shall be free" (emphasis added).

When the summary draft was published in the newspapers, the teachers in the prewar "youth schools" denounced the education article and started a movement to amend it. Youth schools were founded in 1935 as educational institutions that combined technical continuation schools and young men's training schools for young working men. They were intended for the majority of young men and boys who, after graduating from the normal elementary schools, could not go on to middle schools. The schools offered a strict fascist education with military drills. Classrooms and other facilities, compared with those of middle schools, were extremely sparse, but from 1939 this became an obligatory system for boys only. As they faced the return of peace at the end of the war, teachers and students of these schools, who had been continuously discriminated against, quite naturally hoped for an education equal to that provided in the middle schools (equal opportunity of education) as well as free compulsory education.

The summary draft constitution of March 6, 1946, offered no support for their demand for equal opportunity of education, a demand that they had maintained throughout the war. The phrase "obligation to have children receive elementary education" seemed to promise nothing more than [the usual] elementary education, or beginning education, for children. The government's draft was modeled on the MacArthur draft, but the bureaucrats had skillfully limited the period of compulsory education to elementary school, as before the war. MacArthur's draft stated:

"Free, universal and compulsory education shall be established." According to the Foreign Ministry's literal translation—"mushō, fuhenteki katsu kyōseiteki naru kyōiku o setsuritsu subeshi"—the number of years of obligatory (compulsory) education was not specified.

Immediately after the publication of the Japanese draft, a "Conference to Promote National Youth Education" was held in the Kanda district of Tokyo. Teachers of the youth schools who attended the conference criticized the draft and began what they called a "desperate effort" to persuade the Diet to adopt the following amendment: "All people shall be obliged to have youths and juveniles under their protection receive education up to such age as may be determined by law."[64]

Akatsuka Yasuo's *A Study of the History of the Development of the New Middle Schools* provides a detailed account of this movement.[65] It was certainly a "desperate effort" by a few people who were not thought to have a very strong public voice. They organized support groups in every region of the country and went to Tokyo to present petitions to the Ministry of Education. The ministry, as usual, did not give a straightforward answer but told them, "Please take your protest to the political parties and other concerned parties."[66] The teachers naturally turned to SCAP. The section of MacArthur's headquarters in charge of such matters was the Education Division of the Civil Information and Education (CI&E) Section, located on the fourth floor of the Radio Tokyo Building directly across the street from the Ministry of Education.[67]

The teachers' appeals had been going on since March 1946. In July, after the Diet debates on the government's bill had already begun in the House of Representatives, Ukai Kinbachi and other principals of the youth schools in Aichi prefecture visited SCAP's Education Division with petitions to amend Article 24 of the government's bill that had been signed by several hundred city and town mayors, village headmen, principals of youth schools, and parents of students of these schools.[68] Major M. L. Osborne came out to meet them. Osborne had been a teacher of social studies in a high school in Missouri. He had just been assigned to his position as officer in charge of middle schools in the Education Division.[69]

Osborne confronted the petition request directly. He was eager to establish a social studies program in the schools.[70] When he received a petition from the chairman of the council of youth schools in Aichi prefecture, he recommended to the chief of his division, Mark T. Orr, that "at an appropriate stage after reaching a decision on this and before the bill for revision of the Constitution is finally adopted, Article 24 should be rewritten."[71] Orr accepted Osborne's recommendation.

About the time that CI&E was under pressure to make "elementary education compulsory," the House of Representatives Special Committee on Revision of the constitution took up the teachers' demand for an amendment. Ōshima Tazō of the Shinkō Club appealed to his colleagues to make changes.

> Rather than the word "children" [*jidō*] in Article 24, can't we include the youth who are presently in the sphere of compulsory education? This is something that we who are concerned with education feel deeply dissatisfied about. Everyday, I receive numerous telegrams and letters demanding that this part of Article 24 be amended somehow.[72]

Ōshima himself had been a teacher in a middle school in Saga prefecture. With the support of educators of the youth schools of Saga, he had been elected to the Diet in the first postwar general election in April 1946 as a candidate of the Shinkō Club, a political party of Diet members in the field of education. In July of that year the Shinkō Club and some members of the Independent Club formed a new party of educators, the *Shinseikai*.[73]

As a member of the subcommittee on revision of the constitution, Ōshima proposed an amendment to the education provision. However, the subcommittee chairman, Ashida Hitoshi, did not consider the matter very important, noting that the provision required nothing more than a "correction of some wording." To Ashida, the Socialist Party's proposed amendments were far more significant. At the fifth meeting of the subcommittee, the Socialist Party proposed two amendments to Article 24 in the form of a second paragraph: "Higher education for talented youths without resources shall be given at the cost of the State," and "The basic principle of education shall be in accord with the spirit of this Constitution."[74] Although from today's perspective both of these amendments certainly seem important, at the time neither had the support of other parties. Thus the Socialist Party's amendments were never added to Article 24. The second amendment was inserted into the preamble of the Fundamental Law of Education in 1947, but the first, free higher education, is an issue that has yet to be resolved. The situation remains today as it was more than forty years ago. The Japanese government, when signing the International Human Rights Convention in 1978, did so with the reservation that it "will gradually extend free education into higher education."[75]

The debate on this day, July 30, 1946, lasted for many long hours. Ashida was apparently confident that the Socialist Party's amendment would not pass and attempted to move on to Article 25. But Ōshima interrupted him and insisted on offering his own amendment to Article 24.[76] The amendment stated: "All people shall be obligated to have all youths and juveniles under their protection receive education up to such age as may be determined by law. Such compulsory education shall be free." None of the members objected. In fact, they all seemed to think that it was "a matter of semantics." Behind the scenes bureaucrats often suppressed potentially important provisions for the rights of the people by calling them "semantical issues," and Diet members tended to indulge the bureaucrats. In the ensuing debate over whether the word *jidō* (children) in the government draft ought to be replaced by *shitei* (sons) or *shōnen* (juveniles), or whether *seishōnen* (youths and juveniles) was appropriate in the proposed amendment, Ashida engaged in the following word game:

> It would not do to call a boy who frequents cafes "jidō" (laughter). In the association of "shōnen" there are members who are about thirty years old. Regarding "shitei," it would be unsuitable for a wife with a baby on her back. Concerning "seinen," even men thirty or forty years old are admitted to a "seinendan" [young men's corps]. This term has a broad meaning; all men, except old men, are called "seinen."[77]

When the wave of laughter had receded, Ōshima proposed the word *shijo* (boys and girls), and the amendment was approved. In the final version of the bill Article 24 was renumbered as Article 26, and the subcommittee's draft, without further change, became paragraph two of Article 26 of the new constitution:

> All people shall be obliged to have all boys and girls under their protection receive ordinary education as provided by law. Such compulsory education shall be free.

This was a small amendment. Yet when we consider that it extended compulsory education to include middle school, we must recognize its significance at the time. Middle school teachers, who had a much stronger voice on social matters than did the teachers of the youth schools, showed no reaction to the government's draft. Youth school teachers, on the other hand, reacted strongly, vivid evidence of their discovery that their rights were being denied and that the discrimination against them would continue.

The government draft was thus even further "Japanized" in the course of the Diet debates. But the Japanization that occurred during the amending process was not as simple as the Japanization that occurred when the American draft was turned into a Japanese government draft. As the Legislation Bureau prepared the government's draft in early March, it became more of a bureaucratic document than a product of the Japanese nation. Amendments made by the Diet further complicated the matter. For example, the interpretation of *kokutai* and the provisions concerning "the Japanese people" certainly made the draft much more a product of the Japanese bureaucracy and more like the Meiji Constitution. On the other hand, "popular sovereignty" was Japanization in the sense of introducing American legal ideas, while borrowing social rights from the Weimar Constitution and elsewhere was Japanization in the sense of introducing ideas that had not been in the SCAP draft.

Notes

1. Ōe Shinobu, *Sengo kaikaku*, vol. 31 of *Nihon no rekishi* (Tokyo: Shōgakkan, 1976), p. 150.

2. Murakami Ichirō, ed., *Teikoku kenpō kaiseian gijiroku* (Tokyo: Kokusho Kankōkai, 1986), p. 17.

3. Dai 90 kai teikoku gikai kizokuin giji sokkiroku nigō (June 23, 1946), p. 136.

4. Satō Isao, *Kenpō kaisei no keika* (Tokyo: Nihon Hyōronsha, 1947), p. 136.

5. Kanamori Tokujirō, *Teikoku kenpō yōkō*, rev. ed. (Tokyo: Genshōdō Shoten, 1927), p. 179.

6. Kanamori Tokujirō, *Watakushi no rirekisho: bunkajin 15* (Tokyo: Nihon Keizai Shinbunsha, 1984), p. 80.

7. Kanamori Tokujirō, "Kenpō umareshi hi no omoide ni hitaru," *Kokkai* (May 1952): 9.

8. Kanamori Tokujirō, *Kenpō yuigon* (Tokyo: Gakuyō Shobō, 1959), p. 221.

9. Satō Isao, "Shin kenpō o meguru hitobito no omoide," *Yūsei* 2, no. 5 (1952): 13.

10. Hatoyama Ichirō, *Hatoyama Ichirō kaisōroku* (Tokyo: Bungei Shunjūsha, 1957), pp. 23 ff.

11. Shindō Eiichi, ed., *Ashida Hitoshi nikki* (Tokyo: Iwanami Shoten, 1986), 1:267.

12. Satō Isao, "Seiken katei ni okeru Ashida san no omoide," *Tosho* (February 1986): 23 ff.

13. *Ashida Hitoshi nikki*, vol. 1, p. 118.

14. Uchida Kenzō, "Japan's Postwar Conservative Parties," in *Democratizing Japan*, ed. Robert E. Ward and Yoshikazu Sakamoto (Honolulu: University of Hawaii Press, 1987), p. 212. Uchida's study is based on a report by the Political Parties Branch, Government Section, "Japanese Political Parties," vol. 1 (June 20, 1946).

15. Dai 90 kai teikoku gikai shūgiin giji sokkiroku, no. 5 (June 26, 1946), p. 71.

16. Ibid., p. 75.

17. Ibid., p. 83.

18. Dai 90 kai teikoku gikai shūgiin giji sokkiroku, no. 5 (June 29, 1946), p. 122.

19. Dai 90 kai teikoku gikai shūgiin teikoku kenpō kaiseian iinkai giroku (sokki) dai 10 kai (July 12, 1946), p. 166.

20. Ibid.

21. On Miyazawa, see Dai 90 kai teikoku gikai kizokuin giji sokkiroku, no. 23 (August 27, 1946), pp. 241 ff. On Nanbara, see Dai 90 kai teikoku gikai kizokuin giji sokkiroku, no. 24 (August 28, 1946), pp. 245 ff.

22. Dai 90 kai teikoku gikai kizokuin giji sokkiroku, no. 23 (August 27, 1946), p. 241.

23. Kanamori Tokujirō, "Kenpō umareshi hi no omoide ni hitaru," p. 11.

24. Dai 90 kai teikoku gikai shūgiin giji sokkiroku, no. 35 (August 25, 1946), p. 501.

25. *Minshushugi kagaku,* vol. 1, University of Maryland, MacKeldin Library, pp. 87 ff.

26. Nakamura Akira, *Shin kenpō nōto* (Tokyo: Kyōwa Shuppansha, 1947), pp. 49 ff.

27. Nakamura says in *Shin kenpō nōto* that the declaration in English is appended, but it is not.

28. Dai 90 kai teikoku gikai shūgiin teikoku kenpō kaiseian iinkai giroku, no. 3 (July 2, 1946), p. 22.

29. Takemae Eiji, "Bei senryō seisaku no ito," *Chūō kōron* (May 1987): 197.

30. Murakawa Ichirō, ed., *Teikoku kenpō kaiseian gijiroku* (Tokyo: Kokusho Kankōkai, 1986), p. 56.

31. Satō Tatsuo, "Nihonkoku kenpō seiritsushi—'MacArthur sōan' kara 'Nihonkoku kenpō' made," *Jurist* 24, no. 108 (June 15, 1956): 38.

32. *Minpō,* July 7, 1946 *(Hōsei daigaku Ōhara shakai mondai kenkyūsho shozō).*

33. Matsumoto Shigeharu, *Shōwashi e no ichi shōgen* (Tokyo: Mainichi Shinbunsha, 1986), p. 177.

34. "English Translation of the Points at Issue in the Constitution Editorial by Joji Matsumoto in the Mimpo," July 7, 1946, in Katherine H. Giese, "Kenneth Wallace Colegrove Papers," 1977, Northwestern University Library Archives.

35. Thomas A. Bisson, *Nihon senryō kuisōki,* trans. Nakamura Masanori and Miura Yōichi (Tokyo: Sanseidō, 1983), p. 263.

36. Ibid., p. 113.

37. FEC bunsho, kokkai toshokan shozō, microfiche bangō FEC(A)1244.

38. Bisson, *Nihon senryō,* pp. 260 ff.

39. From MacArthur to War Department for WDSCA, July 8, 1946, FEC bunsho, microfiche bangō FEC (A) 1244.

40. Irie Toshio, *Kenpō seiritsu no keii to kenpōjō no shomondai* (Tokyo: Daiichi Hōki Shuppan, 1976), p. 364.

41. Ibid., pp. 366–367.

42. Satō Tatsuo, "Nihonkoku kenpō seiritsushi," *Jurist* 24, no. 123 (June 1, 1956): 38 ff.

43. Kenpō chōsakai, "Kenpō seitei no keika ni kansuru shōiinkai hōkokusho" (1961), p. 376.

44. Mori Kiyoshi, kan'yaku, *Kenpō kaisei shōiinkai himitsu gijiroku—Beikoku kōmonsho kōkai shiryō* (Tokyo: Daiichi Hōki Shuppan, 1983), p. 21.

45. Matsumoto Shigeharu, *Shōwashi,* p. 182.

46. Irie, *Kenpō seiritsu,* p. 368.

47. Dai 90 kai teikoku gikai kizokuin giji (August 27, 1946), p. 241.

48. Satō Tatsuo, "Nihonkoku kenpō seiritsushi," *Jurist* 56, no. 147 (February 1, 1958): 64.

49. Kanamori Tokujirō, *Kenpō ura omote* (Tokyo: Gyakuyō Shobō, 1962), p. 39.

50. *Tokyo Shinbun*, July 22, 1946, Nakamura Akira, Fusao Yasoji to no zadankai.

51. Miyazawa Toshiyoshi, "Shinsei Nihon no dōhyō," in *Shin kenpō*, ed. Mikuni Ichirō, vol. 5, *Shōwashi tanpō* (Tokyo: Banchō Shobō, 1975), p. 161.

52. *Asahi Shinbun*, June 28, 1946.

53. Satō Tatsuo, "Nihonkoku kenpō seiritsushi," *Jurist* 25, no. 109 (July 1, 1956): 64.

54. Mori Kiyoshi, *Kenpō kaisai*, p. 131.

55. Yoshioka Masao and others, *Zainichi gaikokujin to Nihon shakai* (Tokyo: Shakai Hyōronsha, 1984), pp. 141 ff.

56. This English translation was included in the official English translation of the Japanese Constitution and remains unchanged today.

57. Kobayashi Naoki, *Shinpan kenpō kōgi* (Tokyo: Tokyo Daigaku Shuppankai, 1980), 1:286.

58. Dai 90 kai teikoku gikai shūgiin teikoku kenpō kaiseian iinkai giroku, no. 7 (July 7, 1946), p. 103.

59. Ibid., p. 104.

60. Satō Tatsuo, "Nihonkoku kenpō seiritsushi," *Jurist* 40, no. 125 (March 1, 1957): 53–54.

61. Mori Kiyoshi, *Kenpō kaisei*, p. 292.

62. For example, the *Asahi* case in 1957 charged that the livelihood protection standard based on the Livelihood Protection Act violated Article 25 of the constitution. For the Supreme Court's decision in this case, see *Hanrei jihō*, no. 481 (Tokyo: Saikō Saibansho Jimukyoku, 1967).

63. Such cases have recently occurred one after another, including a mother and two children in Sapporo who starved to death in January 1987 after their appeal under the Livelihood Protection Act was rejected, and an elderly woman in the Arakawa district of Tokyo who committed suicide in October 1987 after she was refused livelihood protection assistance. See Terakubo Mitsuyoshi, '*Fukushi' ga hito o korosu toki* (Tokyo: Akebi Shobō, 1987).

64. Akatsuka Yasuo, *Shinsei chūgakkō seiritsushi kenkyū* (Tokyo: Meiji Tosho, 1978), p. 121.

65. Ibid.

66. Ibid., p. 109.

67. Fukushima Yasurō, *GHQ no soskiki to jinji* (Tokyo: Gannadō, 1984).

68. The English language petition was submitted to the Education Division of CI&E. GHQ/SCAP bunsho, kokkai tohsokan shozō, microfiche no. CIE(A)0659.

69. Suzuki Eiichi, *Nihon senryō seisaku to sengo kyōiku kaikaku* (Tokyo: Keisō Shobō, 1983), p. 59.

70. Kubo Yoshizō, *Tainichi senryō seisaku to sengo kyōiku kaikaku* (Tokyo: Sanseidō, 1984), p. 246.

71. Monta L. Osborne, Report of Conference (July 24, 1946), GHQ/SCAP bunsho, kokkai toshokan shozō, microfiche no. CIE(A)0660.

72. Dai 90 kai teikoku gikai shūgiin teikoku kenpō kaiseian iinkai giroku, no. 4 (July 3, 1946), p. 55.

73. Akatsuka Yasuo, *Shinsei chūgakkō*, p. 115.

74. Mori Kiyoshi, *Kenpō kaisei*, pp. 181 ff.

75. Kubo Yoshizō, "Kōtō kyōiku no tayōsei to kaikaku," in *Kyōiku kaikaku no kadai*, ed. Nihon kyōiku gakkai (Kyōiku seido kenkyū iinkai hōkoku, no. 6, September 1988), p. 33.

76. Mori Kiyoshi, *Kenpō kaisei*, p. 192.

77. Ibid., p. 194.

9

Behind the "Ashida Amendment" of Article 9

The Ashida Amendment

Of the amendments made to the government bill in the Diet, the one that aroused the greatest concern was the amendment to Article 9, the renunciation of war. The provision on renouncing war was the focus of much attention from the moment the government's draft was published on March 6, 1946. Yet relatively little debate about the provision occurred in either the Privy Council or the Diet. The majority of questions asked in relation to the provision regarded the right of self-defense and the problem of security. In the Privy Council, for example, Nomura Kichisaburō, a former navy admiral who would soon be advocating rearmament, commented: "What is of special interest to me in this bill is Article 9 of chapter 2, renunciation of war. Since our country exists as a peaceful nation, I believe that a policy of renouncing war is to be expected." He continued in this vein: "We must begin now to make all necessary preparations to maintain the public peace ourselves after the withdrawal of the occupying forces." He argued for the necessity of "something like a coast guard."[1]

Prince Mikasa Takahito, too, offered high praise for Article 9: "To banish military power from the Japanese people may on the contrary help to develop [in them] a sense of justice." As to the maintenance of public peace, he denied that "only military or police forces can accomplish that objective."[2] Perhaps reflecting this kind of debate in the Privy Council, the "Collection of Expected Questions and Answers," which the government prepared before the convening of the House of Representatives, suggested the following:

Question: Is the right of self-defense recognized?
Answer: The provision concerning the renunciation of war does not directly deny the right of self-defense, but since it does not recognize Japan's right to maintain any military forces or the right of the country to engage in war, in

actual fact Japan cannot undertake a real war as an exercise of its right of self-defense.³

In the plenary session of the House of Representatives, however, the government moved a step closer to renouncing the right of self-defense in Prime Minister Yoshida's reply to a question by Communist Party member Nosaka Sanzō. Nosaka divided war into aggressive war and "defensive" war, arguing that "we should renounce aggressive war instead of war in general. Isn't it more accurate to define in this way the war we wish to renounce?"⁴ Prime Minister Yoshida, apparently angered by questions from the Communist Party, replied in the following way:

> I think that the very recognition of such a thing (for a State to wage war in legitimate self-defense) is harmful. (applause) It is a notable fact that most modern wars have been waged in the name of the self-defense of States. It seems to me, therefore, that the recognition of the right of self-defense provides the cause for starting a war.⁵

From our perspective today, the exchange defined positions that have completely changed since. Yoshida's response became known as the official interpretation until self-defense forces were organized in 1954, at which time the government changed its interpretation, claiming that the constitution did indeed permit war in times of self-defense.⁶ The plenary session ended with Nosaka's question and the government's response, and the draft on revision moved from the special committee to the subcommittee. Before discussing the "Ashida amendment," let us first present the wording of the government's draft and the subcommittee's amendments.

> Government draft. War, as a sovereign right of the nation, and the threat or use of force, is forever renounced as a means of settling disputes with other nations.
>   The maintenance of land, sea, and air forces, as well as war potential, will never be authorized. The right of belligerency of the state will not be recognized.
>   Subcommittee draft. Aspiring sincerely to an international peace based on justice and order, the Japanese people forever renounce war as a sovereign right of the nation, or the threat or use of force, as a means of settling disputes with other nations.
>   In order to achieve the purpose of the preceding paragraph, land, sea, and air forces as well as other war potential, will never be maintained. The right of belligerency of the state will not be recognized.

Judging by the subcommittee's minutes, there was very little debate. First of all, the phrase "Aspiring sincerely to an international peace based on justice and order" was added in the subcommittee. The reason was explained by the following comment of Inukai Takeru: "The first part of Article 9 gives the impression that it had to be written this way because of existing circumstances (i.e., because of the defeat). Therefore, I wanted to put in a sentence that would be more positive."[7]

The amendment that later provoked the greatest concern was proposed by Ashida: "In order to achieve the purpose of the preceding paragraph." In January 1951, during the Korean War, Ashida explained how the so-called Ashida amendment was adopted:

> The second paragraph of Article 9 of the Constitution says: "In order to achieve the purpose of the preceding paragraph, land, sea, and airforces, as well as other war potential, will never be maintained." What does "the purpose of the preceding paragraph" refer to? In this case the purpose is "war as an instrument of national policy," or "war as a means of settling international disputes." One cannot interpret it to mean that the use of force in self-defense is prohibited. . . .
>
> It was my amendment that inserted the words "in order to achieve the purpose of the preceding paragraph" at the beginning of the second paragraph of Article 9, and both houses of the Diet adopted it as it was. Consequently, the pledge never to maintain war potential is not absolute, but is intended to be limited to aggressive war. Writing "the right of the belligerency of the state will not be recognized" at the end of Article 9 is not to deny conflict as a means of self-defense. At the present time the U.N. forces are fighting in Korea, but that is called a police action, not war by the right of belligerency. Without doubt, this is an actual case where self-defense or fighting to defend against aggression and the right of belligerency are not indivisible. By recognizing this kind of activity, we can defend the country from aggression. . . .
>
> My argument has been constant and unchanging since the debate on the draft Constitution. Because the new Constitution has as its purpose the building of a peaceful world, our possession of the right of self-defense for the purpose of maintaining peace is acknowledged as an inherent right.[8]

Whether Ashida's argument was "constant and unchanging since the Diet debate" is an issue we will explore later, but it is true that he had held this viewpoint for some time. On November 3, 1946, he wrote in *Interpretation of the New Constitution*, a book that was published on the same day the constitution was promulgated:

> The renunciation of war and the use or threat of use of force in Article 9 refers to a means of resolving an international dispute. If applied to a real case, it would be an aggressive war. Consequently, this provision does not renounce war and the use of force for the purpose of self-defense.[9]

Ashida repeated his argument at a roundtable discussion organized by Japan Broadcasting Corporation on the day the constitution was promulgated: "In this article, the question of the right of self-defense is definitely not included in the renunciation of war."[10]

The Mystery of the Two Great Secret Documents

Ashida had not said that a statement supporting his argument was preserved in the records of the Diet debates on the draft constitution. When the Liberal Party became the Liberal Democratic Party and began to pursue revision of the new constitution in earnest, Ashida's statements began to change, taking on interpretative overtones. The Liberal Party's principal objective in undertaking revision was, at that time, to make the newly formed Self-Defense Forces consistent with the provisions of the constitution. On March 30, 1956, the day after the House of Representatives had passed a bill to establish in the cabinet a "Commission on the Constitution" with the objective of revising the constitution, *Tokyo Shinbun* published a front-page article by Ashida titled, "How the Constitution Was Born—Hidden Historical Facts."[11]

It is easy to understand the special treatment of a contribution by a man who had risen to the post of prime minister. It is more difficult to understand why the newspaper felt the need to provide such a long introduction to the piece. At the time *Tokyo Shinbun* probably wished to add the weight of historical fact to the explanation of the Ashida amendment's origins. But when seen from today's perspective it provides a splendid clue for solving the mystery.

Let us quote the entire introduction:

> The two men who were most intimately involved in framing the Constitution, Shidehara Kijūrō and Matsumoto Jōji, are both dead. Others who were then [February–March 1946] cabinet ministers do not have reliable records. Moreover, the records of the Diet's secret committee (the Subcommittee on the Bill for Revision of the Imperial Constitution) have not been opened to the public. Only one person, Ashida Hitoshi, who was Minister of Health and Welfare at the time (and presently advisor to the Liberal Democratic Party and chairman of the committee on foreign relations), has accurately recorded in his diary the proceedings of the cabinet meetings. The diary was personal from the beginning, and Mr. Ashida had no intention of making it public. Along with the records of the secret committee, which are kept under lock in the National Diet, the diary is one of the two invaluable secret records which verify the details of the framing of the Japanese Constitution. Responding to a request from this newspaper, Mr. Ashida, instead of making public the diary and related memoranda, is publishing detailed historical facts based on that diary.

Following the newspaper's introduction, Ashida gave this account of the origins of the amendment that bears his name:

> Paragraph two of Article 9 placed limits on the maintenance of military power and war potential and pledged not to maintain military power for the purpose of waging offensive war. But the paragraph was born from the desire to leave room for interpreting the exercise of the right of self-defense as being different. I presented the amendment to Article 9 to the subcommittee on July 27. Because the proceedings were secret, the minutes of the meeting have not been made public. But all of this should be recorded in the stenographic record that is sealed and preserved in the National Diet.

Ashida presented virtually the same testimony to the Commission on the Constitution at the end of 1957.[12] Thus, we might confidently conclude that Ashida's version was a historical fact, fully backed by the minutes of the secret subcommittee and his diary. Moreover, after Ashida's death in March 1979, *Tokyo Shinbun* published excerpts from the "Ashida Diary." The March 12 morning edition announced on the front page in large headlines: "The First Publication of the 'Ashida Diary!'" As expected, the diary included an entry to support his earlier claim in *Tokyo Shinbun* that "I presented the amendment to Article 9 to the subcommittee on July 27."

> (1946) July 27 (Saturday). Weather clear. In the debate of articles in the subcommittee of the special committee on revision of the Constitution, I presented the amendment to Article 9. To add at the beginning of paragraph one, "Aspiring sincerely to international peace based on justice and order, the Japanese people. . . ." And added the words, "To accomplish the aim of the preceding paragraph" at the beginning of paragraph two. Because the original wording of paragraph one was abrupt, the amendment was added to express the feelings of the Japanese people who were determined to renounce war. Paragraph two restricted the maintenance of military forces and war potential, and pledged never to maintain military forces for the purpose of waging aggressive war. It emerged from the desire to leave room for interpreting the right of self-defense as something different. In the subcommittee discussion nobody touched especially on the true intention of this amendment. The debate ended with the changing of just a few words.[13]

This passage has been widely quoted to buttress the rearmament argument, which maintains that the purpose of the Ashida amendment was to permit the maintenance of war potential for the purpose of self-defense.

However, when the real *Ashida Hitoshi Diary* was published in 1986, the entry was nowhere to be found.[14] According to a subsequent report based on an internal investigation at *Tokyo Shinbun*, the statement was written by the newspaper's own reporter. The newspaper offered an apology and eliminated what it delicately called the reporter's "composition."[15] Thus one of what *Tokyo Shinbun* had called the "two great secret documents" turned out to be forged by the newspaper's own reporter. What did the other "secret document," the minutes of the subcommittee (the secret committee), say about the "Ashida amendment"? In fact, we have no means of knowing whether or not it is "preserved under seal," as the newspaper said, for to this day [in 1989; in 1995 the minutes were published] it is still being treated as secret.[16]

The Americans did, however, preserve the English translation of the record of the proceedings [submitted to SCAP in 1946]. A Japanese translation was published in 1983. It appears that Ashida was wrong when he wrote in *Tokyo Shinbun* that discussion of the amendment took place on July 27, as the minutes confirm that the date was actually July 29. (Consequently, the "diary" entry forged by the newspaper is also mistaken.) Further, there is nothing in the July 29 discussion of the "Ashida amendment" that says "the exercise of the right of self-defense is not renounced."[17]

Here the mystery only deepens. While the minutes of the subcommittee were supposed to be "secret," they were classified and closed only two months after the *Tokyo Shinbun* wrote in the introduction to Ashida's article of "the minutes of the secret committee which are preserved under seal." On May 10, 1956, the standing committee for management in the House of Representatives classified the minutes as secret when it voted that "only members of the National Diet, with permission of the Speaker of the House" shall have access to the stenographic record of the subcommittee, and "those who consult them shall not reproduce, make public or distribute the records."[18] In other words, until this vote in 1956 the records were not secret.[19] This suggests that when the Commission on the Constitution was established in June 1956 amid growing concern about the details of the constitution's origins and especially about Article 9, the previously open record was deliberately classified and closed to the public.

Subsequently, the chairman of the Commission on the Constitution, Takayanagi Kenzō, appealed to House Speaker Masutani Shūji to open the subcommittee's record of proceedings to the public. But the speaker, citing Article 57 of the constitution, which allowed either house of the Diet to keep its proceedings secret, refused the request. Kanamori Tokujirō, librarian of the National Diet in 1957, and Satō Tatsuo, special consultant to the National Diet Library, criticized the speaker's policy, arguing that there was no longer any reason for secrecy and that making the record available would be in the public interest.[20] A few days later Kanamori wrote a letter to *Asahi Shinbun* urging that "the minutes of the secret committee ought to be made public" and that "there is a rumor making the rounds that a certain Diet member has been saying that he has had such and such an interpretation since that time."[21]

The "certain Diet member" to which Kanamori referred could have been none other than Ashida. For Kanamori, who knew the truth of the matter, Ashida's rewriting of history in his statements must have been unbearable. Despite Kanamori's appeal the record of the proceedings were not opened to the public. Thus Ashida's personal testimony regarding the intention of the Ashida amendment became for many years an unchallenged myth that served a convenient purpose for proponents of rearmament as well as for the government's interpretation of the constitution. Over the years that interpretation has been accepted as fact in the maelstrom of Japanese politics.

One must surmise that behind the forgery of the "Ashida Diary" and the sealing of the minutes of the subcommittee was an immensely powerful political force advancing the government's interpretation of Article 9 and the case for revision of the Constitution.

The "Ashida" or "Kanamori" Amendment?

Let us now return to the question of the meaning of the Ashida amendment. When we consult the record again, we discover an unexpected fact: In reality the Ashida amendment may well have been the "Kanamori amendment." Debate about Article 9 in the subcommittee began toward the end of the third meeting on July 27, 1946. Various views were expressed on all aspects of the draft of Article 9, but the meeting ended without agreement on an amendment. At the beginning of the fourth meeting on July 29, Ashida, drawing on the views expressed at the previous meeting, prepared the following wording:[22]

> Paragraph One. The Japanese people, aspiring to an international peace based on justice and order, pledge not to maintain land, sea and air forces, as well as other war potential, and renounce war as a sovereign right of the nation.
> Paragraph Two. In order to achieve the purpose of the preceding paragraph, forever renounce war as a sovereign right of the nation, or the threat or use of force as a means of settling international disputes.

Ashida's proposal, based on the discussions of July 27, seems to have been the product of mature deliberation. The proposal amounts roughly to a reversal of paragraphs one and two of the government's draft. Paragraph one provided that war potential would not be maintained and that the state's right of belligerence would not be recognized, while paragraph two announced Japan's renunciation of war. Had this proposal been adopted, there probably would have been no room for the argument favoring defensive war potential, which Ashida and the government later devised.[23] But the order of the paragraphs of the Ashida proposal never became an issue in the subcommittee on July 27. After spending time on other wording of the article, the fourth meeting adjourned.

Subsequently, it was Minister of State Kanamori who expressed unease about the Ashida proposal for amending Article 9. At the fifth meeting of the subcommittee on July 30, while the debate was devoted mostly to chapter three (human rights), Kanamori offered the following comment while responding to a question raised by Suzuki Yoshio. Although his comment was deleted from the minutes of the subcommittee, Irie Toshio, director general of the Legislation Bureau, was present at the meeting and recorded Kanamori's statement as follows:

> This (the question of the order of paragraphs one and two) is a very delicate issue. Paragraph one (in the Government draft) uses the words "forever renounce war," and is quite strong. But paragraph two does not use the word "forever." My personal opinion is that paragraph two, which forbids the maintenance of war potential, leaves various points which should be considered in our future relationship with the United Nations. Therefore, the article should be divided into paragraphs one and two [in the government draft] and that which is very clearly permanent should be put in the first paragraph. This was the thinking behind our original draft.[24]

Kanamori spoke indirectly and used vague expressions, but it is clear that he had for some time been thinking about a provision that would make possible the interpretation that Japan was not renouncing the right of self-defense. Yet after his comment the discussion of this issue ended quickly. Article 9 was next discussed at the seventh meeting of the subcommittee on August 1. By that time Suzuki Yoshio appears to have known what Kanamori had in mind, but Ashida seems not yet to have been aware of it. When Suzuki brought up Ashida's proposal to change the order of the paragraphs, Ashida even said: "Changing the order of the paragraphs is a question of personal preference, isn't it."[25] The debate then continued, with most of the members once again supporting a changed order of paragraphs, this time to resemble the government draft. Inukai of the Progressive Party chose this moment to offer his own proposal.

> Mr. Inukai: I think that the composition of the first and second paragraphs should be kept as they are (as in the Government draft),

with only an amendment that inserts the words, "in order to accomplish the aim of the preceding paragraph," as the Chairman
has said. I want to put the words, "aspiring to . . . justice etc., the
Japanese people, etc . . . ," at the beginning of the provision. Are
there any objections to this?

Chairman Ashida: The words, "aspiring to international peace"
should be written in both paragraphs, but in order to avoid such
repetition, it has been decided to write [at the beginning of the
second paragraph], "in order to achieve the aim of the preceding
paragraph. . . ." In short, the intention is to express in both paragraphs the desire of the Japanese people to contribute to world
peace.[26]

With Ashida's statement the proposal took final shape as Article 9 of
the present constitution. To Ashida, inserting the words "in order to
achieve the aim of the preceding paragraph" was intended to express
"the desire of the Japanese people to contribute to world peace." It would
appear, therefore, that not until the subcommittee finished its work on
August 20 did Ashida become aware of the meaning of what Kanamori
had said. The following statement by Satō Tatsuo, the deputy director
general of the Legislation Bureau, supports this:

What I personally remember is that, whichever way it was done, as an
amendment it would have to be taken to SCAP for approval. Therefore I
whispered this to Mr. Ashida. I remember going over to where he was to
whisper in his ear that, if such a provision were in the amendment, saying
"the aim of the previous paragraph" would probably cause SCAP to suspect
that this is a scheme to rearm for the purpose of self-defense. Mr. Ashida
laughed but didn't reply.[27]

Thus according to the minutes of the meeting, in the process of the subcommittee's debate on the amendment, not one member—including
Chairman Ashida—thought that inserting the words "in order to accomplish the aim of the previous paragraph" would be sanctioning war in
self-defense or sanctioning the maintenance of war potential for the purpose of self-defense. Those who did think so, in addition to Kanamori, included only Irie of the Legislation Bureau and his deputy, Satō, both officials of the cabinet. Neither of them, however, made a clear public
statement to that effect. It appears that Ashida began to believe that Article 9 did not renounce Japan's right of self-defense during the period between the end of the subcommittee meetings and September, when he
began writing *Interpretation of the New Constitution* (during the debates in
the House of Peers).[28]

How did SCAP interpret and approve the Ashida amendment? Many scholars and journalists have interviewed Kades and other former SCAP officials about this issue.[29] Kades has replied in every interview that he knew the Ashida amendment would recognize Japan's right of self-defense and that he presumed Japan was thinking of its future participation in United Nations peacekeeping forces.

Kades has said in recent interviews:

> Since we were protecting only fundamental principles, when the SCAP draft was put into a Japanese draft we accepted the Japanese translation of all the articles, including Article 9. We didn't make the so-called Ashida amendment into an issue for that reason. We thought that even if you eliminate from his note the second of MacArthur's three principles—"as an instrumentality . . . even for preserving its own security"—Japan as a sovereign nation possessed the inherent right of self-preservation.[30]

In short, we can interpret Kades's statement to mean that he equated the right of self-preservation with the right of self-defense. But it is difficult to interpret the statement further as recognizing the maintenance of self-defense potential and therefore as rationalizing the government's subsequent interpretation of Article 9, thus making the Self-Defense Forces constitutional. For when the U.S. Department of the Army prepared a plan for "limited Japanese rearmament" in the spring of 1948 and Undersecretary William Draper and George Kennan, head of the State Department's policy planning staff, went to Japan to get MacArthur's views on the plan, he opposed it. MacArthur believed that the creation of a Japanese force after a peace treaty would violate international trust and worsen U.S. relations with the Far Eastern countries. He believed, too, that even if an effort were made to rearm Japan, it could never be more than a fifth-rate power.[31]

Although his last prediction turned out to be off the mark, MacArthur did have good, sound military reasons for his judgment. His idea at the time was to make Okinawa and the main islands of Japan into one strategic unit. In brief, he believed that if Okinawa could be turned into a powerful U.S. base for air operations, "Japan could be made secure against any outside attack without maintaining military forces on the main islands."[32] Consequently, MacArthur continued to oppose the rearming of Japan despite the request of his own government, at least until the Korean War broke out and he realized that his own military judgment had been mistaken.[33]

In 1948 the Department of the Army offered the following interpretation of Article 9: "It is completely rational to interpret Article 9 to mean that creating a high level Japanese military organization exceeding a constabulary force would be unconstitutional, and in the long run [taking this position] would place the United States in the best political position in relation with the Japanese people."[34]

The Chinese Delegate to the FEC Complains

Finally, how did the Far Eastern Commission view the "Ashida amendment"? On August 24, 1946, when the bill to revise the constitution was approved in the House of Representatives and sent to the commission in Washington, an unexpected debate developed.

The FEC did not, of course, refer to the Ashida amendment as such. "The Article 9 amendment problem," as it was called, was first taken up at the twenty-sixth meeting of the commission on September 21. At the meeting the Soviet Union proposed an amendment to bridge the gap between the commission's own policy decision of July 2 and the bill for constitutional revision that the House of Representatives had passed.[35] The July 2 policy decision on the issue of sovereignty was one that we touched on earlier. That decision also included the following: "The Prime Minister and all the State Ministers should be civilians, a majority of the State Ministers [should] be selected from the Diet, and cabinets should be collectively responsible to the Diet." The bill for revision of the constitution passed by the House of Representatives contained the provision about the collective responsibility of the cabinet but not the provision about all ministers being civilians. One of the Soviet proposals for the amendment dealt with the absence of this provision from the bill.

When the Soviet proposal came before the commission, the Chinese representative expressed concern about the civilian ministers provision.

> The Chinese delegation notes that that Article has been so revised by the House of Representatives of Japan as to permit of an interpretation which might in effect permit the maintenance by Japan of land, sea and air forces for purposes other than those specified in the first paragraph of Article IX of the Draft Constitution. . . . [W]e know that, of course, it is necessary for any government to have a police force. But, generally speaking, we don't call a police force an armed force. That is to say, there is a danger, if Japan will be allowed to maintain armed forces for other purposes than those enumerated there, that means there is [a] possibility for Japan to employ such armed forces under certain pretexts, such as, for instance, self-defense.[36]

Chairman Ralph E. Collins, the representative from Canada who explained the position of the Third Committee (which dealt with constitutional and legal reform) at the urging of Commission Chairman McCoy, then said that the omission of the civilian ministers provision was a serious matter.

> Mr. Collins: In Chapter 2, Article IX, on the maintenance of armed forces, it appears to preclude the appropriateness or possibility of any such provision in the draft as it stands. However, from the Japanese text which now is available, it did appear that there might be a loophole and there were definite ambiguities, and that it would be advisable to have this provision inserted in the constitution in the opinion of the Committee.
>
> Gen. McCoy: As prepared by the Soviets?
>
> Mr. Collins: Yes, which is in complete accordance with our original policy statement from the Commission.
>
> Gen. McCoy: I would like to have Mr. Borton, who represents the United States on that Committee, to comment on that please.[37]

Asking Hugh Borton to comment seems to have had special significance. A specialist on the Japan problem, Borton was the acting chief of the division of Japanese affairs in the State Department. He had chaired the group that drafted the document "Reform of the Japanese Political System" (SWNCC 228), the decisive policy document of the U.S. government, which has been called the real origin of the Japanese Constitution. The prototype of FEC's policy statement of July 2 on the necessity of all the ministers being civilians was contained in SWNCC 228. In short, Borton was the father of the provision that all cabinet ministers be civilians:

> That provision was absolutely essential in terms of the present operation of the Japanese Government and in terms of the constitution which is still in effect in Japan. However, under the new constitution, regardless of whether it seems to my Government, regardless of whether or not [the] present Article IX of Chapter 2 could be interpreted in such a way as to allow, as the Chinese representative suggested earlier, for limited military forces of some sort to maintain internal order or for some other reason, regardless of whether that Article can be interpreted in that way, and, consequently, regardless of whether you might have military persons available who might become a Minister of Internal Order, or call him what you will, it has no relation to such things. Since in the Draft Constitution which we have here the cabinet system of responsibility, the prime minister's responsibility to the Diet is made very clear, my Government sees no reason to include a special provision that says that all cabinet ministers must be civilians. However, so long as there appears to be a problem of interpreting Article IX, and I have noticed it and people I have talked to in Washington have also noticed it, but

we don't know why the words are in Article IX in the way that the Chinese representative has said.[38]

Following these remarks, Borton proposed that an inquiry be sent to MacArthur. Responding to this, the Chinese representative Hsuan-Tsui Liu expressed deep distrust of Japan, noting that according to the Ashida amendment, even if Japan engaged in war it would not be called war and probably would not violate the constitution. Finally, he proposed that MacArthur be queried. The British representative, George Sansom, argued that because a variety of interpretations were possible and ambiguities abounded, the amendment set the worst possible precedent. He, too, agreed that MacArthur should be asked about it. The Canadian delegate, George S. Patterson, agreed that a query should be sent to MacArthur and strongly supported the argument for the civilian provision and the necessity of clarifying the relation between that provision and Article 9. Since his point illustrates today's interpretation of Article 9, let us quote at length from his comment:

> It is possible that at some time in the future through appropriate measures, the Japanese will eliminate Article IX from their constitution, and if at that time there is no other provision in the constitution that all ministers shall be civilians, the issue would go by default. But if at that time there is also this additional provision in the constitution, the Japanese people would be fully aware of the issue and in a position to face the issue as to whether they wish to continue the provision that all ministers shall be civilians. . . . The argument might well be raised that [this provision] is not necessary, but I would contend that it is certainly desirable.[39]

When the Australian representative Major J. Plimsoll spoke, his distrust of Japan was almost palpable. He believed that Japan might in the future amend Article 9 so that Japan would "be allowed to maintain armed forces." Once that occurred, he explained, it would be consistent with Japanese traditional practice for officers on active duty to be appointed to the cabinet as ministers of the army and the navy. Therefore, it would be more effective to insert at this juncture a provision specifying that all cabinet members be civilians.[40]

The Civilian Provision as a "Supplement" to Article 9

After these many views had been expressed, the FEC members agreed to submit a proposal to MacArthur on the issue. On that same day, September 22, Assistant Secretary of War Howard Petersen sent a telegram to MacArthur. Petersen recounted in some detail the FEC's debate about the

meaning of the amended paragraph two of Article 9, the necessity of inserting a provision that all cabinet members be civilians, and another
provision requiring universal adult suffrage for the election of public officials.[41] The following morning, September 23, MacArthur sent Whitney
and Kades to see Prime Minister Yoshida.[42] They conveyed this information to him verbally, but Yoshida requested something in writing. That afternoon Shirasu, deputy director of the Central Liaison Office, carried a
letter from MacArthur to Yoshida.

According to Irie, who saw the letter, it said: "Add to Article 15, 'Universal adult suffrage is hereby guaranteed with regard to the election of
public officials.' And add to Article 66, 'The Prime Minister and other
Ministers of State shall be civilians.'"[43] Unfortunately, there was no word
in Japanese that corresponded to the English "civilian." The government
was in a quandary. It hurriedly prepared a draft that read, "The Prime
Minister and other Ministers of State must be persons without military
service," and submitted it to the House of Peers.

MacArthur did not, however, tell Yoshida about the problem of interpreting Ashida's amendment in paragraph two of Article 9. Why did
MacArthur remain silent on this issue? There is no record that clearly
provides an answer, but a clue is offered in the following telegram that
MacArthur sent to Petersen on September 25, two days after he had written to Yoshida:

> In deference to the views of the other [FEC] Governments, I have persuaded
> the Japanese Government to accept the following amendments to the Con-
> stitution: Article 15 by adding the following sentence "universal adult suf-
> frage is hereby guaranteed"; and Article 66 by adding the following sen-
> tence, "the Prime Minister and the Ministers of State shall be civilians." At
> the same time, in view of the delicacy involved in the Government's spon-
> sorship of amendments at this late date, I assured the Japanese Government
> that I would seek no further modifications so long as there is no legislative
> change in the principles embodied in the draft as it now stands.[44]

In a practical sense, to be sure, it was difficult at this "late date" to
make further demands for amendments and insertions. Thus MacArthur
probably thought it would be easier to demand only an insertion. And by
quickly accepting one part of the FEC's request, MacArthur satisfied the
commission and achieved a political victory. Borton wrote on September
26 to John Carter Vincent, director of the Office of Far Eastern Affairs at
the State Department: "The acceptance of the above changes by SCAP
created a favorable atmosphere at the Commission meeting."[45] Although
the Chinese delegate, V. K. Wellington Koo, still felt somewhat unhappy
about Article 9, he expressed in the following comment his "sense of sat-

isfaction" with MacArthur's prompt response to the commission's request:

> The second point related to the wording of Article 9 of the Draft Constitution, which, as it stands, contains implications which could not be acceptable to us. Japan in the past repeatedly used her armed force for aggressions against her neighbors and denied at the same time that she was making war upon them. It should, therefore, be clearly understood that the Commission, in letting this Article stand, intends in no way to overlook the possible danger of Japan again misusing her armed forces for any war-like or aggressive acts any more than for war itself. . . . The Chinese representative, however, notes with satisfaction that the message just received from the Supreme Commander for the Allied Powers reports, among other things, that a provision has been pledged to be made in the Draft Constitution that the Prime Minister and all Ministers of State shall be civilians. This provision, when made, will to some extent serve to preclude the objectionable implications to which I have just referred.[46]

In the meantime, on September 27, the deputy director general of the Legislation Bureau, Satō Tatsuo, went to see Kades and Captain Frank Rizzo at SCAP headquarters with a copy of the government's draft [of the new provisions]. When Satō commented that "essentially this request for an amendment [to Article 66], given the intention of Article 9, is very strange," Kades offered this observation:

> It may seem so now, but in view of the fact that the amendment of Article 9 by the House of Representatives added the words, "for the above purpose," I assume that a misunderstanding has arisen among the Allied nations that if it is for another purpose, Japan could rearm. Or perhaps Japan might be expecting to join the United Nations in the future and might have the obligation to participate in an international constabulary.

Satō was taken aback by Kades's statement. "I recalled [he wrote] what I had whispered into the ear of Chairman Ashida at the House of Representatives' subcommittee meeting when this amendment was made, and I was shocked."[47] The section in which the government had translated "civilian" as "person who has no record of military service" was changed during the debate in the House of Peers to *bunmin,* a newly coined word, and became paragraph two of Article 66.

We can summarize as follows the complicated process that began with the Ashida amendment of Article 9 and ended with the insertion of the civilian provision. The idea that through the Ashida amendment a war of self-defense or war material for self-defense could be made constitutional, as Ashida later contended, was not expressed by either the government or the Diet. The thought was secretly entertained by no more than three or four officials in the Legislation Bureau. Only in the FEC was the possibility discussed that the Ashida amendment might give rise to the self-defense interpretation on which Ashida later insisted. In order to close off that possibility, the FEC demanded that Japan insert in the draft of the revised constitution the civilian provision as an additional safeguard. The Japanese side at this point agreed that it would supplement Article 9 and accepted the insertion. In the words of Miyazawa Toshiyoshi, who engaged in the debate as a member of the House of Peers, "This [civilian] provision was expected to be useless as a way of countering Article 9."[48]

Consequently, one must conclude that there is absolutely no basis for the argument[49] that by virtue of the Ashida amendment war and war potential for self-defense came to be recognized. Nor is there a basis for the supposition that the civilian provision was inserted as a way of preventing this possible interpretation of the Ashida amendment, otherwise known as the "thesis that war potential for self-defense is constitutional."[50]

Still, it is essential to consider anew the meaning of the statement by the Chinese delegate to see through the intention of the Ashida amendment, an intention that bureaucrats of the Legislation Bureau, skilled in legal techniques, had hit upon but that was not noticed by a single Diet member. Clearly, the Chinese statement was based upon China's historical experience of suffering from Japanese aggression in the name of "self-defense."

Not only China, but Canada, Australia, and other countries as well did not believe that by virtue of Article 9 Japan would become a peaceful country at a single stroke. In their belief that Japan would definitely revise Article 9 and eventually possess military forces, they were expressing a deeply rooted distrust of Japan. As we shall see in the next chapter, the whole Japanese nation celebrated the birth of the "peace constitution," but there was another side to this optimistic view of postwar Japan. It is true that there was great rejoicing over the peace that had liberated the nation from a long period of oppression under the wartime regime. At the same time, however, one must not ignore the fact that the ruling group that had encouraged or supported aggressive war and that remained more or less unchanged in power possessed an immature view of the state and of the constitution. Too easily dismissing the very recent aggressive war, they assumed that Japan could change its stripes at once and become a "peaceful country" by relying on the constitution. Furthermore, if viewed from our vantage point today, the Asian and Pacific countries' perception of "postwar Japan" in 1946 was right on target, for Japan has made great progress toward becoming a military superpower without revising Article 9 and without reflecting seriously on its aggressive wars.

Many issues raised in the Diet debates deserve to be explored—the jury system, nationalization of land, and others that are still live issues today. But we must now lower the curtain on the last Imperial Diet. The Ninetieth Imperial Diet, which began with a term of 40 days and was extended four times to last 114 days, approved on October 7, 1946, the new Japanese Constitution.[51]

The day of promulgation was set for November 3, a national holiday celebrating Emperor Meiji's birthday. Since the constitution would take effect six months later, the day for promulgation was not chosen lightly. Yoshida had originally considered August 11, hoping that the constitution would become the supreme law of the nation on February 11, the day on which the Meiji Constitution was promulgated in 1889. It was also the day of *kigensetsu*, the anniversary of the mythological Emperor Jimmu's accession to the throne. But the Diet debates continued longer than expected, thus making Yoshida's plan impossible. He therefore chose for promulgation another day that would have special meaning, November 3. Whitney expressed concern to MacArthur when he heard of this. But the Japanese government had already received approval for the plan from the Supreme Commander. MacArthur supposedly exclaimed to Whitney: "We will fill Emperor Meiji's birthday with our democratic content."[52] It seems likely too that MacArthur had noticed that the day on which the constitution would take effect six months later, May 3, 1947, would be the first anniversary of the opening of the International Military Tribunal of the Far East (Tokyo War Crimes Trials). The "peace constitution" thus took effect exactly one year after the opening of the tribunal, in which the responsibility of those who had waged a war of aggression would be judged. MacArthur must have approved November 3 as the day for promulgating the new constitution, thinking that such a choice historical moment could hardly be contrived.

Notes

1. Murakami Ichirō, ed., *Teikoku kenpō kaiseian gijiroku* (Tokyo: Kokusho Kankōkai, 1986), pp. 188–189.
2. Ibid., p. 190.
3. Satō Tatsuo, "Nihonkoku kenpō seiritsushi—'MacArthur sōan' kara 'Nihonkoku kenpō' made," *Jurist* 24, no. 108 (June 15, 1956): 40.
4. Dai 90 kai teikoku gikai shūgiin giji sokkiroku, no. 8 (June 29, 1946), p. 123.
5. Ibid.
6. Yūhikaku henshūbu, ed., *Kenpō dai kyūjō* (Tokyo: Yūhikaku, 1981).

7. Mori Kiyoshi, ed., *Kenpō kaisei shōiinkai himitsu gijiroku* (Tokyo: Daiichi Hōki Shuppan, 1983).

8. *Mainichi Shinbun*, January 14, 1951.

9. Shindō Eiichi, ed., *Ashida Hitoshi nikki* (Tokyo: Iwanami Shoten, 1986), 7:319.

10. Transcript of the broadcast appears in "Zadankai: Kaisei kenpō o megutte," *Hōsō* 7, no. 1 (January 1947). Participants were Ashida, Inukai Takeru, Miyazawa Toshiyoshi, Suzuki Yoshio, and Shimoyama Seiichi.

11. *Tokyo Shinbun*, March 30, 1956.

12. Kenpō chōsakai dai nanakai sōkai ni okeru kōjutsu, gijiroku, pp. 90 ff.

13. *Tokyo Shinbun*, March 12, 1979.

14. The "Ashida amendment" was made on July 29, not July 27 as *Tokyo Shinbun* reported. It does not appear in the "Ashida nikki" on either of these days. After the diary was published, *Tokyo Shinbun* admitted that it had "supplemented a part of it." *Asahi Shinbun* reported the next day that actually seventy-five lines had been added, making the incident a public issue.

15. On May 31, 1986, *Tokyo Shinbun* apologized that its reporter added seventy-five lines to the Ashida manuscript and said it would delete them.

16. The minutes of the subcommittee were published in 1995.

17. See Mori Kiyoshi, *Kenpō kaisei*. The translator, Mori Kiyoshi, a member of the Liberal Democratic Party in the House of Representatives, acknowledges this in the introduction of the book.

18. Ibid., p. 485.

19. Ibid., p. 502. Mori indicates here that Irie Toshio saw the stenographic record in 1950.

20. *Yomiuri Shinbun*, October 22, 1957.

21. *Asahi Shinbun*, October 24, 1957.

22. Mori Kiyoshi, *Kenpō kaisei*, p. 121.

23. Irie Toshio, *Kenpō seiritsu no keii to kenpōjō no shomondai* (Tokyo: Daiichi Hōki Shuppan, 1976), p. 383. Iric says (p. 387) that "at the time Ashida attempted to establish the premise that this meant all wars, wars of aggression as well as those of self-defense."

24. Ibid., p. 383. In a note Mori quotes this on p. 226 of his book.

25. Mori Kiyoshi, *Kenpō kaisei*, p. 280.

26. Ibid., p. 286.

27. Kenpō chōsakai dai nanakai sōkai ni okeru kōjutsu, gijiroku, p. 109.

28. The editor of *Ashida Hitoshi nikki*, Shindō Eiichi, wrote in the introduction to Satō Isao's volume that "the intent of the Ashida amendment aside, Ashida believed in his heart that under Article 9 Japan could still maintain its 'right of self-defense' and be allowed to keep a certain level of 'military power.'" Satō Isao says: "I essentially agree with Shindō's thesis that the thought process that went into the Ashida amendment is what I call a complicated 'refraction.'" Satō Isao, "Kenpō dai kyūjō no seiritsu katei ni okeru Ashida shūsei ni tsuite," *Tōkai hōgaku*, no. 1 (1987): 47.

29. See, for example, Ōmori Minoru, *Sengo hishi* (Tokyo: Kōdansha, 1975), 5:256; Tanaka Hideo, *Kenpō seitei katei oboegaki* (Tokyo: Yūhikaku, 1979), p. 106; Komori Yoshihisa, "Kenpō dai kyūjō no seiritsu ni tsuite," in *Senryō shiroku*, ed. Etō Jun (Tokyo: Kōdansha, 1982), 3:34; Nishi Osamu, *Nihonkoku kenpō no tanjō o*

kenshō suru (Tokyo: Gakuyō Shobō, 1986), p. 157; Takemae Eiji, "Kades Memoir on the Occupation of Japan," *Tokyo keizai daigaku kaishi*, no. 148 (November 1986): 230; Takemae Eiji, *Nihon senryo—GHQ kōkan no shōgen* (Tokyo: Chūō Kōronsha, 1988).

30. Takemae Eiji, "Bei senryō seisaku no ito," *Chūō kōron* (May 1987): 197.

31. See my "Beikoku no senryōka Nihon saigunbi keikaku," *Hōritsu jihō*, 48, no. 10 (September 1976): 72–73. The quote is from Limited Military Armament for Japan (JCS 1380/48).

32. Ibid., p. 73.

33. MacArthur said in a note to John Foster Dulles just before the outbreak of the Korean War that "Japan will not enter a military alliance with the U.S., but will reject the Soviet Union." When the Korean War began, he ordered Japan to establish a national police force. Memorandum by MacArthur, June 14, 1950, *Foreign Relations of the United States* (1950), 6:1219.

34. Koseki, "Beikoku no senryōka," p. 73.

35. Harumi Nobuyoshi has written a series of articles on the Far Eastern Commission's deliberations on the Japanese Constitution in *Yamaguchi daigaku kyōiku gakubu kenkyū ronsō*, vols. 27, 30, and 32–35. For the article that deals with the Soviet proposal, see "Kyokutō iinkai ni okeru Nihon kenpō sōan shingi (sono ni)," 35 (December 1985): 43 ff.

36. Transcript of the Twenty-Seventh Meeting of the Far Eastern Commission, September 21, 1946, microfiche FEC (A)0085, National Diet Library, pp. 18–19.

37. Ibid., p. 27.

38. Ibid., pp. 27–28.

39. Ibid., pp. 33–34.

40. Ibid., pp. 35–36.

41. Washington (Assistant Secretary of War Petersen) to CINCAFPAC (Personal to MacArthur), W 81154, September 22, 1946, MacArthur Memorial. I have used a copy in the possession of Professor Amakawa Akira, Yokohama National University.

42. Satō Tatsuo gives this date as September 24. Satō Tatsuo, "Nihonkoku kenpō seiritsushi," *Jurist* 52, no. 141 (November 1, 1957): 43.

43. Irie, *Kenpō seiritsu*, p. 420.

44. Transcript of the Twenty-Eighth Meeting of the Far Eastern Commission, September 25, 1946, microfiche FEC (A)0085, National Diet Library, pp. 2–3.

45. Borton to Vincent, September 26, 1946, National Archives 740.00119, FEAC/9–2646.

46. Transcript of the Twenty-Eighth Meeting of the Far Eastern Commission, September 25, 1946, pp. 8–9.

47. Satō Tatsuo, "Nihonkoku kenpō seiritsushi," *Jurist* 52, no. 141 (November 1, 1957): 45.

48. Miyazawa Toshiyoshi, "Bunmin tanjō no yurai," in *Komentaaru-Nihonkoku kenpō—bessatsu furoku* (Tokyo: Nihon Hyōronsha, 1955), p. 332.

49. See, for example, Nishi Osamu, *Nihonkoku kenpō no tanjō o kenshō suru* (Tokyo: Gakuyō Shobō, 1986), especially "Kenpō dai kyūjō seiritsu keii no subete," pp. 104–181.

50. For recent research that offers this kind of interpretation, see Yamauchi Toshihiro, "Sensō hōki—heiwateki seisonken," in *Gendai kenpō kōza,* ed. Yamauchi and others, vol. 2 (Tokyo: Nihon Hyōronsha, 1985).

51. Satō Tatsuo, "Nihonkoku kenpō seiritsushi," *Jurist* 54, no. 145 (January 1, 1958): 76.

52. Thomas A. Bisson, *Nihon senryō kaisōki,* trans. Nakamura Masanori and Miura Yōichi (Tokyo: Sanseidō, 1983), pp. 258–259.

10

Blooming Brightly in May:
Popularizers of the Constitution

Establishing the Committee to Popularize
the Constitution

The Committee to Popularize the Constitution was organized in the Imperial Diet on December 1, 1946, about a month after the constitution had been promulgated on November 3 of that same year. The members of both houses of the Diet were made councillors, and directors were appointed from among the councillors. Scholars and journalists were added to the board of directors. The scholars included Kawamura Matasuke (Kyushu University, constitutional law), Suekawa Hiroshi (Ritsumeikan University, civil law), Tanaka Jirō (Tokyo University, administrative law), Miyazawa Toshiyoshi (Tokyo University, constitutional law), Yokota Kisaburō (Tokyo University, international law), and Suzuki Yasuzō (private scholar). From the field of journalism were the critics Iwabuchi Tatsuo, Obama Ritoku, Hasebe Tadashi, and others. The organization was divided evenly between government officials and private citizens. Ashida Hitoshi was made chairman. An official of the Ministry of Education, Nagai Hiroshi, was named secretary general of the organization.

Under this central organization were created branches or local committees in every metropolitan district and prefecture in Japan. Tokyo was the slowest in setting up its local committee, completing it in March 1947, while other districts and prefectures established theirs in January and February. Except for Kyoto, the district and prefectural governors were appointed to head the committees, and their offices were located in local government offices.[1] SCAP's leadership was, of course, behind this activity to popularize the constitution. It is not clear what leadership was provided at the stage of formation and organization, but certainly it did not reflect "the freely expressed will of the Japanese people" as declared in the Potsdam Declaration. But considering the fact that the FEC had been criticizing SCAP precisely on this point, one can imagine that it was necessary for SCAP to show the outside world that it was making the Japanese government undertake the popularizing activity itself. Moreover, members of MacArthur's staff must have thought it their duty as reformers to popularize the "democratic constitution" in which they had invested so much time and effort.

When the national committee began its activities on January 17, 1947, Alfred R. Hussey and Ruth A. Ellerman of Government Section attended a meeting of the committee (probably a meeting of the directors) at the prime minister's official residence. Ellerman urged the committee to fully educate the Japanese concerning the social and political responsibilities of Japanese women under the new constitution. Hussey stressed that rather than teaching the Japanese people the various articles of the constitution, it was more important for the committee to educate them about the significance of these articles for the people and how the people could use them.[2]

The first task of the national committee was the training of middle-ranking government officials through lectures. The country was divided into ten districts (Tokyo, Kantō, Hokuriku, Kansai, Tōkai, Chūgoku, Shikoku, Kyushu, Tōhoku, and Hokkaido), and training was conducted in each for a period of four to five days. In Tokyo training sessions for 664 middle-ranking bureaucrats were conducted for four days in classroom number 31 of Tokyo University's law school, beginning on February 15, 1947. Each government ministry was required to send fifty officials to participate, and about fifty of the top sixty officials of the Foreign Ministry participated. Surprisingly, even fifty members of the Metropolitan Police Headquarters participated. The Committee to Popularize the Constitution compiled a record of these seminar meetings, publishing them in July 1947 as *Lectures on the New Constitution*. The following excerpt depicts the scene of the seminar:

A special lecture series for 700 middle-ranking officials of the Cabinet and each ministry was held in the auditorium of Tokyo University's School of Law for four days beginning February 15. With 300 students also attending as auditors, some 1,000 people heard the lectures every day. A rare, heavy snow fell during the morning of the opening day, and traffic accidents occurred one after another. Despite this, however, by starting time the hall was already filled to capacity with participants who braved the snow and crowded in. Their enthusiasm was unabated from beginning to end. Every time the lecturer finished his talk, earnest questions and answers occurred repeatedly.[3]

Chairman Ashida Hitoshi's "opening remarks" in front of these "enthusiastic participants" lasted for almost an hour, no doubt annoying the other lecturers who were waiting to speak. The speakers and their topics during the four days are listed below:

> *Opening Remarks (Ashida Hitoshi)*
> *The New Constitution and Politics (Ashida Hitoshi)*
> *Modern Political Thought (Hori Makoto, Tokyo University)*
> *Outline of the New Constitution (Kanamori Tokujirō, Vice Chairman)*
> *On Renunciation of War (Yokota Kisaburō, Tokyo University)*
> *Fundamental Human Rights (Suzuki Yasuzō, Director)*
> *The Diet and the Cabinet (Miyazawa Toshiyoshi, Tokyo University)*
> *The Judiciary and Local Government (Tanaka Jirō, Tokyo University)*
> *The Family System and Women (Wagatsuma Sakae, Tokyo University)*
> *The New Constitution and Socialism (Morito Tatsuo, Diet member)*
> *Closing Remarks (Nagai Hiroshi, Secretary General)*

From the list of lecture topics it is possible to make some generalizations about the seminar's organization and focus. First of all, the constitution was viewed in a broad perspective. Second, no topic directly addressed the issue of the emperor. Third, comments on the machinery of government were rather abbreviated. And fourth, human rights were given special treatment. There is no doubt that from the perspective of the assembled bureaucrats, these lectures were very different from lectures on the Meiji Constitution that they had heard in their college days. Indeed, this series was very different from the college textbooks on the constitution that were published later, which for the most part began with "Chapter 1. The Emperor." In these textbooks, too, one sees the hidden hand of SCAP.

Renouncing War to Become a Leading Nation of Culture

Perhaps only two of the many lectures deserve comment here. One was the lecture on "Renunciation of War" presented by Yokota Kisaburō, the international law scholar who had cooperated eagerly in the effort to write the constitution in the colloquial language. Yokota spoke on Article 9 and focused especially on whether the article had renounced the right of self-defense or defensive war. Though the following quote is very long, it seems justified to include it here considering that Yokota later became chief justice of Japan's Supreme Court and that as a scholar of international law, he greatly influenced the interpretation of the right of self-defense. After commenting that paragraph one of Article 9 provided that "hereafter [Japan] will not settle international disputes" by means of war or use of military force, Yokota spoke about the article's broader applications:

Unless it is a means of settling international disputes, there is no objection to engaging in war, or to the use of force and the threat of force. Therefore, are there occasions to engage in war and use force other than in settling disputes? The answer is yes, of course. For example, there is the case of self-defense. A country appealing to the use of force or war to resist an attacker, or going to war immediately for the purpose of defending against an invasion from a foreign country, is not a means of settling an international dispute. So paragraph one of Article 9 does not renounce war in the sense of self-defense. . . .

But in the case of paragraph two, which does not recognize Japan's right of belligerency, it is not limited or restricted for the purpose of settling disputes. Since it says in general that the right of belligerency of the nation is not recognized, we must understand that paragraph two completely renounces the right to engage in war. . . .

The reason is that in the past Japan actually has often flagrantly committed aggression in the name of self-defense. The Manchurian Incident is an example, as is the China Incident, and recent Pacific War. Consequently, nobody in the world trusts Japan's claims of self-defense. Now, in the Constitution Japan has renounced war for the purpose of settling disputes. But if we say that there is no objection to war for self-defense, then the world will suspect that Japan might intend to repeat such things as the Manchurian and China incidents and the Pacific War. We can understand why Japan is naturally suspected if we look at Japan's activities during the past fifteen years. But since Japan now has no intention whatsoever [of invading in the name of self-defense] there can be no such interpretation of the Constitution that excites suspicions of that sort.

In other words, one reason is that henceforth Japan has no intention of fighting any war, even one of self-defense.

Another reason is that in the future international society no country should be permitted to decide arbitrarily what is self-defense and what is not, and that it is all right to go to war if it is in self-defense. On the contrary, this would be determined by an international organization, and if a certain country commits an act of aggression, other countries must make a concerted effort to prevent it. This will be the direction in which international society will go in the future, and Japan itself must assume the initiative in taking such actions. This is the second reason. For these two reasons, Japan will not henceforth go to war even for the purpose of self-defense.

I know there is the counter argument that says that because it is only natural to defend oneself when attacked, renouncing war even in that case is going too far. And, logically speaking, that argument is not without reason. However, if we see that Japan's past aggressive wars actually were waged in the name of self-defense, and understand that no country should arbitrarily determine this issue for itself, the theory that says it is all right to take military action or to go to war if it is for self-defense is not necessarily justified. Not only this. At the present time the United Nations recognizes the right of self-defense, but that is limited to a period of time until the United Nations itself can take concerted action. Therefore, in case of an attack by a foreign country, the right of self-defense is recognized, but the United Nations will decide whether or not the act of self-defense was justified and will assume responsibility after that. The right of self-defense is recognized only during the temporary period when the United Nations cannot act. I think that nations must conduct themselves in this way in the future, and that no country can arbitrarily act on its own authority because it claims self-defense. Consequently, in Japan's case it is certainly not without reason that she is determined not go to war whether for self-defense or to enforce sanctions. In any case, that is the provision of the latter part of paragraph two.[4]

Thus Yokota expressed his interpretation that Article 9 does not recognize a war of self-defense and only recognizes the right of self-defense with strict limitations. Yokota was fifty years old at this time. He had not resisted fascist authority during the war, but neither had he cooperated with the military. Having great expectations at the birth of the "peace constitution," he gave similar lectures all over the country. For Yokota, the "peace constitution" did not mean merely the "renunciation of war"; it meant the creation of a new nation, a "nation of culture." In this lecture as well as in others he ended by raising high the following grand ideal.

I think that henceforth, by not building military armaments and by not fighting wars the Japanese will be able in a few decades to achieve a very high culture by expending their entire spiritual energy for the purpose of culture. . . . Unfortunately, until now the Japanese people's energy has been spent for the wrong thing by their misguided leaders. But from now on, if the people really make an effort in behalf of culture, ten years from now Japan will, I believe, be able to achieve the status of a leading nation of culture. If we do that, we will win the full respect in the international community as a leading nation, and should be treated as a first class country.

If we try to do this, then the choice of complete pacifism, the complete abolition of armaments and the renunciation of war contained in this Constitution will have indicated the true path which Japan should follow. In this sense I think we must not think that the renunciation of war provision goes a little too far and must not assume a wavering attitude, but must have the faith that this indeed is the true path for Japan to follow and the only path to reconstruction and improvement. And we must practice and achieve it.[5]

It is clear from these words that Yokota, and indeed all of Japan, was trying to pursue an ideal whose pinnacle was the "renunciation of war."

The other lecture that deserves mention was given by Morito Tatsuo, the last lecturer to appear in the series. He was not passionate, but as a member of the Constitutional Research Association he had a long-standing interest in the constitution. When the association's draft was submitted to SCAP, the political adviser George Atcheson, in a message to the

secretary of state, referred to Morito as "a well-known economist and political scientist" and called the draft, which had been written by Suzuki
Yasuzō and others, the "Morito draft."[6]

Morito was responsible for presenting a lecture on "social rights,"
which he called "rights of life." He emphasized the provision on minimum standards of living (Article 25), a provision that had not appeared
in the government's draft. It had been proposed by the Socialist Party, to
which Morito belonged, and inserted in the draft during the Diet debates. He praised that provision as "the most significant article of the
Constitution" and said: "The fact that it made clear that the Government
must guarantee to the people a minimum standard of living makes this
provision, in my opinion, comparable to the democratic revolution in
government, and in some cases is more meaningful to the working
masses than that revolution."

Morito even went so far as to assert that the new constitution "offered
to the people, if they only desire, the means by which it would be possible legally to change the capitalist system into socialism." And further,
"Under the new Constitution the possibility is presented through the
mechanism of parliamentary democracy for capitalism to change into socialism without a violent revolution. That is to say, if the people's confidence in socialism becomes dominant, then the possibility will have been
provided for a peaceful conversion to socialism."[7] As luck would have it,
Morito presented this lecture immediately after the February 1 general
strike had been called off. One wonders what those middle-level bureaucrats and police officials who were listening to the lecture thought about
Morito's comments. Three months later Morito became minister of education in the Katayama cabinet. Since the first minister of education, Mori
Arinori, there probably had not been another who advocated "revolution" and who had the distinction of being expelled from Tokyo University for discussing Kropotkin.

Training sessions of this sort were held in the other nine districts, and a
total of eighteen hundred people heard them.

In addition to this lecture series an explanatory introduction to the constitution was published. The committee printed fifty thousand copies of
its *Lectures on the New Constitution* and distributed them free of charge.[8]
And in November 1946 the Cabinet Legislation Bureau published two
hundred thousand copies of its *Commentary on the New Constitution* (94
pages), also intended as an explanatory introduction.[9] As both books
were officially distributed, it is uncertain to what extent they were actually read, but considering that a book written by professors of Tokyo University, *Studies of the New Constitution,* went through twelve editions and
sold seventeen thousand copies,[10] it is likely that they attracted many
readers.

One further point worth mentioning is that the Committee to Popularize the Constitution led the way in organizing numerous lectures for the general public. In Gumma prefecture, a strongly conservative area of agricultural communities, 382 public lectures were attended by some sixty thousand people. Twelve thousand people in Ishikawa prefecture attended 108 public lectures, and in Nagano prefecture fifty-seven lectures reached fourteen thousand people.

Meanwhile, young people were holding their own small meetings of youth groups, organizing meetings of fifty to one hundred young people in villages and towns. Of those meetings reported, the number of participants reached thirteen thousand.[11]

Twenty Million Booklets

Pamphlets and booklets were published with the aim of popularizing the constitution among all the people of Japan. The number of these booklets reached twenty million, about the number of Japanese households at the time. The booklet compiled by the committee, *The New Constitution! A Bright Light!*, was about the size of a memo pad (14 x 10 cm) and included in its thirty pages the complete text of the constitution in fifteen pages. Ashida Hitoshi, the Chairman of the Committee to Popularize the Constitution, wrote the following introduction titled "For the New Japan" on the booklet's opening page:

> The Japanese people mutually respect individual character. They will correctly practice democracy. With a spirit of love of peace, they will have warm and friendly relations with the countries of the world.
>
> These principles contained in the Constitution constitute the way that the new Japan should live and the fundamental spirit by which we make our lives as human beings worth living. Truly, the new Constitution indicates the highway along which the Japanese people should progress. It is the compass of our daily lives. It is the splendid code which will be woven into our ideals and aspirations.
>
> In order that Japan may be reborn as a good country, we must restore that spirit so that the new Constitution becomes our flesh and blood. Unless the Constitution is put into practice it will be no more than a dead document.
>
> By declaring boldly and frankly that "we will go to war no more" the new Constitution has expressed the highest ideal of mankind. The building of a peaceful world is the only road for Japan's rebirth. Henceforth we must raise high the banner of peace and build a fatherland of culture upon a foundation of democracy.[12]

In the main body of the booklet the basic provisions of the constitution were explained from the viewpoint of people's lives under the heading

"Features of the New Constitution—How They Apply to Our Lives." There were such subheadings as "Japan Reborn," "Toward a Bright and Peaceful Country," "War Never Again," "Everybody Is Equal," "Women and Men Are the Same," "We Also Elect the Prime Minister," and "The Japan That We Rule."

Following the appearance of this booklet, in August 1947 the Ministry of Education issued the well-known supplementary reader for middle school social science courses, *The Story of the New Constitution.* Simpler and more widely available than the Ministry of Education's book, the reader had a much greater influence on the people of Japan. It had been prepared quite carefully. According to a letter that Director General Ryūichi Sakakibara of the committee sent to Hussey (undated, but judging by an enclosed document, probably April 15, 1947), the committee and the Ministry of Education's textbook section prepared the first draft; professors Yokota Kisaburō and Tanaka Jirō of Tokyo University revised it; and Kanamori Tokujirō and Chairman Ashida Hitoshi added their own careful reading.[13] SCAP, of course, did not remain silent in the matter. Hussey himself acknowledged in a letter to the U.S. Army Information and Education Section on June 18, 1947, that he had personally supervised the project.[14]

How were the twenty million copies of this booklet distributed? According to Sakakibara's letter to Hussey, the committee planned to finish distributing them to each prefecture by the middle of April 1947. In terms of numbers, Tokyo received the most, 1.7 million copies, and Tottori prefecture the least, 145,000 copies. As for actual distribution of the booklets to all households of Japan, Sakakibara bragged in his letter to Hussey:

> We used the same method we use in distributing ballots for elections. The Committee's headquarters first sends the booklets to each of its branches. A branch office is located in the government office of each prefecture and metropolitan district, except for Kyoto. Each branch sends booklets to each city, town and village in the prefectures and metropolitan districts. And then the cities, towns and villages distribute them through local town councils to each and every household. If we use the neighborhood organizations (tonarigumi), we can distribute to all households without missing a one.[15]

In Kanagawa prefecture, where 550,000 were distributed, a notification in the name of the county office director of Ashigarashimo-gun was sent to the head of every town and village, suggesting "as one way of helping spread the spirit of the new Constitution, [the] use [of the neighborhood associations] to distribute the booklets to every household.[16]

The letter said further that "500,000 copies of the booklet are being kept for distribution to civilians and soldiers who are being repatriated from the Soviet Union, and will be distributed on board their ships." This systematic distribution also included booklets written in raised letters for the blind.

Given the social and economic conditions of the time, the printing and free distribution of these booklets to all households of the country was considered a tremendous task for a government hampered by severe material shortages. Paper and the coal for its production was in short supply. The Committee for Popularizing the Constitution asked SCAP to increase the allocation of coal to three paper companies with which it had placed orders for the booklets. Hussey, who received the request, consulted with the Economic and Social Section (ESS) and was able to increase the coal allocation by seven hundred tons. It is difficult to imagine this happening today.[17]

This campaign to familiarize and enlighten people with the constitution truly raised the Japanese people's concern about and interest in the constitution. The committee held an essay-writing contest, jointly sponsored with *Asahi Shinbun,* on the occasion of the adoption and promulgation of the constitution, and many people showed a strong interest in entering the contest. The Society received 1,038 entries from around the country.[18] On May 3, 1947, the day the constitution took effect, the judges—Ashida Hitoshi, Kanamori Tokujirō, Sekiguchi Tai, Miyazawa Toshiyoshi, and Yokota Kisaburō—selected "The New Constitution and Democracy" by Hayashi Matabei of Ishikawa prefecture as the best essay, and on the following day his essay was published in *Asahi Shinbun.* Hayashi was a forty-five-year-old employee of the Komatsu Manufacturing Company whose refreshing youthfulness and passion imbued his whole essay. His essay, considering the new constitution from the perspective of democracy, discussed the relationship of democracy to the emperor system, human rights, and pacifism, and closed with the following sentence:

> In the Preamble to the new Constitution the Japanese people have sworn to the world that "we pledge our national honor to accomplish these high ideals and purposes with all our resources," destroying every obstacle and plot against democracy. The course that we now should follow is, judging correctly the new trends of the world, to abandon such cowardice as trying to escape from the bloodless revolution of reconstructing our homeland and quickly to educate and cultivate ourselves so that we will never again repeat the disgrace and chaos of our recent history.[19]

Contest entries were collected at all the branch offices of the committee. While it differed from place to place, most prefectures arranged for joint sponsorship with a local newspaper. The committee's office in Miyagi prefecture, for example, jointly sponsored the contest with the *Ka-*

hoku Shinpō, which then published the winning essays over a period of four days in May 1947. The Yamagata office of the committee solicited from teachers "educational essays to commemorate the promulgation of the new Constitution" and published them in the local newspaper. The committee's branch in Kanagawa conducted a contest jointly sponsored by *Kanagawa Shinbun* but did not publish the essays in the press. And, of course, some prefectural branch offices of the committee held no essay contests at all.

Before their war wounds had even healed, several thousand average citizens took to their desks to compose essays on the birth of the constitution at a time when writing paper was in very short supply. In the one hundred years of Japan's modernization, except for the "people's rights" movement in the late nineteenth century, the Japanese people had experienced nothing like this before.

Movies and "Constitution Songs"

Efforts to popularize the constitution included a great variety of activities. There was the production of a documentary film, "The Making of the New Constitution," which dealt with the framing process.[20] The Committee to Popularize the Constitution subsidized the films "Fierce Passion" (*Shōchiku*), "Political Drama" (*Daiei*), and "War and Peace" (*Tōhō*). In addition, there were short films, cards, puppets, picture-story shows for children, and a collection of songs called "Peoples' Songs to Commemorate the New Constitution," including "Our Japan" and the following "Constitution Song." In short, all the media of the time seemed to be mobilized for this purpose.[21]

> *The old hat woven from grass (clap, clap, clap),*
> *We have gotten completely rid of it.*
> *New hat woven from flowers,*
> *Will be worn by the new Japan of peace.*
> *Flying over and coming in,*
> *Bush warblers and sky larks.*
> *As they sing their songs of hope,*
> *A Rainbow appears in the sky (yea, yea, yea).*
> *Isn't it wonderful (clap, clap, clap),*
> *Isn't it wonderful!*

Even today there must be elementary school teachers somewhere who taught this "Constitution Song" and children who learned it.

The day the constitution became law, May 3, 1947, finally arrived after an extended period of such popularizing activities. Some fifty years later this day is generally remembered in one particular photograph, the picture of the emperor and empress standing on a platform in front of the imperial palace listening to the cheers of the assembled crowd. But this was actually the scene that immediately followed the celebration of the first constitution day. The emperor and empress did not attend, nor was the official national anthem ("Kimigayo") sung at the celebration.[22] Instead, the song "Our Japan," from the people's songs to commemorate the first constitution, was performed.

> *The glory of peace fills the heaven,*
> *Power of justice springs from the earth.*
> *We are a people of freedom,*
> *Full of hope for the new age.*
> *Let's rise anew before the world!*

On this day "Our Japan" took the place of the national anthem. In the same way that the new constitution as a declaration of rights could not be expressed in literary Japanese, "Kimigayo" would have been out of place at an event celebrating the birth of a new constitution that made the people sovereign. This formal ceremony was not the only event held on this day. In Tokyo and Osaka and every place in the country public lectures and oratorical contests were held. At 1:00 P.M. in Kyoto all the temples and shrines of the city rang their "bells of peace."[23] Not only the constitution but also all newly enacted fundamental laws of the nation, such as the Diet Law, the Cabinet Law, the Local Autonomy Law, and the Supreme Court Law, took effect on this day. There is little doubt that this was a historic day for Japan.

It was all the more historic because, to those who had believed in "the everlasting law" [the Meiji Constitution], this day was indeed "the day the nation died." It is a little known fact that Shimizu Tōru, a scholar of constitutional law who taught at Gakushūin University and elsewhere and who had served as an adviser to the Committee to Study Constitutional Problems and as the last president of the Privy Council, killed himself at the end of September by jumping from a cliff into the ocean at Atami. He left the following words in his last will and testament, which was written on the very day that the Meiji Constitution was buried: "I have to be greatly concerned about the future of the Emperor System. . . . I wish to commit suicide and strive to achieve my purpose [protecting the emperor system] from the realm of the dead."[24]

But the passionate experience that lasted for the six months from the promulgation through the popularizing activities to the day the constitution took effect was soon forgotten by the Japanese people themselves, leaving little trace even in the history books. What could this possibly signify?

The period of the first Yoshida cabinet was one of tumultuous change in the old power structure, with the political purge, the dissolution of the *zaibatsu,* and the land reform, on the one hand, and, one the other, workers forming labor unions amidst the policy of democratization and beginning to organize the labor movement. Many of the people and intellectuals were involved in this "democratic revolution," and attempted to make the constitution an issue in their activities. SCAP would not permit it, however. Consequently, the leaders of the "democratic revolution," though not indifferent to the constitution, had no way of taking an active hand in its reform and thus did not attempt to become involved. Their active involvement in forming the "group to protect the Constitution" came some ten years later, in the mid-1950s, when the conservative government embarked on a campaign to revise the constitution.

Most intellectuals were on the side of the supporters of the "democratic revolution." They lived their postwar lives feeling deep remorse for their failure to prevent fascism in prewar Japan. To borrow the words of the scholar of civil law, Kainō Michitaka, scholars who "could only cry to console themselves"[25] during the war obtained freedom after the war and attempted to live with the masses. They engaged in "self-criticism" of their prewar and especially wartime scholarly activities and sought together a new way of living and working as scholars. It was what Maruyama Masao called the "formation of a community of remorse,"[26] a time when it seemed natural to abandon their narrow specialties, to debate their methods of research and talk of revolution, and then to advance toward the "enlightened activities" of workers and peasants who were the carriers of the "democratic revolution."[27]

The Committee to Popularize the Constitution was quite different in character from this "democratic revolution" movement—more like a semi-public and semi-private organization, or rather an "official" organization—and could not have existed without SCAP backing. The committee was an organization that never questioned the past and never sought to understand individual lives, but tried only to popularize the newly written constitution among the Japanese people, and this only for one year, until October 1947. Therefore, the intellectuals who cooperated with the committee were people of various persuasions who had related to the war in different ways, well-educated people who during the war gladly and without thinking repeated the irrational, barbarous military slogans of "Better Death than Surrender!" and "The Divine Land Is Indestructible!" They were people who neither resisted nor felt any particular pang of conscience while somehow surviving the war and afterward speaking of peace. And their vacillations had not been criticized by those around them.

Katō Shūichi pointed to certain scholars of literature in the introduction to his book, *1946: A Literary Study*, and referred to them as the *seikin-ha*, a new romantic school of poets who wrote of love in reference to stars and violets.[28] It would be fair to say that the scholars of constitutional law who gathered around the Committee to Popularize the Constitution were similar to these romantic poets. Products of their time, they participated in the activities of the committee, and as the times changed their own positions changed accordingly. And yet the shifts in their positions never were so extreme as to make them the bearers of the government's banners or, on the other hand, to place them at the head of the masses.

Yokota Kisaburō was an example of such a scholar. After claiming that Article 9 of the constitution "completely renounces war," Yokota revised this interpretation immediately after MacArthur stated in early 1950 that the constitution did not deny the right of self-defense. Yokota then quickly published his book, *The Right of Self-Defense*, just two days after the peace treaty and security treaty were signed in 1951. Yokota asserted first that the constitution says nothing about the right of self-defense. He argued that if we assume that "in international law nations generally have the right of self-defense, this means that Japan possesses the right of self-defense." However, "because Japan has the right to defend herself, we must not think that she can immediately arm herself or resort to the use of arms or go to war." He advocated "the right of self-defense without military force."[29] On the other hand, concerning the security treaty with the United States that permitted the stationing of U.S. troops in Japan, he said that Article 9 "neither renounces nor denies the seeking of military assistance from other countries in case Japan is the object of attack or of aggression from a foreign power." Consequently, "it should be said that the placing of foreign forces or bases in Japan does not violate any provision of the Constitution."[30] He thus made clear his position on the constitutionality of the security treaty. Was this the reason, perhaps, that he was appointed chief justice of the Supreme Court by the Ikeda cabinet in 1960, one year after the Tokyo District Court ruled that the security treaty violated the constitution?

Miyazawa Toshiyoshi was much like Yokota. As the one-sided peace began to take shape, several intellectuals organized a "Symposium on the Problems of Peace" at the end of 1949 and took the lead in calling for a comprehensive peace. Miyazawa did not participate in the symposium.[31] However, when the Liberal Party organized the Committee to Investigate the Constitution in 1954 and began actively agitating for revision of the constitution, Miyazawa, as we have seen, neither supported nor opposed the revision of Article 9 when he appeared at a hearing of the committee.[32] It was only after the creation of the Committee for the Study of Constitutional Problems in June 1958 that, making clear his stance of protecting the constitution, he resisted the government's own Commission on the Constitution.

Yet another example of a committee member with vacillating views is Morito Tatsuo. Morito, who had called for "revolution," displayed a wider range of attitudes than either Yokota or Miyazawa, advocating years later as chairman of the Central Education Council "the development of a new kind of human being."

Thus the activities of the Committee to Popularize the Constitution faded quickly from people's memories. A glance at the career of the secretary general of the committee, Nagai Hiroshi, who was at the center of this activity, offers the best illustration of the changing views of those who were behind these popularizing activities when the constitution was in its infancy. The following letter from a Japanese woman sent to SCAP's Counter-Intelligence Section raised some disturbing questions about Nagai's background:[33]

> Dear General MacArthur:
>   To acquaint the people with the new Constitution, I hear that a Committee to Popularize the Constitution has been organized, and a great deal of money has been spent making Ashida Hitoshi chairman and setting up a central office on the fourth floor of the Ministry of Education and appointing as secretary general Nagai Hiroshi, a retired official of the Ministry. This man Nagai as chief of the student mobilization bureau during the war cooperated in rounding up and mobilizing innocent students for the war effort. He later became the governor of Kumamoto Prefecture, and although he should have been on the list of political purgees, he managed to escape the purge net and become the secretary general of the Committee to Popularize the Constitution. . . .
>   (I hear that they are having a spree with public money and) when I hear these rumors I as one citizen who lost a husband on the battlefield and am left alone to raise our child, am beside myself with anger. . . .
>   I think you should investigate those special restaurants and the cinema world and completely sweep out Ashida and Nagai and their subordinates and make a just and honest Committee to Popularize the Constitution, or otherwise it would be better for the country to be completely rid of such a Committee. . . .
>   (Signed) A Female Patriot

It is unclear whether the committee was involved in corrupt financial activities, but it is true that Secretary General Nagai served as director of the Ministry of Education's Bureau for Student Mobilization from June to September 1945 and was later appointed governor of Kumamoto, serving from January to July 1946. The ringleader who—just over a year before—had exhorted students to participate in a sacred war and had sent them to the battlefields was suddenly in charge of popularizing the "peace constitution." Was there ever another false ideological convert who could compare with this one? Under the guidance of Nagai the "Stars and Violets School" spoke of the beautiful ideals of the constitution and the Japanese people danced to the music of the "Constitution Song." Though not a bad dream, perhaps it is understandable that it was quickly forgotten.

It is interesting to note that certain ideals have lived on, no matter who taught the ideals of the constitution through the popularization campaign. Despite the fact that opinions were later revised, people are still born today who continue to share the emotions and ideals that existed at that time. Perhaps Nozaki Yoshiharu, who was involved in the well-known Eniwa incident in 1962, was one of those people. Nozaki, a dairy farmer who lived at the time in Eniwa village in Hokkaido, felt that his life was threatened by the Ground Self-Defense Forces' repeated use of a firing range nearby. In December 1962 he and his older brother cut the communication wires used at the firing range and were later indicted for violating the Self-Defense Law. During his trial in the Sapporo District Court in January 1967, Nozaki justified his act:

I was educated by reading a book with the title, *The Story of the New Constitution*. The teacher taught us that there would never again be war. If the prosecutors and the judges studied law after the war, they should have been taught that Article 9 of the Constitution says that Japan shall not possess any military forces.[34]

Both Nozaki Yoshiharu and his brother were acquitted of the charges that had been brought against them.

Notes

1. We should consider the local committees to be official organizations. Kenpō fukyūkai, comp., *Jigyō gaiyō hōkokusho* (December 1947), pp. 4–5.
2. Hussey Papers, reel no. 6.
3. Kenpō fukyūkai, comp., *Shin kenpō kōwa* (Tokyo: Seikai Tsūshinsha, 1947), p. 5.
4. Ibid., pp. 117–120.
5. Ibid., pp. 147–148.
6. Hussey Papers, reel no. 5.
7. Kenpō, comp., *Shin kenpō kōwa*, p. 321.
8. Kenpō, comp., *Jigyō gaiyō hōkokusho*, p. 34.
9. Hussey Papers, reel no. 6.

10. *Shin kenpō no kenkyū* (Tokyo: Yūhikaku, 1947). See Sakamoto Yoshikazu, "Hyakunen shūnen o mukaeta kokka gakkai," *Shosai no mado,* no. 374 (May 1988): 15.

11. Kenpō, comp., *Jigyō gaiyō hōkokusho,* p. 101.

12. Kenpō fukyūkai, comp., *Atarashii kenpō akarui seikatsu* (May 3, 1947), in the private papers of Takano Takechiyo, Koganei-shi, Tokyo.

13. Hussey Papers, reel no. 6.

14. Ibid.

15. Ibid.

16. Kanagawa ken, comp., *Kanagawa kenshi* (shiryōhen), 12:475.

17. Hussey Papers, reel no. 6.

18. Kenpō, comp., *Jigyō gaiyō kōkokusho,* p. 58.

19. *Asahi Shinbun,* May 4, 1947.

20. For a review of these films, see my "Eiga 'shin kenpō no seiritsu' o miru," *Asahi Shinbun,* September 5, 1986, evening edition.

21. Kenpō, comp., *Jigyō gaiyō hōkokusho,* pp. 36 ff.

22. *Asahi Shinbun,* May 4, 1947. According to the report, following Kanamori's words of welcome opening the session, the national anthem, "Kimigayo," was played as the emperor made his entrance to shouts of "banzai!"

23. *Kyoto Shinbun,* May 4, 1947.

24. Shimizu Tōru, "Shimizu Tōru no yuigon," *Chōryū* (November 1947): 49.

25. Kainō Michitaka, "Watakushi no hōritsugaku," *Hōritsu jihō* (August 1975): 124.

26. Maruyama Masao, "Kindai Nihon no chishikijin," in *Kōei no ichi kara* (Tokyo: Miraisha, 1982), p. 114.

27. Ushiomi Toshitaka, ed., *Sengo no hōgaku* (Tokyo: Hyōronsha, 1968), pp. 24 ff.

28. Katō Shūichi and others, *1946: Bungakuteki kōsatsu* (Tokyo: Fusanbō, 1977), pp. 6 ff.

29. Yokota Kisaburō, *Jieiken* (Tokyo: Yūhikaku, 1951), pp. 187–188.

30. Ibid., pp. 205–206.

31. "Sengo heiwaron no genryū," *Sekai,* special edition, no. 477 (1985). The same group issued a research report at the end of 1950 titled "Mitsutabi heiwa ni tsuite." Ukai Nobunari wrote the third chapter of the report, "Kenpō no eikyū heiwashugi to Nihon no anzen hoshō oyobi saibusō no mondai."

32. Miyazawa Toshiyoshi, "Kenpō kaisei no zehi," *Saiken* (Jiyūtō chūō kikanshi), 8, no. 7 (September 1954): 48.

33. U.S. National Archives, Record Group 331, Box 235. I have used a copy in the possession of Professor Sodei Rinjirō of Hōsei University.

34. "Eniwa jiken," *Hōritsu jihō* 39, no. 5 (1967): 342.

11

Yoshida Shigeru's Counterattack

Preserving the Crime of High Treason

Thus Japan's new constitution was born at last. This meant a sweeping change in the nation's supreme law, but in a sense it was only a change on paper. No matter what laws were passed under this new constitution or what laws under the Meiji Constitution were revised, in a sense it was only from such changes in the existing laws that the true worth of the new constitution could be measured. The basic law under the new constitution, Japan's Criminal Code, still embodied the true principles of the Meiji Constitution. The sacred nature of the emperor enacted in Article 3 of the Meiji Constitution appeared in the Criminal Code's "crimes against the Imperial House." These crimes were high treason (Articles 73 and 75) and lese majeste (Articles 74 and 76). Because the debate in the Diet about the *kokutai* ended in confusion while the SCAP bill on revision of the constitution was passed, it is perhaps not surprising that the conservative ruling class wished to preserve these "crimes against the Imperial House" with the aim, to use Yoshida's words, "of assuring the tranquility of the Imperial House."

While the debate on the bill for revision of the constitution was going on in the Diet, revision of the Criminal Code was under way in the temporary committee to investigate the legal codes. Prime Minister Yoshida served as chairman and State Minister Kanamori Tokujirō as vice-chairman of this committee. By the end of October 1946 a bill had been drafted on a "Law to Revise a Part of the Criminal Code." This bill considered ways of reconciling the code with the provisions of the new constitution, such as deleting the crime of adultery in accordance with Article 24 of the new constitution, which provided for the equality of husbands and wives. But on high treason and lese majeste the bill offered only the following change: "Number Five. In provisions on crimes against the Imperial House make clear the significance of crimes of lese majeste against the Emperor and the Imperial Family."[1]

This clearly contradicted Article 14 of the constitution, which provided for equality under the law. In the spirit of the constitution there is no logical basis for only the emperor and imperial family to receive special protection under the Criminal Code. For that reason SCAP directed the Japanese government to delete "Crimes Against the Imperial Household" (Articles 73–76) when revising the Criminal Code. Upon learning this, Prime Minister Yoshida wrote to MacArthur on December 27, 1946, saying he wanted to retain the revisions contained in the outline of the legislative bill.

> I desire to address you specially with regard to the Criminal Code now in the process of revision. Mr. Kimura, Minister of Justice, was informed orally on December 20 by Brig[adier] Gen[eral] Whitney, Chief of Government Section, to the effect that you had instructed the deletion of Articles 73 and 75 relating to high treason as well as Articles 74 and 76 relating to lese-majeste. As to Articles 73 and 75, however, there are several reasons which necessitate their retention.

He then gave three reasons. Because these reveal most clearly Yoshida's views of the emperor and the imperial house, the whole text is quoted here:

> In the first place, under the new Constitution the Emperor's position is that of "Symbol of the State and of the unity of the people," which is in accord with the traditional faith that has been held firmly by the Japanese nation ever since the foundation of Japan. It is truly a high and lofty position. Moreover, it is undeniable that the Emperor is ethically the center of national veneration. That an act of violence against the person of the Emperor, occupying such a position, should be considered of a character subversive of the State, and deserving of severe moral censure and a severer punishment than any act of violence against the person of an ordinary individual is quite natural from the standpoint of Japanese national ethics. It is similar to the case of acts of violence against the person of one's parent or ancestor, which is considered as deserving of a severer punishment than an act of violence against the person of an ordinary individual.
>
> Secondly, the same is true of the members of the Imperial Family. As long as acts of violence against the person of the Emperor are to be punished with special consideration as above, it follows that a member of the Imperial Family, occupying an important place in respect of succession to the Throne, should be placed in a position different from ordinary individuals.
>
> Thirdly, the fact that all the countries under monarchical systems such as England have special provisions relating to acts of violence against the per-

son of the Sovereign demonstrates beyond dispute the truth of the above statement.

Accordingly, I believe that the retention of Articles 73 and 75 of the Criminal Code will fall in line with the sentiments and moral faith of the Japanese nation. I earnestly hope that the matter will receive your reconsideration in light of what I have stated above.[2]

After an extended delay MacArthur sent his reply on February 25, 1947. It is unclear why it took almost three months for him to do so, but perhaps some time was required to investigate the English legal system. When the investigation was completed, MacArthur wrote a long letter to Yoshida—much as a college professor might lecture a student on the new constitution—and completely rejected his appeal.[3]

Concerning Yoshida's first point, MacArthur criticized it as follows:

As to your first point, it would appear that to consider an act of violence against the person of the Emperor as "of a character subversive of the State" would be undesirable and inconsistent with the spirit of the new Constitution. As the symbol of the State and of the unity of the people, the Emperor is entitled to no more and no less legal protection than that accorded to all other citizens of Japan who, in the aggregate, constitute the State itself. To hold otherwise would violate the fundamental concept, clearly and unequivocally expressed in the new Constitution, that all men are equal before the law. . . .

As for your second point, I feel that there is even less basis for rationalizing a special position for other members of the Imperial family. The elevation of these members to a higher status under the law could only be construed as a discrimination based upon family origin, the essence of which is repugnant to the emergence of a free and democratic society.

As for your third point, there is no statutory provision in British law comparable to Article 73 and 75 of the Japanese Penal Code.

MacArthur noted further that although no comparable provision in British law existed, there had been such a provision during the reign of Edward III, but "that statute of 600 years ago" was "revised 100 years ago."

Shortly after this incident Yoshida left office when the Liberal Party suffered defeat in the general election of April 1947, but he did not give up on this issue. But neither did SCAP change its policy of deleting these provisions from the Criminal Code.

Thus the Katayama cabinet submitted the bill on the revision of the Criminal Code on July 26, 1947, to the judiciary committee of the House of Representatives. In accordance with SCAP's directive, the bill completely deleted all mention of "Crimes against the Imperial Family." Vice-Minister of Justice Satō Tōsuke, when explaining the reason for submitting the bill, hinted that it was being done at the direction of SCAP. After saying that the focus of the reform was the deletion of provisions on "Crimes against the Imperial Family," Satō explained that "We proceeded taking into account the fact that the existence of these provisions as a part of the problem of Japan's democratization is the object of concern to the Powers."[4] Responding to this, Kitaura Keitarō of the Liberal Party said: "I would like to hear whether or not the ordinary people of this country, with advice from those of knowledge and experience, approve or disapprove of Japan, with its 2,600 years of history, deleting the crime of lese majeste in the American style."[5]

The Issue of Lese Majeste

The conservatives were not ready to accept this change. The Liberal Party mounted a strong counterattack as the summer began. Because Yoshida's arguments for preserving the law on high treason were not accepted, party members changed their tactics, opposing the part of the government's reform bill that concentrated on preserving the crime of lese majeste, which was easy for most people to accept.

When the Diet convened at the end of September, Kitaura and others presented an amendment to the government's provision on the crime of lese majeste by limiting "Crimes Against the Imperial Family" to "Crimes Against the Emperor." Their amendment read: "Anyone who has committed an act of libel or insult against the Emperor shall be subject to imprisonment of not less than three months and not more than five years."[6] This revision limited the prohibition of lese majeste to the emperor, as the prohibition had previously applied to the imperial family as well, and changed it from "a person who has committed an act of lese majeste" to "a person who has committed an act of libel or insult." The penalty remained unchanged. This revision was almost identical to the bill proposed by the Provisional Committee on Legal Investigation. For the Liberal Party it was without question its maximum concession, but securing the support of a majority within the Diet appeared hopeless, despite support from the Socialist and Democratic parties for the government's reform bill.

The Liberal Party was desperate to preserve in the Criminal Code at least the crime of lese majeste. In many incidents of the time there were indications of apparent "disrespect" for and "insults" to the emperor. In May 1946, for example, there was the placard incident that would become famous. A placard was displayed on "Food May Day" by a member of the Communist Party that read: "I, the Emperor, am eating to my heart's content. You, my subjects, are starving to death." In October of that same year an article in the Communist Party's newspaper, *Red Flag*, was thought to have shown disrespect for the emperor but was disposed of without an indictment.

The magazine *Shinsō* (Truth) had just begun publication in January 1946, calling itself an "expose magazine." It chose to test the lengths to which the government would go to protect the emperor from "acts of libel or insult." At the time the emperor was making regular trips throughout the country, and wherever he went the roads and facilities were quietly repaired and put in good order. In September 1946 *Shinsō* wrote in a sarcastic article: "If [the Emperor] rides even in a small car around the entire country, Japan will indeed become a beautiful country and this will be helpful to the national tourist industry."[7]

Liberal Party member Akerai Kisaburō and others were outraged at this article and on October 4 brought a charge against *Shinsō* at the Tokyo Prosecutor's Office.[8] They were too late, however, as the Liberal Party's amendment to the reform bill was defeated in the judicial committee on October 3 and voted down again the next day in the full House. Despite this setback, Yoshida was not reconciled to accepting the change that SCAP had ordered. He next attempted to enlist the authority of SCAP in his effort. On October 6 he sent an envoy to see Kades at SCAP headquarters to attempt to revive the lese majeste law. He was not successful.[9] Although Yoshida fought to the very end, the revised Criminal Code, with "Crimes Against the Imperial House" deleted, was promulgated on October 25, 1946.

Howard Meyers, chief of SCAP's Criminal Division, Legal Section, who oversaw revision of the Criminal Code, wrote that "the fact that a certain political group attempted to make a comeback as protectors of the old Emperor system through the debate on revision of the Criminal Code, indicates that this issue is not dead and that it might raise its head sometime in the future."[10] The deletion of "Crimes Against the Imperial House" from the code would have been unthinkable without SCAP's firm insistence.

Perhaps nothing better than this revision of the Criminal Code indicates just how attached Yoshida and his Liberal Party were to the emperor system and how intellectually committed they were to the Meiji Constitution, even after the new constitution had taken effect. This attachment was not limited to Yoshida and the Liberal Party, however. The Japanese people were similarly attached. The continuing influence of the emperor system can be seen in the process by which the National Holidays Law was amended immediately after revision of the Criminal Code.

Trying to Preserve the Traditional
National Founding Day

The Japanese government began making preparations in December 1946 to revise the National Holidays Law. At the outset it considered issuing an Imperial Edict, as it had in the past, or an executive order. But realizing the significance of holidays to people's lives, the government decided to establish national holidays through statute and made preparations by organizing a "Conference for Those Concerned with National Holidays." The invited participants were "Appropriate Officials from the Prime Minister's Deliberative Council, the Imperial Household Agency, the Ministries of Education and Foreign Affairs, and Committees of both House of the Diet."[11] The following policy for revision was formulated during this conference:

> Abolish those festival holidays having their origins in Shinto but with little re-
> lation to people's lives. Reexamine those with weak historical foundations. . . .
> Adopt those which are consistent with the spirit of the new Constitution and
> which promote the goal of building a peaceful and cultured Japan.

This statement gives the impression that the adoption of new holidays was being considered, but this was not the case at all. The conference issued a report on January 20, 1948, listing the following nine days considered to be "suitable as national holidays."

1. January 1–3, New Year's Holiday.
2. February 11, *kigensetsu*, to be called national founding festival, national founding day, or memorial day for the founding of the country.
3. Vernal equinox, to be called *higan*, *higansai* [traditional Buddhist holidays], or the first day of spring festival.
4. April 29, to celebrate the birth of the Emperor.
5. May 1, to celebrate labor and to be called labor festival, labor memorial day, May day, or labor thanksgiving day.
6. Autumnal equinox, to be called autumnal equinox day, autumn day, or autumn festival day.
7. November 3, to celebrate promulgation of the new Constitution, and to be called Constitution day, Constitution memorial day, or Emperor Meiji's birthday.
8. November 23, the traditional farm day for celebrating the new harvest, to be called the new harvest day, or harvest thanksgiving day.
9. December 25, Christmas, to be called the celebration of Christ's birth, or the day of international friendship.

Other candidates that were considered for honored status as national holidays included: March 3 as traditional dolls day for girls; April 1 as first day of school; May 5 as traditional boys day; November 15 as children's day, children's festival, or loving and protecting children's day (the traditional day for children aged three, five, and seven to visit the local Shinto shrine); April 10 as lady's day or women's day (when women first exercised their suffrage rights); and a day yet to be determined as peace day or peace memorial day.

What deserves attention here is that November 3 was designated Constitution memorial day. As we know, this was because Prime Minister Yoshida wished to promulgate the new constitution on Emperor Meiji's birthday. He apparently did not consider the day the constitution took effect (May 3), which coincided with the beginning of the Tokyo war crimes trials in 1946, as a memorial day for the constitution. Next, there was *kigensetsu* to consider. The conference report commented passively about this day:

> [Although many accounts describe February 11 as the day the first emperor, Jimmu, ascended the throne,] there appears to be little scientific evidence for this, but it is the conventional historical theory. Yet we have not been able to find another appropriate day on which to remember the founding of the country. February 11 has long been known to the ordinary Japanese [as the day of national founding.]

To learn the preferences of the public for national holidays, the conference decided to invite people to submit letters to newspapers and radio stations with their ideas. The conference record shows that 137 letters were received from the public, although nothing is known of their contents. On the other hand, in January 1948 the *Jiji Tsūshin* wire service conducted personal interviews of a stratified, random sample of Japanese. The poll provided detailed statistics on the issue.[12] The total sample included 6,097 people, a fairly large number. According to the poll, the three most popular "current national holidays" (all established by Imperial Ordinance in 1927) that the Japanese people wished to retain were: New Year's Day (January 1), 92.1 percent (keep), 7.9 percent (abolish); Emperor Meiji's Birthday (November 3), 91.3 percent (keep), 8.7 percent (abolish); and National Founding Day (February 11), 89.0 percent (keep), 11.0 percent (abolish).[13] Thus immediately after the new constitution took effect, an overwhelming majority of the Japanese people believed that the traditional National Founding Day (*kigensetsu*) should be preserved.

On February 4, 1948, the conference's report and the result of this poll were submitted to William K. Bunce, chief of the Religions Division of SCAP's Civil Information and Education Section (CI&E).[14] Thereafter the government's proposal for establishing national holidays took a meandering course. On April 15 the government proposed to SCAP a provisional bill to designate February 11 as "National Origins Festival." SCAP immediately rejected it.[15]

Bunce and Donald R. Nugent, the head of CI&E, wrote in a memorandum dated May 27, 1948, titled "Abolition of Certain Japanese National Holidays":

> Present Japanese national holidays are not very old, most having been created by the Meiji Government. . . . Of the eleven that are now celebrated, ten of them have their origins in Shinto. They are formally celebrated as Shinto festivals. . . . Continued observance of these holidays would not only violate the principle of religious freedom but would also constitute a violation of the directive abolishing governmental sponsorship and perpetuation of Shinto (December 15, 1945). . . . It is recommended that the Japanese Government be directed to abolish those national holidays which have their origin and significance in State Shinto . . . and that the Japanese Government be encouraged and guided in the selection of new national holidays more in keeping with democratic ideals.[16]

It was in such circumstances that *kigensetsu* was abolished, despite the public's preference, and the National Holidays Law was promulgated on July 20, 1948. What, one might ask, did the public think of removing the section "Crimes Against the Imperial House" from the Criminal Code? That is unclear, but it is likely that public opinion on this was not very different from opinion on the National Holidays Law. Perhaps that was the inevitable result of adopting a constitution that disregarded the traditions and desires of individual Japanese. In other words, even after the constitution had taken effect, the Japanese people's feelings about the emperor had changed very little. And Yoshida's conservative political power, based on those popular feelings, resisted SCAP with all its might in order to protect the system.

The new constitution achieved a fundamental shift from the principle of sovereignty of a "sacred and inviolable Emperor" to the principle of sovereignty of the people. In spite of all the fanfare surrounding the new constitution, however, there had been no fundamental intellectual conversion in the area of basic rights. What about pacifism and Article 9, the other fundamental doctrine of the new constitution?

A Military Force of One Hundred Thousand

When the constitution was enacted in 1946, the government took the position that Article 9 renounced all forms of war, including wars of self-defense, and told the youth of the country that "Japan will not possess troops, ships, airplanes or anything else that is for the purpose of war." But it changed this public interpretation of Article 9 after the United States, with the development of the Cold War and the outbreak of the Korean War, changed its own policy toward Japan and ordered the creation of a National Police Reserve. The conventional wisdom is that, therefore, government thinking about Article 9 had changed, perhaps unavoidably because of the change in U.S. policy toward Japan or perhaps simply reflecting that change. But is this type of postwar consciousness or the conservative government's view of Article 9 really justified?

W. Macmahon Ball, who was in Tokyo as the British Commonwealth representative to the Allied Council of Japan when the constitution took effect, made the following observation in a book he published in 1949:

> The psychological atmosphere in Japan everywhere suggests that the armed forces are not dead, but dormant. The Japanese are acutely aware of the hostility between the United States and Russia. This clash of interests between the two great powers sets the tone of everything that happens in Japan. The restoration of the Japanese fighting forces in some form or other is sympathetically discussed at Allied social gatherings, and this is well known to the Japanese. It was, therefore, not surprising that early in 1947 the Japanese Foreign Office informally sounded out Allied representatives on the prospects of being allowed a standing army of 100,000 men and a small air force. It is sometimes said that the Japanese have come to hate war and their war leaders. I think it would be more correct to say that they hate losing a war, and are glad to repudiate the particular military leaders they blame for the defeat.[17]

This is a rather harsh view of Japan. But if one tries to get behind some of the facts that appear only faintly in this book, one might come to the conclusion that Ball's view of Japan was perhaps understandable. The informal proposal that Japan should possess a standing army of 100,000 and a small air force reappears in an official telegram that Ball sent from Tokyo to the Australian Ministry of External Affairs. The telegram was dated April 16, 1947, only two weeks before the constitution legally took effect. This was also the time when the campaign to popularize the constitution was under way throughout the country and when people were loudly shouting about "building a peaceful country." Ball reported to his government:

1. Asakai Kōichirō, a senior Japanese Foreign Office official, called on me this afternoon. He was anxious to draw me out about my ideas of the Peace Treaty. He is himself engaged in preparing draft proposals for the Japanese Government.

2. He pointed out that if all Allied troops were to be withdrawn from Japan on the signing of the Treaty, this would leave a vacuum in Japan. In particular Japan had to be protected against illegal entry of people and goods from Korea and Asia. Moreover, there was always the danger of a general strike which would create economic chaos. At present this police work is being done by Allied forces but the work must still be done after their withdrawal.

3. I asked Asakai what kind of forces he thought they needed. He said that what he had in mind was a Japanese military force of 100,000 strong with some aircraft for patrols.

4. I pointed out that Japan had renounced armed forces in her new Constitution. Asakai said that, of course, Japan would prefer to be without armed forces but there was no blinking the necessity for the kind of forces he had in mind.[18]

Ball was a political scientist as well as a diplomat. Born in 1901, he graduated from Melbourne University in 1923 and studied at the London School of Economics. Following service as a government official, he was appointed professor at Melbourne University in 1945 and attended the United Nations founding ceremony as a member of the Australian delegation. In April of the following year he arrived in Tokyo as the British Commonwealth's representative to the Allied Council for Japan. He stayed in Tokyo until August 1947, after which he returned to his teaching post at Melbourne University, where he was professor of government and politics from 1949 to 1968.[19]

Even to a man as experienced in politics as Ball, the Asakai proposal must have come as a great surprise. When Asakai said that a defeated Japan needed one hundred thousand troops, Ball apparently recalled that the one hundred thousand troops that Germany had been allowed after World War I had been used later by the Nazis to build a large army. Ball ended his telegram with a response to Asakai:

> I said that personally I felt my Governments would not be sympathetic to this proposal. I added jokingly that if the Japanese Government seriously intended to make this proposal, it might be prudent to ask for 95,000 or 105,000 since the mention of 100,000 might remind people of the request made by the German Government after World War I. Asakai thanked me for this advice.

Asakai himself was a career diplomat who had entered the Foreign Ministry after graduating from Tokyo Commercial University (presently Hitotsubashi University). At the time of his conversation with Ball, he was the head of the General Affairs Section of the Central Liaison Office in the Ministry of Foreign Affairs. He later served as Japanese ambassador to the United Kingdom and to the United States.[20]

Although Asakai was a young diplomat, he dealt with the Allied occupation personnel in a confident manner, and has been judged to have been at the "point of contact between the Japanese Government and the Allied forces during the early period of the Occupation."[21] Although he met Macmahon Ball three times,[22] he did not leave a record of the meeting that Ball recorded in such detail. That meeting appears to have been unofficial. Was Asakai's proposal, then, just a casual suggestion? Certainly not. It was, it seems, an idea that he got from Prime Minister Yoshida. This is evident from an April 1984 interview with Asakai by a Kyōdō news correspondent:

> Question: Was your rearmament proposal official policy of the Japanese Government?
> Asakai: I had no authorization from the Government, but since I was a member of the Government, I felt strongly the atmosphere that prevailed in the Government. But it was my own idea to sound out [Ball] by making the proposal.
> Question: What do you mean by atmosphere in the Government?
> Asakai: I think Mr. Yoshida (Prime Minister Yoshida Shigeru) also had the same idea (rearmament). I listened to what he said. That was one source of the atmosphere I spoke of. And then there were the meetings of top officials in the Foreign Ministry.[23]

The very same proposal for rearmament was made a month later, in May, to Canada's representative in Japan, E. Herbert Norman.[24] Yoshida himself carefully avoided making a rearmament proposal directly to SCAP, an act that would have constituted a rejection of the "renunciation of war" that MacArthur strongly advocated. Yoshida thought, no doubt, that he would begin by first seeking the views of such influential diplomats as Ball and Norman. His conclusion from this effort was that there was no possibility that the proposal would be accepted and that he should continue waving the flag of "pacifism." From Ball's point of view, however, the incident indicated that Yoshida was nothing less than "an untrustworthy conservative politician" and it contributed greatly to his distrust of Japan.

At this time an official "Preparatory Committee for the Peace Settlement" was set up in Australia to prepare for a peace treaty with Japan. Ball's report to the committee included the following evaluation of Japanese politicians' views of the constitution:

> I don't think that important Japanese groups of whatever political persuasion have given serious consideration to the new Constitution. Educated po-

litical leaders first praise the new Constitution, then offer a series of qualifications on the interpretation that will mollify Japanese without arousing SCAP. Of these qualifications, conservative political leaders point out, for example, that the nation's legal system has changed but the nation's policy has not, that the Meiji Constitution was also democratic, that if they know the new Constitution has serious defects it can quickly be revised, and that in any case it was approved by the Diet with the realization that internationally it was necessary. . . . I am convinced that many socially influential Japanese believe that before long the Americans will permit Japan to rebuild some military strength in order to assist the United States in protecting its strategic interest in the Japanese islands from Russian aggression. In these circumstances it is not surprising, as I have already reported, that it was proposed to me by a high-ranking official of the Japanese Foreign Ministry that the peace treaty should allow 100,000 Japanese troops and a small number of aircraft.[25]

Australia apparently believed that Japan had no intention of observing the pacifistic provisions in the constitution, and was therefore very apprehensive about the rebirth of the Japanese military. For Australia, the Japanese military was the same threatening force it had always been. Australia thought that if the pacifistic constitution could not prevent the revival of Japanese militarism, then perhaps a peace treaty could do so. In May 1947 the preparatory committee decided on a number of provisions for a draft peace treaty with Japan: Japan's responsibility for the war was to be stated in the preamble of the document; thorough demilitarization of Japan; complete disarmament; the achievement of democratization; Japan must prohibit all military organizations, special police, armaments industry, and state Shinto; the peace treaty must include the complete implementation of the purge of all militarists from public office; and restrictions on shipbuilding, educational reform, breakup of the *zaibatsu*, and other reforms already decreed by the Allied occupation. Moreover, as it was dangerous to leave the implementation of these reforms to the Japanese government, a supervisory commission would be established by the Allied powers in Japan to continue overseeing those reforms for twenty-five years.[26]

Thus Australia believed from the day the new "peace constitution" took effect that Japan was unlikely to observe it. At this very moment the people of Japan, under the slogan "Building a Peaceful Country," were dancing to the music of the "Constitution Song," or perhaps more accurately, were being forced to dance to it.

Neither Yoshida nor the Liberal Party nor indeed most of the Japanese people were much changed by the new constitution. It was not that Yoshida eagerly set about strengthening the emperor system and rearming his country after the U.S. policy toward Japan changed from democratization to anticommunism. But he refrained from advocating these goals openly and publicly only because SCAP was still encouraging the policy of democratization and the Japanese people generally were still supporting it. In other words, the Yoshida government's talk of "building a peaceful country" as the constitution took effect in 1947 merely served the cause of expediency. In that sense, the U.S. government's change of policy in Japan from democratization to anticommunism was a blessing for Yoshida because he was then free to shift the responsibility for the change in his own policy to the Americans. Yoshida was already attempting to mount various challenges to the new constitution before the shift in U.S. policy, but these failed in the face of SCAP's opposition. As John Dower has written, the first Yoshida cabinet, which lasted almost exactly a year, from April 1946 to May 1947 "did not make a deep impression on anyone, including Yoshida himself."[27]

In the April 1947 general election, held just before the new constitution became law, the longtime bureaucrat Yoshida stood for election for the first time in Shikoku. Accompanied by Kanamori Tokujirō, he appeared in Kōchi to give a speech. At the inn where they were staying, Kanamori began writing poems on colored paper. As we have already seen, Kanamori had quite a talent for poetry and painting. He also wrote several simple introductions to the new constitution, one of which, *Random Thoughts on the Constitution*, included a note saying "illustrated by the author."[28] He had drawn a chrysanthemum [symbol of the Imperial Family] on the cover, had written the title with a brush, and had drawn a *daruma* doll as a frontispiece. The binding conveyed a warmth that was certainly uncharacteristic of a book written by a legislative bureaucrat. The one-stroke sketch of a *daruma*, a figure commonly associated with elections in Japan, was particularly apt. With the meaning of "never count me out," it was an especially good omen. Kanamori also sketched a *daruma* on colored paper. Yoshida himself did not make any sketches, but he did write on the paper the characters for "Liberal Democrat." He then wrote two characters that are read *Sowai*, much as one would write a pen name. It is said that he used this word as an approximate Japanese pronunciation in English of his initials, "S.Y." While he was watching Kanamori skillfully sketch *darumas* on colored paper, Yoshida picked up a brush in a joking fashion and began writing on the side of the round *daruma* figure the two characters *nanakorobi* (seven falls), from the expression *nanakorobi yaoki* (seven falls, eight rises), or vicissitudes of life associated with the *daruma*. However, Yoshida changed the last of the four characters to read *shitten battō*, which means writhing in agony.[29]

Notes

1. "Rinji hōsei chōsakai ni okeru shimon dai ichigō ni taisuru tōshinsho." Irie Toshio bunsho, National Diet Library, kokkai toshokan shozō.

2. Sodei Rinjirō, trans. and ed., "MacArthur-Yoshida ōfuku shokan (1)," *Hōgaku shirin* 77, no. 4 (March 1980): 118.

3. Ibid., pp. 121–122.

4. Dai ikkai kokkai shūgiin shihō iinkai gijiroku, no. 6 (July 28).

5. Dai ikkai kokkai shūgiin shihō iinkai gijiroku, no. 9 (July 31).

6. Dai ikkai kokkai shūgiin shihō iinkai gijiroku, no. 44 (October 3).

7. *Shinsō*, no. 11 (September 1947).

8. *Asahi Shinbun*, October 5, 1947.

9. Sodei Rinjirō, "Sengo minaoshi no genten: Yoshida-MacArthur shokan," *Hōgaku seminaa* (November 1979): 28.

10. Howard Meyers, "Revisions of the Criminal Code of Japan During the Occupation," *Washington Law Review and State Bar Journal* 25, no. 1 (February 1950): 134. Japanese officials in the Ministry of Justice paid this article close attention. A summary by Takahashi Masami was published in *Hōsō jihō* 2, no. 11 (November 1950).

11. Sōrichō kanbō shingishitsu, "Shukusaijitsu ni kansuru kankeisha kaigi hōkokusho," January 20, 1948, GHQ/SCAP bunsho, Kokkai Toshokan Shozō, microfiche CIE (A)08641.

12. Jiji Tsūshinsha, "Shukusaijitsu ni kansuru yoron chōsa," February 1948, GHQ/SCAP bunsho, Kokkai Toshokan Shozō, microfiche CIE (A)08643.

13. "Abolition of Certain Japanese National Holidays," May 27, 1948, GHQ/SCAP bunsho, Kokkai Toshokan Shozō, microfiche CIE (A)08643.

14. From S. Shima (Secretary of the Prime Minister's Office) to W. K. Bunce, February 4, 1948, GHQ/SCAP bunsho, Kokkai Toshokan Shozō, microfiche CIE (A)08642.

15. Ibid. In this "provisional plan" that was submitted to SCAP in Japanese, the section that read "February 11, Festival of the Beginning of the Country" had been scratched out.

16. "Abolition of Certain Japanese National Holidays," May 27, 1948, GHQ/SCAP bunsho, Kokkai Toshokan Shozō, microfiche CIE (A)08643.

17. W. Macmahon Ball, *Nihon—teki ka mikata ka,* trans. Nakayama Tatsuhei (Tokyo: Chikuma Shobō, 1953), pp. 140–141.

18. CRS, A 5466/T 1, Item CCT 5-A, Australian Archives, Canberra. See also my "Soto kara mita heiwa kenpō no genten," *Hōritsu jihō* 56, no. 6 (May 1984).

19. Alan Rix, ed., *Intermittent Diplomat: The Japan and Batavia Diaries of W. Macmahon Ball* (Melbourne: University of Melbourne Press, 1988), p. 9.

20. "Asakai Kōichirō ryakureki," in *Shoki tainichi senryō seisaku: Asakai Kōichirō hōkoku,* comp. Gaimushō, vol. 2 (Tokyo: Mainichi Shinbunsha, 1978).

21. Ibid., p. 267.

22. Ibid.

23. *Shinano Mainichi Shinbun*, April 30, 1984.

24. CRS, A 5466/T 1, Item CCT 5-A, Australian Archives, Canberra.

25. Paper by Mr. W. Macmahon Ball on the Progress of the Occupation in Japan, Post-Treaty Controls and the Machinery of Control, June 10, 1947, PCPS 1/57, CRS, A 5469 Item 3, Australian Archives, Canberra.

26. Kikuchi Tsutomu, "Australia to tainichi sōki kōwa no teishō," *Kokusai mondai* (September 1983).

27. John Dower, *Yoshida Shigeru to sono jidai,* trans. Ōkubo Genji (Tokyo: TBS Britannica, 1981), 2:44.

28. Kanamori Tokujirō, *Kenpō zuisō* (Tokyo: Miwa Shobō, 1947).

29. Kudō Yoshimi, *Ruporutaaju—Nihonkoku kenpō* (Tokyo: Yūhikaku, 1987), p. 4.

12

The Forgotten Sequel

A Chance to Review the Constitution

Under pressure from MacArthur, the constitution was thus born in full view of an "agonizing" Yoshida. *Daruma* could not arise until the United States reversed its policy for the occupation of Japan. It was not that there was no chance of rebounding. Immediately after Yoshida sent his letter at the end of 1946 asking MacArthur not to eliminate the treason law from the Criminal Code, he received on January 3, 1947, the following letter from MacArthur:

Dear Mr. Prime Minister:

In connection with their consideration of political developments in Japan during the course of the past year, the Allied Powers have decided, in order to insure to the Japanese people full and continuing freedom of opportunity to reexamine, review, and if deemed necessary amend the new constitution in the light of experience gained from its actual operation, that between the first and second years of its effectivity it should again be subjected to their formal review and that of the Japanese Diet. If they deem it necessary at that time, they may additionally require a referendum or some other appropriate procedure for ascertaining directly Japanese opinion with respect to it. In other words, as the bulwark of future Japanese freedom, the Allied Powers feel that there should be no future doubt that the constitution expresses both the free and considered will of the Japanese people.

These continuing rights of review are of course inherent, but I am nevertheless acquainting you with the position thus taken by the Allied Powers in order that you may be fully informed in the premises.

With cordial best wishes for the new year,

Most Sincerely,

Douglas MacArthur[1]

MacArthur was offering another chance for the Japanese freely to amend the constitution. It is very interesting to see how Yoshida replied.

Before we hasten to a conclusion, however, let us first examine the background of MacArthur's letter.

Recall that MacArthur had hastily scheduled the first postwar general election for April 1946, soon after the Japanese government had published a summary of its draft constitution on March 6. He quickly had the draft sent to the Imperial Diet for deliberation. In response to this, as we have seen, the FEC had confronted MacArthur, objecting that such a procedure for enacting the constitution violated the pledge made by the Potsdam Declaration concerning the "freely expressed will of the Japanese people." Later, on October 17, 1946, the FEC adopted a policy providing for a review of the new constitution after two years. MacArthur's letter to Yoshida, then, relayed the FEC decision made two and a half months earlier. But MacArthur's letter said "the Allied Powers have decided," instead of saying that the FEC had done so. Furthermore, it is very significant that his letter completely omitted the following section of the FEC decision: "The Far Eastern Commission shall also review the constitution within this same period (from May 3, 1948, to May 2, 1949)."

This FEC policy decision was taken at the request of Australia and New Zealand,[2] but the U.S. government strongly opposed the idea of informing Japan of the decision. As soon as the policy was adopted by the FEC, Assistant Secretary of War Howard Peterson told Assistant Secretary of State J. H. Hilldring that he "feared that announcing the Commission's policy decision would undermine the prestige of the constitution."[3] SCAP quite naturally agreed. General Whitney, head of Government Section, wrote in a private letter to Professor Kenneth Colegrove that "announcing the FEC decision at the same time the Constitution is promulgated would be the worst possible thing."[4]

Amidst these developments, MacArthur sent a letter to the army chief of staff strongly opposing any public announcement of the FEC policy decision to the Japanese government. He wrote:

> Announcing the Commission's decision would not only invite the collapse of the Constitution as a result but would bring about a tremendous worsening of conditions in the whole country. The objectives of the Occupation and the results achieved thus far would unnecessarily be put in jeopardy.

He said at the same time: "I agree that the Prime Minister should be informed formally of the Far Eastern Commission's decision of October 17."[5]

MacArthur's letter to Yoshida was thus sent against this background. How, then, did Yoshida respond to the letter? We might expect, from the perspective of one who was "agonizing" because [the constitution] was "imposed" on him, that Yoshida would leap at the glad tidings, but such was not the case. Three days later, on January 6, Yoshida sent the following reply:

> My dear General:
> I acknowledge receipt of your letter of January 3rd, and have carefully noted the contents.
> Yours very sincerely,
> (signed) Shigeru Yoshida[6]

Nothing more than this. There is a common expression, "three and a half lines" [meaning a letter of divorce]. Yoshida's letter was even shorter; the original was no more than two lines. Why did he send such a brusque reply? Why did he not take advantage of MacArthur's proposal? It would appear that his view of the new constitution, his view of the occupation, and his whole understanding of postwar Japan at the moment were compressed into his reply to MacArthur.

As MacArthur had wished, then, the FEC decision was not announced to the Japanese until March 20, 1948, the following year. The Japanese press reported it on March 30, though the story was not given major treatment. It was, however, reported on the first pages of *Asahi Shinbun* ("The Constitution to Be Reviewed—A Popular Referendum Being Considered") and *Yomiuri Shinbun* ("A National Referendum on the Constitution"). There was little immediate reaction to the news.

Preparing for a Constitutional Review

The review of the constitution became an issue in Japan in August 1948, after the formation of the Ashida cabinet. On June 20, a year after the constitution had taken effect, in accord with the FEC ruling, the Attorney General (or Minister of Justice), Suzuki Yoshio, acting for Prime Minister Ashida, told Matsuoka Komakichi, the Speaker of the House of Representatives: "I would like to request that you undertake a study to determine whether or not the Constitution should be amended."[7] By August every newspaper was playing up the issue of constitutional amendment. *Yomiuri Shinbun*, the first to take up the question, published Suzuki's following statement under the headline "Constitutional Amendment—To Be Submitted to the Regular Session of the Diet?"

> In view of the fact that the Supreme Commander has issued a directive on the problem of amending the Constitution, I have already relayed that to the Speakers of the House of Representatives and the House of Councillors and requested that they select members to serve on a committee to amend the Constitution. There doesn't seem to be much enthusiasm for it in the Diet.

However, we hope very much the Diet will begin its debate on revising the constitution at the next regular session, which begins in December. At the moment I am not considering the question of whether or not the future of the Emperor System should be determined by a national referendum. Nor do I intend to seek a referendum on the Emperor's abdication, for I believe that should be decided independently by the Emperor himself. Therefore, I would like to propose an amendment to the Imperial House Law, along with a plan to revise the Constitution, which would permit the Emperor to abdicate. . . . The revision would be largely a technical matter and would probably not touch on fundamental issues of the Constitution. For example, we would like to change Article 89, which prohibits the expenditure of public funds to private religious, charitable, educational and benevolent enterprises, so that the Government can provide assistance to private schools.[8]

Acting on Suzuki's statement, the Legal Affairs Office and "administrative officials of the Diet" began to consider which provisions of the constitution required a "re-examination." The following are some of the "items for re-examination" selected by the "administrative officials of the Diet" (exactly who they were is unclear; even the newspapers reported it in this way).

Article 1. Clarify the fundamental attitude concerning the retention or abolition of the Emperor System and Constitutional position of the Emperor in case he is retained.
Article 28. Guarantee of the right of workers to organize and to bargain and act collectively when the public officials law is revised.
Article 67. Clarify the procedure for designating the Prime Minister.
Articles 69 and 70. Clarify the rules for en masse resignation of the Cabinet.

Chairing a committee in the Legal Affairs Office, Kaneko Hajime put together the issues for consideration. Kaneko himself said that they had waited for the completion of a proposal for revision by a constitutional research committee of Tokyo University, of which he was a member, before deciding the exact policy.[9]

Thus at the same time that the points for revision were being precisely determined, the procedures for debate were beginning to be concretely defined by those working with Speaker of the House Matsuoka. Matsuoka described his plan in this way:

[The plan] is to establish a committee of inquiry of about 20 representatives of all the parties in the two Houses of the Diet and to study the amendment issues quietly. . . . If domestic or foreign conditions change and new events develop, the committee of inquiry would be disbanded and a new special committee would be created by decision of the Diet.

The emperor's abdication seems to have been a major concern in the discussion of amending the constitution. Consideration was being given to a revision of the constitution that would simultaneously include revision of the Imperial House Law.[10]

How did the public react as the government and the Diet took up the issue of constitutional amendment? Although Speaker Matsuoka indicated a concrete procedure for constitutional revision, he said that "I am not thinking of revising the Constitution at the present time. I have talked to the leaders of the major political parties and they share my view completely."[11] This and other statements indicate that he was very opposed to the idea. The newspapers published conversations with so-called well-informed sources—Kanamori Tokujirō,[12] Suzuki Yasuzō,[13] Abe Yoshinari,[14] Asai Kiyoshi,[15] and others who were instrumental in enacting the constitution—and all were similarly opposed. Editorial opinion followed the same line. *Mainichi Shinbun*, after a rather careful survey of the deficiencies of various articles of the constitution, raised doubts about "whether or not it is necessary to conduct a national referendum and revise the Constitution if all that is being raised are small, technical issues."[16] *Asahi Shinbun* was also lukewarm. Perhaps revision was necessary "in order to consolidate interpretations of opaque provisions," but at the same time it seemed like "a useless effort" in the sense of "presenting an opportunity to popularize the fundamental ideas of the new Constitution among the people."[17] In other words, *Asahi* saw the significance of a revision as an opportunity to popularize the constitution.

Satō Isao's words summarize well the conditions of the time:

> Those things in the Constitution which are considered objective and fundamental principles are permanent. Even if the issue of amending the Constitution comes up again, these will not be questioned. I think any amendment would be limited to small points, things which over two years have proved to be an impediment or an inconvenience, such as, for example, the procedure for designating the Prime Minister, or the conditions under which the Diet would be dissolved.[18]

From the mid-1950s Article 9 (renunciation of war) was always mentioned whenever the topic of constitutional revision was broached. In 1948, however, not one person, including members of the Liberal Party, spoke publicly of revising Article 9. Moreover, no one expressed the opinion that the constitution should now be submitted to a national referendum or that the free will of the Japanese people had not been expressed upon its adoption.

A few legal scholars did suggest, however, that revision should be undertaken in order to advance further the fundamental principles of the constitution. These were scholars who had not played a positive role during the framing process, yet only two years after the new constitution became law, they had achieved the ability to criticize it. The reasons are interesting: first, the new constitution intellectually liberated them from the Meiji Constitution; and, second, senior law professors who had achieved their status and authority through the Meiji Constitution now lost that authority because younger scholars were able to express their views freely.

Proposals to Review the Constitution

One proposal for revising the constitution came from the Public Law Forum in March 1949.[19] As this group had been studying the issue since the spring of 1948—the same time that the FEC published its policy decision to review the constitution—it seems certain that the FEC's decision caused the group to begin its study. The forum's "Views on Constitutional Revision" offered concrete revisions with reasons listed for each, but these did not constitute an expression of the group's views on the entire constitution. Probably there was little time to prepare such an expression. The document contains the notation: "We are hastily publishing here only the part through chapter three."

Here are a few of the forum's numerous ideas for amendments:

Change the words "Nihon kokumin" [Japanese people] to "Nihon jinmin" [Japanese people, "jinmin" being a word for "people" favored by the Socialists and others on the left] throughout the Constitution.

Article 1. Add a new provision "Sovereignty resides in the Japanese people."

Article 2. Change the existing Article 1 to "The Emperor shall be the emblem of the Japanese people."

Article 9, paragraph one. Delete "as means of settling international disputes," and insert a new provision which prohibits individual participation. In paragraph two change the words, "In order to accomplish the aim of the preceding paragraph," to "For whatever purpose."

The reason for changing "symbol" in Article 1 to "emblem" was explained as follows:

The word "symbol" in Article 1 of the existing Constitution contains a mythological element; moreover, its legal meaning is not clear. Some people interpret one who is a symbol to mean someone who is elevated to the position of sovereign. Since symbol was a word originally used to indicate a ceremonial existence, to make it much clearer, emblem should be used. Emblem also is equivalent to the concept of an ensign or flag mark. It is a newly coined word and expresses well, we think, the ritual existence of the Emperor.

Explaining their reason for revising Article 9, the group wrote:

Paragraph one of Article 9 is a declaration of the renunciation forever of aggressive war and the threat or use of force. Paragraph two is a provision which denies the right to maintain any armaments or to wage any kind of war. Despite the fact that the spirit of the original provision was a declaration of complete pacifism renouncing all war, including wars in self-defense and wars for imposing sanctions, the wording of this article contains various restrictions which can be misinterpreted and should be completely rewritten.

Another proposal for revision was issued by the Constitution Research Committee of Tokyo University. Titled "Problems of Constitutional Revision" and numbering over one hundred pages, this proposal was prepared by a group of young scholars in the Faculty of Law.[20] Tanaka Jirō (administrative law) wrote the introduction, Ishii Akihisa (labor law) the section on basic economic rights, and Hirano Ryūichi (criminal law) the section on habeas corpus.

In his introduction Tanaka wrote that "there is probably little difference among us with respect to basic positions and fundamental principles." While accepting the basic principles of the new constitution—popular sovereignty, permanent pacifism, and respect for human rights—they proposed fundamental revisions in its organization.

The majority opinion of our research group was that the topic of chapter one should be general provisions or matters pertaining to the Japanese state. That is to say, among the general provisions popular sovereignty and permanent pacifism should be clearly stated. Perhaps provisions concerning the Japanese people, the territory, the flag and so forth should be placed here as well.

The renunciation of war (chapter two) should be included in chapter one, the provisions concerning fundamental human rights of the people (chapter three) in chapter two, and provisions on the emperor (chapter one) should be moved to chapter three.

This proposal for revising the constitution shares several common features with that of the Public Law Forum.

The SCAP draft had consciously followed the organization of the Meiji Constitution in including "The Emperor" as the first chapter, but this had also been challenged as inappropriate in a constitution that located sovereignty in the people. These criticisms are significant even today, for among the arguments in support of constitutional revision advanced in the political maelstrom of the late 1950s, there was little room for revisionist views like these, nor has there been to this very day.

While the question of amending the constitution was a serious problem for some, it was never so for the Ashida cabinet. The Shōwa Denkō scandal had been revealed by the press following the arrest in June 1948 of the president of Shōwa Denkō for bribing government officials to obtain loans for investment and reconstruction. High officials in the Finance and Trade ministries were also arrested, as were the director of the Economic Stabilization Board (presently the Economic Planning Board) and even Prime Minister Ashida himself [for questioning]. Thus the Ashida cabinet collapsed after only eight months, without presenting any conclusions on the issue of constitutional review. In place of Ashida, Yoshida Shigeru returned to power.

If viewed purely as a question of revising the constitution, it might seem fortunate that Yoshida, who had earlier received a letter directly from MacArthur concerning this issue, again became prime minister. But subsequent events certainly do not support this view. For ten months after he became prime minister Yoshida did not address constitutional revision. In the meantime, at the end of April 1949, facing the FEC's deadline of "two years from the time the Constitution becomes law," Yoshida responded as follows to a question about the issue at the House Foreign Affairs Committee:

> I know nothing about a decision by the Far Eastern Commission. I am not aware of it, but the Government has no intention at the present of amending the Constitution. And if the Ashida Cabinet planned to revise the Constitution, I have not heard about it.[21]

A very surprising answer indeed! It is difficult to believe that he forgot to "bear in mind" his reply of "two and a half lines" to MacArthur's letter. Rather, we see in his apparently arrogant reply Yoshida's own sense of resignation about the constitution. There can be no doubt that he had learned much while agonizing [over the constitution]. Certainly he had attempted in a variety of ways to resist SCAP, and not without some success. But it was impossible to change the basic principles of the constitution so long as the military occupation continued. Moreover, with respect to revision of the constitution, Japanese public opinion was diametrically opposed to the idea of revision. It seems certain that he was aware of this and had become resigned to it. For now he had to accept the constitution silently. Eventually the occupation would end, and then it would be time to consider constitutional revision. Herein lies Yoshida's new view of the constitution, as well as his view of postwar Japan.

Consequently, Yoshida thereafter did not publicly reject the new constitution, for that would have involved disowning both the first and second Yoshida cabinets as well. And Yoshida no longer took the position that the constitution had been imposed on Japan. In his 1957 memoirs he wrote about the period when the SCAP draft was presented to the Japanese.

> It is quite true that, at the time of its initial drafting, General MacArthur's headquarters did insist, with considerable vigor, on the speedy completion of the task and made certain demands in regard to the contents of the draft. But during our subsequent negotiations with GHQ there was nothing that could properly be termed coercive or overbearing in the attitude of the Occupation authorities towards us. They listened carefully to the Japanese experts and officials charged with the work, and in many cases accepted our proposals.[22]

Politicians who believed that the constitution was "imposed" were, like Yoshida, intellectually conservative; and when Yoshida was "agonizing" over the issue, many of them were being indicted for war crimes, being purged, or were young members of the Yoshida "school." One would have to say that the "imposed constitution" thesis was no more than an easy assertion by those who watched the clash of ideas from the sidelines during the military occupation that followed Japan's defeat.

Be that as it may, why has this thesis survived for so long, now more than forty years after the occupation? There was, after all, an opportunity to revise the constitution. The chance was offered to Yoshida. While fleeing from the opportunity presented to them, the would-be revisionists, by continuing to harp on the theme, have perpetuated the thesis that the constitution was "imposed." The point must be made that even recent studies of constitutional revision and textbooks on postwar Japan have not mentioned the fact that Yoshida was given an opportunity to revise the constitution.

Change in Occupation Policy

The Japanese government thus made it clear that it would not attempt to revise the new constitution. But what of the FEC, which had made the policy decision to review the constitution within two years of its taking effect? As this question was becoming an issue in the Japanese press, the

U.S. delegate and FEC chairman, Frank McCoy, sent an urgent letter to the Assistant Secretary of State for Occupied Areas, Charles F. Saltzman.

> I do not propose [he wrote] to initiate this review in the Commission. Other members, however, may do so, since the subject has recently been under discussion by some of them, and the Commission has a standing committee on the Japanese Constitution. The leaders of the two Houses of the Diet, also, according to press reports, have recently agreed to appoint a joint committee to study the Constitution with a view to its possible revision. . . . May I query whether you might deem it advisable to initiate within the Department a study of the Japanese Constitution in order to determine the views of the United States as to its revision and as to any specific amendments?[23]

Saltzman quickly replied that "steps [would be taken] towards determination of a U.S. position in the matter."[24]

But at this time, the fall of 1948, the State Department's policy toward Japan was on the verge of major change. The Chinese Communist Party had expanded its power from the villages of China to the cities, and a Communist government had been established in the northern part of Korea. The State Department's Policy Planning Staff under George F. Kennan was beginning to formulate a policy for Japan giving top priority to economic recovery to prevent the spread of communism in Japan. This policy document, "Recommendations with Respect to U.S. Policy Toward Japan," or NSC 13/2, was adopted by the National Security Council on October 9, 1948, and became the basis of U.S. policy toward Japan. The document undertook a comprehensive reexamination of U.S. policy, including the question of a peace treaty, security matters, the regime of control, and occupation policies. It described the U.S. position with respect to the FEC as follows: "The United States Government should take the position that conditions of surrender set forth in the Potsdam Declaration have been substantially fulfilled."[25] In other words, policies of demilitarization and democratization need not be pushed any further. This meant, in effect, that there was no need to review or reexamine the Japanese Constitution, the very symbol of demilitarization and democratization. Saltzman argued that the policy of democratization was not an obstacle to the stabilization of Japan and should be pursued, but he eventually gave in to Kennan and others [on the Policy Planning Staff].[26] Given these circumstances, Saltzman wrote to McCoy on December 3 that the U.S. government's position was that the "Far Eastern Commission should as inconspicuously as possible and with a minimum of debate review promptly the Constitution."[27]

On the other hand, Australia, which of the FEC countries most favored reviewing the new constitution, had already begun to study the matter in its Preparatory Committee for the Peace Settlement under the direction of Sir Frederic William Eggleston. Eggleston, a lawyer and politician, had been appointed ambassador to the United States in 1944 and represented Australia the next year at the founding conference of the United Nations. Born in 1875, he was Australia's most senior diplomat.[28]

Eggleston initiated a serious investigation of Japan's new constitution. He asked Professor G. Sawer of Melbourne University to review it,[29] and based on Sawer's findings, made a careful study of all aspects of the constitution himself. Meanwhile, Australia's diplomatic mission in Tokyo sent Eggleston reports on conditions in Japan. The chief of the mission, Patrick Shaw, translated and sent with his report *Mainichi Shinbun*'s editorial of August 16 and *Tokyo Minpō*'s editorial of August 18.[30] *Mainichi* indicated a need for technical revisions to the constitution but not for fundamental changes. *Tokyo Minpō,* however, offered an essentially different evaluation than did other newspapers. In an editorial titled "Constitutional Revision and Conservative Political Forces," it argued that the government mentioned constitutional revision in the first place because it saw it as a way of blocking a sharp advance of democratic forces "following the Government's executive order depriving public employees of their right to strike." And second, with the issuing of judgments by the Tokyo War Crimes Tribunal, "the Government expects the question of the emperor's [war guilt] will subside. . . . Revision of the Constitution and the Imperial House Law would provide a way [for the emperor] legally to abdicate."[31] Shaw's enclosure of these editorials with his report is evidence of Australia's strong distrust of Japan's conservative government that had continued ever since Ball was in Tokyo.

Most of the Australian reports from Japan concerning constitutional revision were pessimistic. The acting mission chief, T. W. Eckersley, in reporting on Attorney General Suzuki's views on constitutional revision, wrote:

> (In a Yoshida cabinet) there would no longer be any socialists. Suzuki's views do not appear to be taken seriously. A conservative spokesman had little to say about it, and there seems little likelihood that the Yoshida Government will seriously examine the revision issue any time soon.[32]

In spite of Eggleston's intense study of the constitutional issue, neither the United States nor Japan were keen on undertaking a review, and so Australia's proposal for a review never had much chance of being realized. MacArthur then reported to the army chief of staff on January 22, 1949, that "no action should be taken by the Allied Powers at this time to force upon the Japanese people a review of their constitution with the view to its modification."[33] In a plenary session on April 28, the FEC decided "not to issue a new directive concerning Japan's new Constitution."[34] With this, the opportunity for carrying out the FEC's decreed review of the constitution was formally lost.

No doubt MacArthur was delighted that the constitution that was drafted and adopted on his initiative had been accepted without undergoing a review. On May 3, 1949, on the second anniversary of the constitution, he announced proudly to the Japanese people:

> The achievements of these two years have indeed been enormous. During this period you have come to understand what is provided in the Constitution and to apply it in your daily lives. . . . The goals of the Allied Powers set forth in the Potsdam Declaration have already been achieved in most important areas.[35]

This boastful statement, so much like Washington's NSC 13/2 document mentioned earlier, relegated the Potsdam Declaration to the past. It was MacArthur's way of conveying to the Japanese people that his government's policy toward Japan had changed.

On this same day in Washington, Charles Kades formally submitted his resignation to the Department of the Army.[36] Beginning with the first draft of the constitution, Kades, as the American with the major responsibility in the matter, had poured his heart and soul into its birth. Now, aware of his government's change of policy toward Japan, Kades made perhaps the wisest choice by submitting his resignation on the day that the constitution was finally accepted without being reviewed.

Questions Remaining

The road along which the new constitution would travel thereafter would be increasingly dangerous. As the Cold War between the United States and the Soviet Union developed, Japan was increasingly incorporated into a security relationship with the United States from the time of the Korean War to the signing of the Security Treaty in 1951. Within that relationship views about the Japanese Constitution alternated between demands for "enacting an independent constitution" and defending the "peace constitution." The constitution survived such anachronistic concepts of revision as limiting fundamental human rights and making constitutional the Self-Defense Forces and the emperor as head of state. Perhaps this was the kind of path that had to be travelled by a constitution that contained a bill of rights that the Japanese people themselves certainly could not have enacted without a revolution from below. Consequently, perhaps we can see the nearly fifty years since the constitution became the supreme law as a redemptive process of the legacy of this burden, which continues today.

Moreover, during this process the mosaic pattern that originally characterized the Japanese Constitution has been completely lost. The constitution had included provisions adopted without sufficient discussion from the American draft, provisions that during the Japanization process bureaucrats attempted to model as closely as possible on the Meiji Constitution, provisions that used declaratory or vague expressions that would not give rise to concrete references to rights, and provisions in which new human rights stipulations based on Japan's prewar experience were incorporated. There were also provisions that simply disappeared or were removed silently. This diversity vanished completely from the constitution as it faced the demands of the revisionists and the protectionists. This whole process was indeed "postwar democracy" itself. One cannot speak of what was given Japan by the occupation, what Japan itself produced, or what was lost without making a sharp distinction between the work of these two forces.

The energy that produced the Japanese Constitution did not by any means emerge solely from the power of the victor over the vanquished or of one nation against another. Whether that energy contributed more or less to the framing process, it came, essentially, only from the views of individuals about the constitution and their ideas about human rights. Inherent in the Japanese Constitution are constitutional views and notions of human rights that transcend both state and race. As Article 97 of the constitution says, these are indeed the "fruits of the age-old struggle of man to be free."

Just as the new constitution did not emerge from the struggle of nation against nation or race against race, a new constitution in the future will not be born solely from "thinking only of one's own country" or from asserting that the Japanese race is distinctive.

Can we not proclaim that we have given up living passively in a period of "protecting the constitution" and welcome an era in which we live under a "shadow constitution" that has incorporated such new human rights as the right to a safe environment, racial equality, and freedom of information? The problems that were not thoroughly explored or that were abandoned when the new constitution was born have much to teach all of us who live in such an age.

Notes

1. Sodei Rinjirō, "MacArthur-Yoshida ōfuku shokan (1)," *Hōgaku shirin* 77, no. 4 (March 1980), p. 119.

2. George H. Blakeslee, *The Far Eastern Commission*, Department of State, 1953. The Japanese translation of Chapter 5, "The New Japanese Constitution," published in *Reference*, no. 48, was reprinted in Kenpō chōsakai jimukyoku, *Kenshi sōdai nigō* (1956).

3. Memorandum for General Hilldring by Ernest A. Gross, September 18, 1946, U.S. National Archives, copy in possession of Professor Amakawa Akira of Yokohama National University.

4. Letter from General C. Whitney to Dr. K. W. Colegrove, November 5, 1946, Herbert Hoover Presidential Library.

5. Kenpō chōsakai jimukyoku, *Kenshi sōdai nigō*, p. 29.

6. Sodei Rinjirō, "MacArthur-Yoshida ōfuku shokan (1)," p. 120.

7. *Asahi Shinbun*, August 22, 1948.

8. *Asahi Shinbun*, August 13, 1948.

9. *Asahi Shinbun*, August 16, 1948.

10. *Asahi Shinbun*, August 14, 1948.

11. Ibid.

12. *Asahi Shinbun*, August 29, 1948.

13. *Asahi Shinbun*, August 30, 1948.

14. Ibid.

15. *Asahi Shinbun*, August 25, 1948.

16. *Asahi Shinbun*, August 16, 1948.

17. *Asahi Shinbun*, August 28, 1948.

18. "Zadankai: Kenpō o kokumin no mono e," *Chūō kōron* (May 1949): 35. Participants were Kainō Michitaka, Satō Isao, Fujita Tsugio, and Hani Setsuko.

19. Kōhō kenkyūkai, "Kenpō kaisei iken," *Hōritsu jihō* 31, no. 4 (April 1949): 56–61.

20. Tokyo daigaku kenpō kenkyūkai, "Kenpō kaisei no shomondai," *Hōgaku kyōkai zasshi* 67, no. 1 (June 1949).

21. Daigō kokkai shūgiin gaimu iin kaigiroku, dai nanagō (April 20, 1949).

22. Yoshida Shigeru, *Kaisō jūnen* (Tokyo: Shinchōsha, 1957), 2:50.

23. The chairman of the Far Eastern Commission (McCoy) to the Assistant Secretary of State for the Occupied Areas (Saltzman), October 25, 1948, *Foreign Relations of the United States* (hereafter, *FRUS*) (1948), 6:876.

24. Ibid., footnote on p. 876.

25. Ibid., pp. 858–862 for text of NSC 13/2. The Japanese translation is in Ōkurashō zaiseishishitsu, *Shōwa zaiseishi* (Tokyo: Tōyō Keizai Shinpōsha, 1976), vol. 3 (fuzoku shiryō), pp. 20–25.

26. Igarashi Takeshi, "George Kennan to tainichi senryō seisaku no tenkō," in *Tennō ga baiburu o yonda hi,* ed. Ray A. Moore (Tokyo: Kōdansha, 1982), p. 191.

27. Memorandum by the Assistant Secretary of State for Occupied Areas (Saltzman) to the United States Representative on the Far Eastern Commission (McCoy), December 3, 1948, *FRUS* (1948), 6:913.

28. *Australian Encyclopedia*, p. 344.

29. Letter from Sawer to Eggleston, July 21, 1948, Eggleston Papers, The Rare Books and Manuscript Room, Australian National Library.

30. Departmental Despatch No. 187/1948, "From Australian Mission in Japan," August 27, 1948, Eggleston Papers.

31. *Tokyo Minpō,* August 18, 1948, Hōsei daigaku Ōhara shakai kenkyūsho shozō.

32. Departmental Despatch No. 226/1948, "From Australian Mission in Japan," October 29, 1948, Eggleston Papers.

33. General of the Army Douglas MacArthur to the Department of the Army, January 22, 1949, *FRUS* (1949), vol. 7, part 2, p. 627.

34. *Asahi Shinbun*, April 30, 1949. Transcript of the 151st Meeting of the Far Eastern Commission, April 28, 1949. I have been unable to confirm this because the microfiche copy of the record in the National Diet Library is illegible.

35. *Asahi Shinbun*, May 3, 1949.

36. Takemae Eiji, "Bei senryō seisaku no ito—moto GHQ minsei kyokuchō Kades ni kiku," *Chūō Kōron* (May 1987): 294.

About the Book and Author

This 1989 Yoshino Sakuzō prize-winning book is essential reading for understanding Japan's postwar constitution, political and social history, and foreign policy. The most complete English account of the origins of Japan's constitution, it analyzes the dramatic events of 1945–1946 that led to the birth of Japan's new constitution. Koseki Shōichi challenges the simplicity of the current interpretation that General Douglas MacArthur in February 1946, faced with inept Japanese efforts at constitutional reform and Soviet interference through the Far Eastern Commission, secretly ordered his staff to write a constitution in seven days and then imposed it on Japan. Differentiating between the adoption procedure and the framing process, the author argues that the latter was varied, complicated, and rich, going beyond the actions of two nations and their representatives. It involved the clash of legal ideas, the conflicting efforts of individuals of different cultures and different political persuasions, and significant contributions by people with no connection to government.

Drawing on Japanese, American, and Australian archives as well as recent scholarly research, Koseki presents new and stimulating interpretations of MacArthur's actions, the Ashida amendment of Article 9, Yoshida's role, and much more. Criticizing Japanese conservative defenders of the old order, he explores Japanese liberal and socialist ideas on constitutional reform and reevaluates the Far Eastern Commission's influence on MacArthur's policies and on the shaping of the basic principles of Japan's antiwar constitution.

Koseki Shōichi is professor in the Faculty of Law at Dokkyō University and has authored several studies of early postwar Japan and Japanese-American relations. **Ray A. Moore** is professor of history and Asian studies at Amherst College and is coeditor of the forthcoming book *The Japanese Constitution: A Documentary History of Its Origins.*